AFRICA
AND THE WORLD

EDITED BY
ROBERT K.A. GARDINER
M.J. ANSTEE
C.L. PATTERSON

ADDIS ABABA
OXFORD UNIVERSITY PRESS
1970

OXFORD UNIVERSITY PRESS, ELY HOUSE, LONDON W.I
GLASGOW NEW YORK TORONTO MELBOURNE WELLINGTON
CAPE TOWN SALISBURY IBADAN NAIROBI DAR ES SALAAM LUSAKA ADDIS ABABA
BOMBAY CALCUTTA MADRAS KARACHI LAHORE DACCA
KUALA LUMPUR SINGAPORE HONG KONG TOKYO
OXFORD UNIVERSITY PRESS P. O. BOX 1024 ADDIS ABABA ETHIOPIA

PRINTED IN ETHIOPIA BY COMMERCIAL PRINTING PRESS

CONTENTS

Message from His Imperial Majesty

We take great pleasure in extending our wishes for the success of the international conference on 'Africa and the World' organized by the Haile Selassie I Prize Trust. We established this organization in 1963 and entrusted it with the responsibility of recognizing outstanding achievements in Ethiopia and the rest of Africa and to strengthen the spiritual and cultural bonds between our people and the peoples of the African continent and of the whole world.

We are pleased to witness that such distinguished scholars as those assembled here have readily co-operated and accepted the invitation extended by this organization. This gathering provides an opportunity for so many people who have studied Africa to share views and knowledge. It will also help in strengthening the foundations of African unity.

We have consistently supported the view that adequate channels and opportunities should be established at all levels to facilitate the exchange of ideas and thoughts. Leaders and their people can utilize enlightened thinking that may result from such exchange. As you well know, the Organization of African Unity has enabled leaders to consult as well as act together.

You meet as scholars concerned with the present and future of our continent. You meet to discuss critically and objectively some of the major areas of concern, namely history, politics, economics and education.

You are gathered to comment on specific African problems and air considered views on the courses of action that the continent should best follow in its dealings outside its continental boundaries.

As academic people it is essential that your discussions should not be fettered by considerations of promotion of any kind of bias but rather pervaded by scholarly integrity and a positive outlook. Furthermore, you must focus on the future rather than solely on the past.

We look forward to seeing the proceedings in published form and we wish the conference every success.

Preface

The present volume, Africa and the World, *the result of a symposium sponsored by the Haile Selassie I Prize Trust, contains nineteen addresses delivered in October 1966 at the offices of the Trust, with three summaries prepared by the three commissions set up by the symposium on History and Politics, Economics and Trade, and Education, respectively.*

The previous symposium entitled Man and Africa *was the first of its kind to be held in Ethiopia and was conducted at the same venue in 1964, under the joint auspices of the CIBA Foundation and the Haile Selassie I Prize Trust. The first symposium set the tone and provided a framework for future meetings of this kind. The change in title for the second gathering is important, in that it marks a new development and contains a new emphasis. Whereas in 1964 attention was focused on man and the African physical environment (climate, resources, transport and communications, population, socio-economic factors and education in economic and social modernization), on this occasion the accent has been placed on Africa's relationship with the world as a whole. In the interval between 1964 and 1966 Africa's role in the international scene had become clearer and an assessment was therefore timely. The post-independence imperatives, not only of Africa but of the developing world as a whole, had become a matter of worldwide interest and concern. Quite appropriately, the contributors to the symposium were persons with different racial and national backgrounds, men and women who had been exposed to different academic disciplines and held different ideological concepts. The fact, too, that papers read were submitted by Africans as well as by non-Africans with or without professional interests in Africa, emphasized the importance the organisers of the symposium attched to its basic aim, namely, 'the promotion of the objective and scholarly study of the relations of Africa with the rest of the world'. It should be noted, in passing, that the object was not to draw up a blueprint for action, but to direct attention to African problems and suggest some approaches to their solution.*

The general trend of the discussion on historical and political questions indicated that in spite of the degree of political liberation achieved in Africa, there still remain many problems to be solved, not the least of them being the elimination of the vestiges of colonialism. This is basically a psychological problem, implying a new and forward-looking attitude towards the many positive tasks of development, rather than indulgence in endless recrimination over evils suffered in the past. Africa is involved in world currents of develop-

ment and has to meet the challenge of playing her full part in the new international role she has assumed. Africa can take pride in the fact that although Europe and the world generally have made a positive contribution to many aspects of her life, she has much to offer which will reflect her intrinsic qualities and her cultural heritage.

At this particular point in her history, Africa's essential task is nation-building, which calls for realistic appraisal of facts, the responsibilities of independence being to a large extent international and basically different from those of pre-independence days. The existence of the Organization of African Unity provides a framework for the co-ordination of policies, and for strengthening the collective support of governments and masses for Africa's views on, and reactions to, international events. In a world in which distance is rapidly being eliminated by scientific progress, isolation has become a thing of the past. African development is, therefore, bound to reckon with multi-racial organizations, and what is needed in international organizations is consensus rather than majority decisions.

The discussion on economics and trade emphasized the fact that Africa is at present passing through a critical phase in her economic development. This crisis stems from the geographical distribution of the new countries, the inherited structure of their economies and from the patterns of trade. Fluctuations in commodity prices generally operate against Africa's interests, while the cost of imported manufactured products keeps rising. The increasing use of synthetics, the tariff protection of similar or competing primary commodities in temperate zones, and the slow growth in the increase of demand for primary goods in relation to manufactures point to the deterioration, if not the total disintegration, of the relations between manufacturing and raw-material-producing countries. Even more significant and disturbing is the increasing dependence of predominantly agricultural countries on industrialized countries for food imports. There is need, therefore, for a reorientation of economic policies to permit balanced economic development which will include concurrent promotion of agriculture and industry.

Another problem confronting the emergent national economies in Africa is the high income differentials as between the salaried worker and the wage-earner, and the tremendous disparity in the living standards of the urban dweller and the inhabitants of the rural areas, due to the predominance of urban interests. Widening class differentiations and the wastefully conspicuous habits of the elite underline the urgent need for action to secure a better distribution of incomes and thus speed national development. Progress in rural areas depends upon changes in the techniques and structure of agriculture, on the creation of institutions for finance and marketing, and for research and the application of the results of research, and above all, on physical improvements which will permit a free flow of goods and the emergence of enlarged markets for agricultural products. But all these developments postulate an understanding of the social milieu which will permit changes in traditional institutions such as land tenure and notions of familial or tribal social security. Of supreme importance also is the need to change the mentality of the rural farmer by practical demonstration of the advantages to be gained by scientific methods of farming. Important though these measures are as a means towards promoting agricultural development, such development by itself is not enough. There must be a local market made up of wage earners and salaried workers in urban and industrial areas to absorb agricultural products. This means that agricultural development must go hand in hand with industrial development.

In the discussion of both agriculture and industry, attention was drawn to the very great shortage of manpower and skills. Here the need is for training programmes to meet the requirements of planned development. Africa is still a net importer of skills, but as a result of the attainment of independence in many countries, experienced personnel—especially expatriate scientific and technical personnel—have been lost. Moreover, a fair proportion of Africans trained abroad have been attracted to jobs in countries with more lucrative openings or better facilities, not to mention those who for political reasons have chosen to be exiles. These are essentially the characteristics of the 'brain drain' in Africa.

One way of dealing with the problem might be by 'bonding' graduates, which would ensure that they give their countries of origin a period of service before emigrating to other lands. In the circumstances, investigation should be conducted into ways in which full use can be made of refugees from the Republic of South Africa, and in this the Organization of African Unity can play a part.

Present-day conditions demand that aid should rely mainly on the provision of managerial and technical skills to launch projects and programmes for the training of local personnel to man them, rather than on transfers of capital alone. Most of the African states are too small in terms of population and resources to provide viable industries and sufficiently large markets in themselves. Some form of regional grouping or multi-national approach is necessary to combat this disability. In such an arrangement it would be necessary for the more advanced developing countries to make concessions to the less developed ones. The content and range of such concessions would have to be negotiated and this is bound to be a difficult and long-drawn-out process. The trade policies of the countries associated with the European Common Market, those who enjoy Commonwealth Preferences as well as those having links with other economic groupings also have to be harmonized: the establishment of a common external tariff will be necessary to protect and encourage intra-African trade in manufacture.

The sustained growth of any economy depends on the quality of the people as much as on that of institutions and the constant reference in the papers and in the ensuing discussions to the dearth of trained human resources repeatedly brought home the catalytic role that education must play in African development. But the role of education is not restricted to providing men to perform economic functions. Apart from equipping men to earn a living, education must fit them for living. This raises the question of the cultural and social environment in which Africans find themselves today—their reaction to their former status as members of peripheral societies has led to the cult of the African personality and nègritude. *In this search for identity in politics, economics and human relations, the OAU can assist by encouraging the compilation of cultural documentation such as the recording of oral history and the publishing of unpublished African material contained in individual theses.*

Africa needs to re-define the structure, content, objectives and processes of education in relation to her recognized needs. Educational planners would do well to conduct comparative studies into educational practice as it obtained in such countries as Japan, Australia, Canada, Scandinavia, the USSR, Eastern Europe and the Chinese Republic. There is still room for foreign teachers but teachers recruited to posts in developing countries should be persons of a special quality, prepared to learn in order to teach. They should, in short, be ready to adapt themselves to their environment, to study its needs and plan their teaching accordingly, rather than try to transfer to Africa wholesale techniques, methods and content quite remote from and irrelevant to the African context. A preliminary orientation course would help them to adapt better to their environment.

In supplying the deficiency of skills in Africa, or, to state the point more positively, in facilitating their acquisition, an attempt must be made to move away from the purely literary type of education to one in which means are sedulously adapted to ends. It is therefore most necessary that provision should be made for the working population, that is, for those above the school-age group. One last point. The need was expressed for identifying useful research projects and co-ordinating such work with that of outside research institutions and academies, a course of action which necessarily implies travel and contact.

In recent years there has been a considerable expansion in primary education, but primary school-leavers without pre-vocational or vocational training can make little or no contribution to the economy. There is need, therefore, to relate the expansion of educational facilities to economic requirements. In other words, educational and manpower planning should be undertaken concurrently. There may be a short-term justification for increasing the emphasis on the transfer of skills in the stated educational objectives of each country. The predominance of liberal arts courses in African educational systems will have to give way to vocational, technical and scientific training. It was also recognized that the developing academies of arts and sciences in African countries and the research institutions which they sponsor need to have permanent relations and frequent contacts with similar bodies in foreign countries.

This preface would not be complete without a word of grateful thanks and appreciation to His Imperial Majesty, Haile Selassie I, Emperor of Ethiopia, through whose foresight, wise judgment and munificence the Haile Selassie I Prize Trust was founded. In the contemporary world, procedure by dialogue has become commonplace, and is being increasingly used. As always, the end result of any phenomenon is the sum-total of many elements, some of them unspectacular, the importance of whose role it is not always easy to determine. Nevertheless, I feel sure than when the time comes to take stock of the many factors or agencies that have contributed to Africa's development, a place of honour will be reserved for the Haile Selassie I Prize Trust.

Finally, we the members of the Editorial Panel, would like to record our gratitude for the opportunity given to us to participate in this most rewarding task

R. K. A. Gardiner
M. J. Anstee
C. L. Patterson

AFRICA AND THE WORLD

by

ROBERT K. A. GARDINER

Your Excellencies, Ladies and Gentlemen,

I would like to take this opportunity to express my appreciation and gratitude to the Haile Selassie I Prize Trust for the honour they have paid me in asking me to preside over this meeting; and also to welcome all the participants to the Second African Conference to be held under the aegis of the Trust.

I would also like to add that each participant will speak in his personal capacity and with full intellectual freedom.

Two years ago (October 1964) the first of these meetings took place in the Offices of the Prize Trust under the auspices of the Haile Selassie I Prize Trust and the Ciba Foundation. The object of that meeting was to 'Survey the problems and potentialities of Africa as a whole'. It was understood then that the meeting was to be the first of a series which would bring together the people of Africa and students of African affairs to examine matters of interest to the continent. I do not have to justify the need to undertake this exacting task or to prove it worthwhile. The wisdom, foresight and munificence which have made these meetings possible are characteristic of His Imperial Majesty in all that he has done and continues to do, and in all that he stands for and means to Africa.

The theme of the present meeting is 'Africa and the World'. The task of the participants, as I see it, is at least twofold: to try and see Africa through the eyes of the world and to see the world from the African point of view. I think it might be useful to define 'Africa' before we relate it to the rest of the world.

A definition is given in the terms of reference of the Economic Commission for Africa: 'the geographical scope of the Commission's work shall be the whole continent of Africa, Madagascar and other African islands'. This definition is comprehensive and precise. Other UN organizations have adopted less comprehensive definitions. FAO treats the United Arab Republic, Libya, Sudan and Somalia as parts of the Near East. WHO's administrative arrangements place Libya, UAR, Sudan, Tunisia, Ethiopia and Somalia in its Eastern Mediterranean Region with headquarters in Alexandria, and Algeria and Morocco in the European Office with its headquarters in Copenhagen. The CCTA, a non-United Nations organization, which has now been taken over by OAU, simply ignored Africa north of the Sahara and concentrated on the rest. These divisions reflect differing attitudes to Africa. The ECA, it seems me, owes its comprehensive definition to the fact that it came into being when a growing number of African territories were becoming independent and continental consciousness was on the increase.

The geographical identity of Africa is gradually beginning to be recognized. I recall that at school our geography teacher once asked us to discuss the statement that 'the Sahara, and not the Mediterranean, is the northern boundary of Africa'. I was horrified. My reaction was that if we kept on throwing away pieces of our continent, soon Africans would belong nowhere. This desire to divide away the very existence of Africa appears not only among geographers but also among historians and students of politics.

According to Mr. Silbert, the author of an article dealing with the 'Panorama géopolitique des Afriques'[1] *(geo-political panorama of the Africas) which appeared in 1958, the Mediterranean and the Atlantic portions of Africa are more or less extensions of Europe; they are virgin lands in which the influence of Greece and Rome, in ancient times, and that of France, England, Portugal and Spain, in modern times, have been dominant. The Red Sea, he claims, makes northeast Africa part of the Middle East. The eastern and southern parts of Africa he considers to have been 'Indianised' by influences moving in across the Indian Ocean. Mr. Silbert concludes that 'the history of Africa, at least as much as its geography, proves that it has never been the monolithic isolated continent it is so often said to be'. This process by which parts of Africa are described as appendages to other continents and its identity in the minds of men is destroyed, could, I believe, be applied to other continents. Using the same kind of arguments, we could, no doubt, arrive at several 'Europes' and 'Asias' and even 'South Americas'.*

Africa has never been a monolithic isolated continent, but it has never been divided into water-tight compartments, and its identity is well established in the African mind. According to the Foreign Minister of Senegal, the Moroccan empire extended from the shores of the Mediterranean to the borders of Senegal. Mr. Doudou Thiam concludes 'there is, then, no neat, clear-cut separation between the two parts of Africa, the north and south'.[2] *The same thesis is implied in Algeria's claims to portions of the Sahara desert.*

It is, however, true that, after the drying up of the Sahara basin, some six thousand years ago,[3] *a major barrier developed between north Africa and Europe on the one hand and the rest of Africa on the other. The Mediterranean was easier to cross and recross than the Sahara desert. But the Nile Valley and caravan routes provided channels of communication. Goods and persons continued to move across the desert and also across the continent from east to west, along the semi-arid belt which stretches from the west coast to Somalia. Furthermore, there was traffic between the continent and its adjacent islands. I feel, therefore, that we need have no hesitation in taking as the subject of this meeting that Africa which is made up of the entire continent and of the islands around it.*

Africa's image and relations with the world are influenced, if not determined, by those who speak for her. Until recently, Africa's principal spokesmen have been foreign travellers, missionaries, traders, and colonial administrators. In recent years anthropologists and other scholars have undertaken to explain Africa to the world. At the end of the Second World War only four areas in Africa had what may be described as international identity. These four countries, Ethiopia, Liberia, Egypt, and South Africa, were signatories to the Charter of the United Nations and thus became members by adherence rather than by admission. The rest of Africa, consisting of colonies and Trust Territories, came within the provisions of Chapters 11, 12 and 13 of the Charter; they were represented in the world organization by the ruling powers, not by Africans.

There was only one departure from this tradition by which outsiders spoke for Africa: petitioners from Trust Territories and other persons who had issues to raise in the interest of the inhabitants of these territories were given the right to be heard before the Trusteeship Council. However, in return for their agreement to observe the principle of international accountability for colonies and to allow petitioners from Trust Territories to appear before the United Nations, administering powers were provided, in Article 2, paragraph 7, with protection against interference with their sovereign rights. According to this Article, 'Nothing contained in the present Charter shall authorise the United Nations to intervene in matters which are essentially within the domestic jurisdiction of any state or shall require the members to submit such matters to settlement under the present Charter'. This has been the juridical basis of Britain's refusal so far to refer the Rhodesian dispute to the United Nations.

The brief history of the Economic Commission for Africa and of representation at its meetings throws an interesting light on this question of Africa's voice in the world. By its original terms of reference, membership was open to states 'responsible for their own international relations'; metropolitan countries with territorial responsibilities in Africa were also granted full membership. But the administering powers could sponsor dependencies for admission as Associate Members. The result was that representation at the early sessions of the Commission was predominantly non-African.

By a resolution of the Commission's second session, each administering authority was invited to ascertain whether its dependencies wished to become Associate Members. The Commission later expressed a specific wish to see Africans representing those dependent territories which had become associate members. This decision was followed by a resolution that non-African states responsible for the international relations of non-self-governing territories in Africa should have the status of Associate Members. France, Spain, and the United Kingdom are Associate Members; Portugal's membership of the Commission has been terminated; the Republic of South Africa has been excluded from active participation in the Commission's work; and Rhodesia has withdrawn. This means that all Africans, except those in the so-called Portuguese provinces, in the Republic of South Africa, and in Rhodesia, now participate directly in the work of the Commission. I would add only that Resolution 94 of the sixth session of ECA requested that representatives of the non-

self-governing territories of Angola, Mozambique, and South West Africa be invited to participate in the sessions of the Commissions. But up to the present, Member States have not been able to determine which of the many rival political parties in these territories should be invited.

This evolution which I have described—amounting to a reversal of the original arrangements for representation as set out in the 1958 Terms of Reference of the Commission—has resulted in the formal transfer of powers to Africans to manage the affairs of the Commission.

But who are Africans? As is true of most other continents, no hard and fast lines can be drawn between the peoples of Africa. Anthropometric measurements and even blood groups fail to establish such lines, and as Seligman very rightly points out, 'language—however helpful it may be—by itself is not a sure guide to race'. The conclusion of J. S. Huxley and A. C. Haddon, in their study of racial types in Europe entitled 'We Europeans', *is that there is no such thing as a European type. We can apply that lesson to Africa. Indeed, we may profitably apply to Africa the thesis of the authors of the Monroe Doctrine that 'nature by making us inhabitants of one continent, has likewise united us in the bonds of a common patriotism'.*

But the facts of geography, physical anthropology and history, do not remove doubts and susceptibilities that have taken root in the minds even of Africans themselves. Not so long ago, if we are to go by the accounts of non-African chroniclers, Africa was a continent which was not a continent, contained cultures and civilizations which were neither cultures nor civilizations, and peoples who were not a people, having no past and hardly any future. Under the shock of defeat, enslavement, and subjection, Africans tended to lose faith in themselves and to accept alien dogmas about their nature, aptitudes, and capabilities. It is no surprise that some Africans should have been driven to imitate alien ways of life and to dissociate themselves from the dubious image of things African which had been so assiduously promulgated by non-Africans. Some even welcomed the idea of being regarded as 'assimilated Europeans'. In some territories it was considered more dignified to be regarded as a member of an immigrant race than as a native. Some Africans—inhabitants of the continent of Africa for many generations and centuries—prefer to be regarded as Arabs, Hamites, or Semites rather than as Africans. But the situation has been changing in recent decades. In French-speaking Africa, nationalism began 'the day when the Africans discovered that assimilation was an illusion'.[4] *There is now a growing continental consciousness, which is having a perceptible influence in favour of the development of an African continental community.*

Paul Laurence Dunbar and Leon Damas have demonstrated the process of self-rediscovery of the African. Dunbar writes:[5]

We wear the mask that grins and lies
It hides our cheeks and shades our eyes —
. . . Why should the world be over-wise
In counting all our tears and sighs?
Nay, let them only see us, while
We wear the mask.

I hope we shall remember the grin of Dunbar's mask when next we hear it said that the African is a very happy creature. He is always smiling and laughing. The mask became, for a while, part of the African's facial features. Not unlike that of the mystic dreamy Slav who turned in 1917 into the 'bloodthirsty' Bolshevik. Or the little, excessively polite 'yellow men' who now defy the greatest military powers on earth. Wearing of the mask is not deceit but a biological adaptation for survival, and those who wear it may be as unconscious of it as a member of a parachute unit wearing his camouflage uniform in the main streets of a city. But Damas demands:[6]

Give me back my black dolls to play
The simple games of my instinct
To rest in the shadow of their laws
To recover my courage
    my boldnes
To feel myself m elf
    a new self from the one I was yesterday
        Yesterday
Without complications
        Yesterday
When the hour of uprooting came.

The struggle for self-rediscovery has left emotional scars. Fortunately—for Africa and the world—scars are not hereditary. They may not show on the bodies of our children. These scars are perhaps more noticeable in Africans abroad who first felt the need to struggle and went through the most difficult times. W. E. Dubois claims that the Negro in America has developed a double-consciousness which makes him see himself 'through the eyes of others and by the standards of a world which looks on him in amused contempt and pity'.[7] *But the scars are present and very real also in Africans at home. Richard Wright noticed this double-consciousness in the pronouncements and behaviour of the Afro-Asian participants in the Bandung Conference. He described it as the 'frog perspective: someone looking from below upward, a sense of someone who feels himself lower than others'.*[8] *Dubois, who succeeded to an astonishing degree in identifying himself with the lot of the disinherited African, described his plight in this way. 'Between me and the other world there is even an unasked question: unasked by some through feelings of delicacy; by others through the difficulty of rightly framing it—they approach me in a half-hesitant sort of way, eye me curiously or compassionately—instead of saying directly, 'How does it feel to be a problem'?*[9] *At the core of the nationalism of Africans, as in that of most dependent peoples, there is an urge to free themselves from this state of mind. Africa, in her relations with the rest of the world, is searching for her identity: in scholarship, art, literature, drama, dance and, indeed, in all forms of self-expression.*

The outside world chose to make Africa a problem all its own—in fact the notion of the 'white man's burden' was coined to give currency to this idea. To the conscientious student of African history, it is the outside world which has been a problem to Africa, and it is the African who has had to carry the 'white man's burden' for centuries. Africa has been the colonial continent par excellence, *governed and exploited in the exclusive interest of a small handful of European powers. The independence that most African countries have recently acquired has brought with it enormous problems. The whole continent is made up of developing nations, quite a few at the very first stage of growth. Moreover, states have often been built out of heterogeneous ethnic groups, and African leaders now have the problem of converting them into nations. There is an increasing appreciation among African states of the intractability of these problems of social and economic development and of political integration.*

But in this process of re-awakening a new issue is being raised which may prove to be largely irrelevant to the solution of the real problems, the issue of the 'gap' between rich and poor countries. We are not in sight of anything like catching up with the industrialized countries. I do not believe that closing this gap can be, per se, *the primary aim of economic development anywhere. Such limited perspective can too easily lead to a sense of frustration, bitterness and envy on the part of Africans. As it is, the efforts African states are already making to transform their colonial economies into structures capable of sustained growth are often misrepresented, or misunderstood as being directed against this or that interest, when the truth is that the only aim is the interest of Africa itself. It is better to concentrate on the more positive view of African development which has been well summed up in His Imperial Majesty's statement of the purpose of the Trust:*[10]

to encourage the activities and proficiencies of Our People particularly in the advancement of health, prosperity, and the exercise of the fine and applied arts, and also to strengthen spiritually and culturally the bonds between Our People and the peoples of the African continent and of the whole world . . .

In the programme which this statement implies African governments will have to play an active part and, indeed, take the lead in economic development. The state apparatus played a similar role in building up the economies of many of the present-day capitalist countries. It is clear, for example, that the exploration and mobilisation of natural resources, which must be the foundation of African economic development, cannot be left exclusively to private initiative—especially to foreign private initiative. Again, state action is essential in order to stabilize the prices of the principal export commodities as well as to prevent the costly drain of the earnings of mining and industrial enterprises from the new states. Above all, the state will have to play a vital role if the infrastructure on which further development depends is to be built rapidly.

I am sure other speakers will deal with the economic strategy of African states; but the point which I wish to stress here is that there is nothing in the manner in which African countries are trying to achieve economic development which is inherently or necessarily hostile to the interests of foreign countries.

On their side Africans should accept the development of their continent as a challenge to themselves and not as an excuse for endless recrimination against ex-colonial exploiters; after all, there is no chance now that Africans can be brushed aside like the Red Indians of America, the Eskimos of Canada, the Amerindians of South America or the Aborigines of Australia. Africans should look upon the development of Africa as a task which is primarily theirs, and should cease to regard foreign aid as a form of political bribery or blackmail. With a change of heart on both sides a firm basis will be laid for healthy and mutually profitable international economic co-operation.

In the political field, certain facts determine the attitude of African governments, individually and collectively, towards the rest of the world. Most African states face the problem which the late President Olympio of Togo described as 'serious discontinuities arising from the existence of different ethnic groups and language differences'.[11] *The same problem is expressed in the observation that 'Africa is a continent rich in nationalisms and poor in nations'.*[12] *The political leaders of the newly independent states are aware that they preside over very fragile structures recently put together by foreign powers, and every African government has to strike a delicate balance, not only between political and regional interests, but, even more important, between linguistic, cultural, traditional and emotional factionalisms. Moreover, these weaknesses of the newly born African states present to outsiders a temptation—which may sometimes be too great to resist—to upset these delicate balances. The fear created by this precarious situation is, in its turn, partly responsible for the intolerance of political opposition and the resort to one-party rule which have characterized political life in some African states in the post-independence years. Rulers who live under the constant threat of removal tend to be hypersensitive to criticism.*

The existence of tribal groups also poses difficulties in relations between African states. The fact that most colonial boundaries took no notice of ethnic or linguistic distributions has created conditions which can very easily lead to frontier disputes and wars. Even where, as in Latin America, there were no tribal problems to plague the leaders of newly independent states, more than a hundred years were wasted on frontier disputes and fighting. It is true that, under the Charter of OAU, the chances of frontier fighting have been considerably reduced, and provision has been made for the peaceful settlement of controversies which have already arisen. But this arrangement also can be upset by external influences; for example, large scale transfers of arms—and nearly always obsolescent arms, at that—by developed countries to rival African states. Such arms now provide a screen behind which cold-war infiltration and subversion can take place and lead to so-called popular uprisings and guerilla wars. The Charter does not appear to have provided safeguards against this danger. Already, the expenditures of African governments on arms are out of proportion to their means; they cut into other urgent needs which the governments have to meet.

Thus, African governments have to protect their independence against dissident forces at home; they have to deal with disputes with their neighbours; they have to safeguard their existence against subversion from countries versed in sabotage. These dangers incline them to favour neutralism or non-alignment.

But neutralism is never a popular policy with partisans to any dispute. 'The hottest places in hell', we are told, 'are reserved for those who, in a period of moral crisis, maintain their neutrality'.[13]

Even when they have gained their independence through negotiation, states still feel that it is a prize to be guarded zealously. The attitude of these states to some of the ex-metropolitan countries, is as a consequence, an uneasy blend of suspicion and appreciation of the necessity of international co-operation. Co-operation is important, among other reasons because, prior to independence, all the services had been run by personnel from the metropolitan countries and no African country seems to have been so well prepared for independence as not to require assistance from foreign personnel subsequently.

In economic matters, the new states still, inevitably, somewhat resentful of their former status as appendages to metropolitan countries and of the exploitation of the past, are nonetheless obliged to maintain many links with their former rulers. The facts of the situation—unless countries opt for the painful and difficult road chosen by, for example, Guinea and Mali—may seem to demand such association; but this makes it no less galling for all that. This observation may come as a surprise to some of my audience; because perhaps they assume that the form of economic co-operation in which the recipient countries do all the pleading—the right word may be begging—is a pleasant exercise. A countryman of mine used to say that when Africans are asked to co-operate, those who invite them assume that they will do all the operating while the African does the 'co-ing'.

African states also realize that they have been made far too dependent on former metropolitan countries by such institutional arrangements as preferential tariffs, monetary zones, shipping, air services, telecommunications and other forms of services. Even where these arrangements are technically efficient, they work primarily, if not exclusively, in the interests of the colonial powers; in any case they are yet another reminder to African countries of how new and how essentially incomplete is their independence. Added to this is the fact that most states need some form of defence agreement with foreign countries to secure the supply of arms or even, as has happened, the direct intervention of foreign forces to put down internal revolt. These are some of the components of the crisis of independence.

The bitterness of this crisis is not lessened by reminders from developed countries that newly independent states which are, in fact, client states or states by diplomatic courtesy, should not claim, at the same time, the right to judge the conduct of great powers; they should not speak as if they have equal sovereign rights with these latter, and then expect to turn to them for aid. The attitude of some Great Powers is that the new states should recognize the realities of the international situation and learn to live in the world as it is. The new states, on the other hand, though aware of their own weaknesses and sometimes of their mistakes, find that in international relations 'life is, on the whole, easier for the rich than for the poor'.[14]

The foreign policies of African states aim at the elimination of colonialism from the continent, the defeat of apartheid *and all forms of racial discrimination, and an end to the situation in which foreign influences can decide the fate of Africa. In the Congo (Kinshasa) international finance is demonstrating its unwillingness to allow Africans to live peacefully on any other terms but its own. In the case of the so-called Portuguese provinces, the collective inertia or outright resistance of the major powers has held such influences at bay. The use of paragraph 7 of Article II of the Charter, added to their own military weakness, has baulked African states in the case of Rhodesia. The economic interests of major powers have rendered* apartheid *almost impregnable. It is becoming increasingly clear that Afro-Asian resolutions, even if adopted by United Nations bodies, without the concurrence of the Great Powers remain largely inoperative. And yet, in the eyes of African populations their governments are sovereign and collectively responsible for whatever happens in Africa, and to Africans. This is a disconcerting combination of accountability without power. In these circumstances, African states are obliged to adopt what is known in diplomatic parlance as 'attitudes of expediency'.*

The appearance of African states on the international scene is a novelty which confuses both Africa and the world at large. There are doubts abroad about the will of Africans to pursue their declared objectives. The odds are obviously against Africa, and empty threats and the raising of false hopes of quick results should be avoided at all costs. In the language of the National Association for the Advancement of Coloured People, during its difficult years, Africans must be prepared to 'inch' their way towards their goal, if need be. The walls of this Jericho are not likely to come tumbling down at one trumpet blast.

How do conditions in the continent look? Some people see only confusion and instability; others spotlight ineptitude and corruption, and try to explain these in racial terms. Institutionalized crime under the aegis of a legally constituted authority seems to be spectacular because it is new to Africa. In other parts of the world this type of development has long been associated with political machines—the 'shakedown', the 'rake off' patronage, and contribution to party funds.

The controversial Italian film Africa Addio *puts its emphasis on the failure of independent Africa. This is an international counterpart of the American* Birth of a Nation *which was released after the First World War during a time of Negro agitation. It was a caricature of the reconstruction period in America designed to discredit Negro claims to full citizenship.*

There is no doubt that the 'wind of change' in Africa has given way to the turbulence of transition. Africa must cease to be merely a continent in a hurry, and act as a continent with a purpose. Unless states fix for themselves certain basic directions and purposes, they run the risk of functioning incoherently, being torn apart by egoistic scrambles for internal power, and becoming, in the graphic words of Arthur Schlesinger, a 'government by epilepsy'.[15]

Meetings such as the one we are holding today should enable Africa to determine its purpose and re-evaluate it periodically in the light of changing circumstances. The world, too, shculd be interested in Africa's purpose and progress, because the speed of a convoy is determined by its slowest vessel, and, in a caravan, by its slowest camel. Africa, in any case, has been slow in joining the modern convoy or caravan; but there is no evidence that she will be slow in action.

REFERENCES

1 Silbert, Alfred, in *Revue Politique etrangere*, No. 6, 1958, quoted by Doudou Thiam in *The Foreign Policy of African States*, London, 1965.

2 Thiam, Doudou, *The Foreign Policy of African States*, London, 1965.

3 Bohanan, Paul, *African Outline*, London, 1964.

4 Thiam, Doudou, op. cit.

5 Dunbar, Paul Lawrence, *The Negro Caravan*, New York.

6 Damas, Leon, *Black Orpheus*, January, 1958. Ibadan, Nigeria, quoted by Colin Legum, *Africa: A Handbook to the Continent*, London, 1966.

7 Du Bois, W.E.B., *The Souls of Black Folk*, New York.

8 Wright, Richard, *White Man Listen*, New York, 1957.

9 Du Bois, op. cit.

10 Wolstenholme, Gordon and Maeve O'Connor, eds. *Man and Africa*, London, 1965.

11 Quigg, Philip W., ed. *Africa*, New York, 1964.

12 Touval, Saadia, *Somali Nationalism: International Politics and the Drive for Unity in the Horn of Africa*, London, 1963.

13 Schlesinger Jr., Arthur M., *Thousand Days: John F. Kennedy in the White House*, New York, 1965.

14 Vare, Daniele, *Laughing Diplomat*, London, 1953.

15 Schlesinger Jr., Arthur M. op.cit..

COMMISSION A

HISTORICAL AND POLITICAL SITUATION

THE IMPACT OF THE AFRICAN STATES IN THE UNITED NATIONS

by

GWENDOLEN M. CARTER

The independent African-controlled states form just over one-third of the total membership of the United Nations. No other closely associated group can wield so much influence through its votes so long as these votes are used with some consistency and constructiveness. So far, those issues in which African states have had a noticeable impact are, not surprisingly, directly related to developments on their own continent. The way is open, however, to their wider influence on all international questions when African regimes acquire a knowledge and insight into issues outside their continent that can compare with what they possess about issues within Africa itself.

Four characteristics of the international setting within which the African states achieved their independence have aided them in acquiring an influence not earlier possessed by small countries in a power-conscious world. The first factor has been the relative stalemate in Great Power politics due to the fear of a nuclear war. In the second place, the focus of international discussions has been broadened by the fact that, apart from the Cuban crisis and, to a lesser extent, the Viet Nam situation, no action by a great power has directly threatened another in recent years. Thirdly, the evenness in the strength of rival blocs has given special importance to the votes of the uncommitted countries. And lastly, there is the virtual universality of the United Nations, particularly as compared with the League of Nations, and the growing practice of using international, rather than national, mechanisms in particularly sensitive situations.

Striking examples of this international approach have been the peace-keeping operations of the United Nations in providing neutral forces to patrol the borders between Greek and Turkish Cypriots in Cyprus, between Israel and the Arab states, and between Pakistan and India in Kashmir. It is no less significant that it is the middle and smaller countries, like Sweden, Canada, Austria, and New Zealand, that have provided most of the current peace-keeping forces. Similarly it was countries like these and the African states that provided the United Nations forces for the Congo.

From the first, the independent African-controlled states have affirmed their regard for the United Nations as the crucial element in the formulation and execution of their foreign policy aims. Partly this has been because its Charter embodies those principles of self-determination, the equality of states, and economic development that are their chief objectives. Partly it is because the United Nations brings them into a world forum, thereby visibly recognizing their international significance, and permits them maximum opportunity for influence on the issues that concern them most.

Already at the Conference of Independent States at Accra in April, 1958, its eight participants asserted their intention to project 'a distinctive African personality' in foreign affairs, and to establish permanent machinery at the United Nations for this purpose. This machinery was set up a month later. In the succeeding year, the independent African-controlled states campaigned vigorously, though unsuccessfully, for the removal of the ban on the proscribed nationalist party of the French Cameroons and for a subsequent election supervised by the United Nations before that country gained independence.

The African states were still more active on behalf of self-determination for the Algerians. Diplomatic missions were sent to Latin America and Scandinavia, and resolutions were pressed in the General Assembly. Even though these resolutions failed by narrow margins to secure majority support, the African efforts provided the FLN with an international platform, and led many states to take an active interest in the Algerian struggle which had previously not done so. African pressure also played a role in the rejection of the proposal by the United Nations Good Offices Committee for a partition of South West Africa and helped to persuade a number of countries, including the United States, to support the critical resolution of that year against South Africa's racial policy instead of merely abstaining as in the past.

In February, 1960, as the great wave of independence began, Dag Hammarskjold, Secretary General of the United Nations, declared of the Africans that 'the United Nations is now, or will be, their Organization'. The striking increase in the number of independent states in Africa from 1960 to 1967—the admission of Botswana (Bechuanaland), and Lesotho (Basutoland) in the 1966 Assembly brought the number to 39—has led, in practice, both to greater influence and to major problems in maintaining African unity.

In March, 1960, African and Asian states secured a special meeting of the Security Council to consider the shooting by South African police at Sharpeville of peacefully-demonstrating Africans. Despite the protests of Great Britain and France, this South African action was condemned as a potential threat to peace by a majority of the Council members, including the United States. The breakdown of law and order in the Congo followed shortly after and the African states, unanimous in this regard, supported the assumption of major responsibility by the United Nations in this area, as the alternative to great power rivalries. But sharp differences over policy regarding Katanga secession, and the political rivalry between Lumumba and Kasavubu, coupled with the division of African states between the Brazzaville and Casablanca groups (each of which formed its own organization at the United Nations) greatly weakened African influence in international discussions and decisions.

As the tense situations in both the Congo and Algeria began to ease in 1962, so did the rivalries between the groups of African states. The establishment of the Organization of African Unity in May 1963 in Addis Ababa led gradually to the dismantling of the rival blocs, to re-establishing the common caucus machinery at the United Nations, and to growing co-ordination and thus more influence for African policies in international relations. Pressure for more representation in United Nations organs led eventually to an enlargement of the Security Council from eleven to fifteen members and of the Economic and Social Council from eighteen to twenty-seven. Earlier, the African states had secured an enlargement of the General Committee (steering committee) of the General Assembly, and of many of the committees of the Economic and Social Council whose size was not dependent on an amendment to the Charter. Side by side with these efforts have gone their continuing efforts on behalf of their major political objectives: the speedy and full liquidation of colonialism, particularly in the Portuguese territories of Mozambique and Angola; and the self-determination of African majorities in southern Africa—notably in Rhodesia and in South Africa—through international action against the entrenched control of their white resident minorities.

The most distinctive new emphasis introduced into international relations by the Afro-Asian states is that colonialism in itself is a type of aggression. Since these states acquired the right to conduct their own foreign relations by successfully ending foreign rule, it is not surprising that they put colonialism—the control of one people by another—on the same level as conquest. Historically we know that many colonial situations did not result from the use of force and were not maintained by force. Nonetheless, self-determination is now widely accepted as a principle of international morality. Thus the political control by one state over an outside country against its people's will is commonly condemned. This is particularly the case when the majority population of the dominated country, as in Mozambique and Angola, is of a different race and colour from those who dominate. Even when a territory like French Somaliland votes (1958 and 1966) for association with an outside power, there is wide sympathy for subsequent pressure for a change in status.

The rapid transfer in the period from 1956 to the present by three democratic European colonial powers—Great Britain, France and Belgium—of ultimate political authority in African territories to local leaders supported by majority parties has provided by far the greatest mass liquidation of colonialism in history. The control still exercised in Africa by two non-democratic European countries—Portugal and Spain—brings out the difference between governments that are subject to the pressures of domestic and international public opinion, and regimes that are not susceptible to such influences.

No less intractable, as we well know, has been the situation in southern Africa where entrenched white minorities remain politically, economically and socially dominant over unwilling African majorities. The situation that exists in South Africa and in Rhodesia can legitimately be termed 'domestic colonialism'. Indeed, the controls over Africans in those countries are far more rigorous and the discrimination suffered by Africans far more severe than existed in many of the colonies that have gained independence. But because change in the basic pattern of race relations threatens so wide a range of local interests, and because of the immense strength of the South African economy and the solidarity in support of their privileged position of the three and a half million South African whites, 'domestic colonialism' has proved far more difficult to change than was the traditional external colonial control of the three democratic European countries.

From their first serious intervention in United Nations affairs, the African states have sought to mobilize international public opinion and action against South Africa and Portugal for their discriminatory racial policies and the exclusion of their African majorities from political influence. 1958–59 marked the first watershed in United Nations voting on the perennial South African issue as the United States from that time on has voted affirmatively in condemnation of apartheid. In 1963, another watershed was achieved when a General Assembly resolution in July called on all states to cease immediately 'the sale and shipment of arms, ammunition of all types, and military vehicles to South Africa', and a further resolution in November extended the ban to equipment and materials for the manufacture and maintenance of arms and ammunition. The United States agreed in the autumn of 1963 to institute this comprehensive boycott. Since that time, the American government has refused export permits for a progressively enlarged number of items for South Africa that could potentially be used against the African population. The effect of this American action has been less great than had been hoped, however, since the British did not institute a similar ban until late 1964, the French have continued to sell arms to South Africa, and that country has become increasingly self-sufficient in the production of munitions.

OAU countries have instituted their own sanctions against South Africa. They have denied South African aircraft the right to overfly their countries, thereby forcing them to adopt a new (and not unattractive) route via Portuguese and Spanish controlled territories. Some African countries have placed barriers of various kinds on the travel of white South Africans. Some have instituted more or less complete boycotts of South African goods, but those countries, like Zambia and Malawi, that are on the borders of southern Africa have been unable to detach themselves from dependence on South African production. More revolutionary action is envisaged through the support by the OAU's Liberation Committee of African efforts to organize sabotage and armed attacks in southern Africa, particularly where, as in northern Mozambique, there is a common frontier with an independent African state. But none of these approaches has yet shown signs of inflicting serious damage on the dominant regimes in southern Africa.

Since South Africa is a sovereign state, its discriminatory domestic racial policies do not provide a legal justification for organizing international punitive measures against it unless these racial policies lead to an open breach of the peace. In South West Africa, however, the international obligation to promote the wellbeing of the inhabitants of that territory that South Africa accepted as Mandatory at the end of World War I, offered an opportunity to seek a judicial decision on whether such an obligation was compatible with the policies of apartheid that had been instituted in that territory. In the most constructive approach yet made to the South African situation, the Ethiopian and Liberian governments launched litigation before the World Court to secure a judgement on that issue and also a clear statement of the right of the United Nations in regard to South West Africa, which South Africa, unlike all other Mandatories after World War II, had refused to place under trusteeship.

The General Assembly had been advised in 1957 by its special committee on South West Africa that in a dispute 'of any nature' providing 'it related to the interpretation or application of one or more of the clauses of the Mandate or to the effect of the Mandate as a whole', former members of the League could invoke Article 7 of the Mandate which provides that 'the Mandatory agrees, that if any dispute whatever should arise between the Mandatory and another Member of the League of Nations relating to the interpretation or the application of the provision of the Mandate, such dispute, if it cannot be settled by negotiation, shall be submitted to the Permanent Court of International Justice provided for by Article 14 of the Covenant of the League of Nations'. When the Good Offices Committee (consisting of the United Kingdom, United States and Brazil) failed to find any basis of agreement on South West Africa that was acceptable to both South Africa and the United Nations, and the South African government began to speak of the Mandate as 'lapsed', the Afro-Asian group at the United Nations explored the feasibility of judicial recourse. In June 1960, the Second Conference of Independent African States, meeting in Addis Ababa, concluded that the 'international obligation of the Union of South Africa concerning the Territory of South West Africa should be submitted to the International Court of Justice for adjudication in a contentious proceeding'. On behalf, therefore, of all the African states, Ethiopia and Liberia instituted proceedings before the World Court in the South West Africa case.

The frustrating final judgement of the Court on July 18, 1966, in which it took refuge in a technicality that had apparently been settled by its own advisory decision forty-four months before, should not blind us to the fact that the African states made a forward-looking move in international relations by instituting judicial proceedings in this much-disputed issue.

Had the Court lived up to the expectations raised by its majority decision on its own jurisdiction in 1962, the world might have had a clear-cut legal decision on the morality or immorality of South African apartheid. And this in turn might have injected into international relations the two components that the African states have tried to add in their brief period as participants in foreign relations: the emphasis on universal humanitarian principles as the guiding springs of international action; and recourse to judicial inquiry and adjudication in a sensitive political issue.

It is worth noting how close we came to having the principal judicial organ of the United Nations take a significant role in the handling of a vital and potentially explosive international issue. Only because of the double vote of its president, Sir Percy Spender, did the Court refuse to deal with either of the issues referred to it.

That this refusal came as a complete surprise to the defendants as well as to the plaintiffs and outside observers is evidenced by the South African government's mammoth efforts in this case. Through volumes of written pleadings and the testimony of numerous witnesses, the South Africans tried to prove either that the Mandate was no longer in existence or, if the Court held it was still in existence, that South Africa was not subject to international supervision or was not in violation of the Mandate because of the apartheid policies it had instituted in South West Africa. Because the Court, in my view, abrogated its responsibilities, the issue was plunged back into the political arena with no formal guide lines for future action.

In some respects the Rhodesian situation is a prototype of the situation as a whole in southern Africa. Placed in a different legal position because Great Britain does not accept the claim that sovereignty has been attained by its unilateral declaration of independence, the white minority regime in Rhodesia has been under legal, financial and economic pressure since November 11, 1965, the day of the declaration of UDI. That the economic pressure, including the oil boycott, has been ineffective so far is due to the establishment of a *de facto* economic unity in southern Africa as far as the flow of supplies is concerned. My personal observations in Rhodesia this past summer indicate, however, that the impact of restrictions on selling to outside countries, particularly the all-important tobacco harvest, has affected and can affect Rhodesia's economic situation far more deeply than the boycott on oil. The latter has simply made the price of petrol exorbitant for supplies coming daily from South Africa. Moreover, economic sanctions have driven Rhodesia, under its present regime, much closer than before to South Africa in educational policy, which is crucial for extension of the African franchise but begins to look unpleasantly like Bantu education, and in policy for the rural reserves, which bears all too many similarities to South African separate development.

Yet the relative international solidarity in the imposition of economic sanctions, particularly the oil sanction, against Rhodesia makes it apparent that only the connivance of South Africa and the Portuguese are nullifying its purpose. Indeed, rather than repeat the high degree of criticism levelled by the African states at the organization of sanctions against Rhodesia, it would be well to compare the latter with the colossal failure of the only other major attempt at such international action—sanctions against Italy in 1935 to dissuade it from its attack on Ethiopia—when even the attempt to institute oil sanctions failed.

While it is clear that it would be a mammoth task to organize sanctions against the whole of southern Africa—perhaps the only way in which maximum pressure could be exerted against its weakest link, Rhodesia—there is evidence of capacity for such an effort. It is in this perspective that the African states and many of their liberal supporters in the United Kingdom, the Commonwealth and beyond, pressed to have the Rhodesian issue transferred to the United Nations so mandatory sanctions could be voted. Prime Minister Wilson's request for selective mandatory sanctions when the Rhodesian regime did not come to terms by December was both too little and too late. Only if South Africa and Portugal are confronted with the implications of their support for Rhodesia, and also face penalties if they continue to provide it, can a reasonable settlement be secured. And even though Great Britain and the United States would have to carry the brunt of such an extension of sanctions—involving a cost proportionately far greater for Britain than for the United States—the United Nations as a whole would be involved in a total confrontation in southern Africa. Such a confrontation is inevitable sooner or later, and it is difficult to imagine a more favourable situation in which to force it. Whatever happens the way ahead in this most serious of political struggles is full of dangers. No issue in our generation—as Americans well know—is more sensitive or more difficult to solve than the relations inside countries between persons of different race and colour.

The international community is divided into big powers, that can if necessary stand on their own; middle powers (whether through numbers or resources) that are strong enough to invoke nationalism in their own interest; and small powers that must depend on international sentiment and support. The principle of one state—one vote (which may seem at first sight to contradict the African emphasis on one man—one vote) is well justified as a means of making large countries listen to small ones. Yet it is clear that listening is not enough to mould policy. Only when the attitudes adopted and the policies promoted by the smaller countries have the quality to promote respect and to offer the hope of breaking international log-jams can the words of the smaller powers have full and continuing effect. And while the increasing number of the smaller states provides them with impressive voting power, it is only as they combine their votes in support of such constructive purposes that they can have genuine effect. Beyond this, the smaller states must themselves follow the principles that they hold up before the larger states if their words are to be influential.

In one particular respect smaller states have often played a distinctive and influential role. That is through providing outstanding statesmen for international organizations. Some of the most distinguished of international jurists have been from Latin America and Africa. Successful Presidents of the General Assembly have included Alex Quaison Sackey of Ghana. Most significant has been the fact that the two most distinguished, courageous and influential Secretary-Generals of the United Nations have come from small states: Dag Hammarskjold from Sweden, and U Thant from Burma. Outstanding Africans, including ECA's Robert Gardiner, have been mentioned as possible successors to U Thant. The impact of such individuals on the international community and the distinction thus bestowed upon their country and continent of origin are far-reaching.

The greatest potential strength of African-controlled countries is their unity in support of constructive objectives. As President Julius Nyerere pointed out in a remarkable speech at the installation of President Kaunda as Chancellor of Zambia University in July, 1966, African-controlled Africa is not united , as the leaders of its drive for independence had dreamed it would be, but is composed of a great number of different nationalities, one for each of its thirty-nine independent states. Everyone can appreciate the dilemma that he delineated so clearly. To quote his words:

> *Pan-Africanism demands an African consciousness and an African loyalty; on the other hand is the fact that each Pan-Africanist must also concern himself with the freedom and development of one of the nations of Africa.*

Confronted with the still present danger that ethnic rivalries might lead to still further subdivisions of the existing African states, it is particularly necessary for each of these states to organize economically, socially, politically, and constitutionally in the interests of its own unit, and to build a sense of common loyalty within its boundaries.

But can such necessary efforts be kept compatible with the broad Pan-African aim of the past and with the objective of African leaders to be a major factor in the moulding of international life?

A United States of Africa is not the immediate, and perhaps not the long-range objective of African states. It need not be. But it is important to note that the influence in international affairs of the African states seems in direct ratio to both their cohesiveness and their internal stability. Their influence in international relations is somewhat diminished every time one of the independent African states has an internal upheaval, or an exodus of refugees, or one African leader attacks another. The best evidence that the African states genuinely believed in the process of international adjudication when they placed the South West Africa case before the International

Court would be for them to use judicial processes or conciliation to settle the boundary and other disputes between themselves rather than making them a source for disunity and even conflict.

A major justification for increased external economic aid channelled through the agencies of the United Nations, which is a further objective of the African states, is that it will then be possible to plan regionally for most effective use of available and potential resources. Some states will always be wealthier than their neighbours, but the question is whether these differences shall be intensified by undue concentration on local needs or whether the broad interests and growth possibilities of larger areas will be used as the basis for joint planning by several African countries.

When the Organization of African Unity was established in Addis Ababa in 1963, its first purpose was clearly stated as being 'to promote the unity and solidarity of the African States'. It is their decisions alone that will determine how far this goal will be secured. My purpose is simply to point out that the more this unity and solidarity is achieved, and maintained, the greater the impact of the independent African states in international relations. Their international objectives for extension of human rights, greater equalization of the opportunities for development of all states, more influence in international affairs for the smaller states, and peaceful processes in international disputes, are both valid and far-sighted. The degree to which the independent African states themselves act according to these principles will determine in considerable measure how effectively they can persuade other states to do likewise.

CONSTRUCTIVE DISENGAGEMENT

by

B. T. G. CHIDZERO

The most phenomenal development in Africa in the last decade has been the collapse of the citadel of colonialism and, *pari passu*, the attainment of political independence by over thirty African countries. Not unexpectedly, indeed necessarily, this historic development, as yet incomplete, has suddenly presented Africa with an entirely new species of problems and challenges, while at the same time inevitably making new demands on whatever world order there was or is. It has not only placed Africa in the limelight and in a context totally different from that which existed before 1950, but, what is more, it has telescoped Africa's past, present and future problems at a period of great material expectations, rolling the many problems into one ball and bequeathing Africa the enigmatic double-face of Janus. While in itself by no stretch of the imagination the unbolting of the gateway to immediate stability and prosperity, political independence nonetheless constituted, and constitutes, the momentous and absolutely necessary assumption of the instruments of power by Africans. The alternatives are to go back to atavistic fashion, which is possible but wholly catastrophic; to stand still in passive content or in the grip of paralysis generated by too great a challenge, which is fatal; to move forward with decisiveness and resoluteness of purpose, which is the true challenge—the challenge to give political and economic substance and meaning to independence, so that freedom is at once the unleashing and harnessing of constructive human forces, the condition for establishing a new socio-economic order consonant with the continent's realities and aspirations.

Paradoxically, the attainment of political independence is both negative and positive. Negative, in so far as it necessarily connotes and must mean the removal of all forms of human bondage and foreign domination. In this sense it must destroy in order to create. Positive, for it is immediately a new challenge requiring positive confrontation in order to harness hitherto stifled energies and talents, to establish a new social order. The former, the negative, is probably the easier; it is also ephemeral, neo-colonialistic considerations notwithstanding. The latter, the positive, is the more difficult and lasting task. It clearly calls for what the Romans meant by '*virtus*'. The odds are formidable, but as a famous historian has succinctly put it: 'Ease is inimical to civilization'. By an extrapolation of Toynbee's theory, the proposition may be held that in the dialectic of nationalism and independence the constructive synthesis consists in the dynamic confrontation of a ceaseless flow of multifarious challenges on the one hand and positive responses on the other, whether at the individual, national or international level. In the process, fear or failure of positive confrontation is the negation of meaningful independence while in a positive confrontation—in grasping the nettle—realism is of the essence. This leads to the subject of this paper: 'constructive disengagement'.

In examining the concept of 'constructive disengagement', three main aspects of the question—or is it variations on a theme?—seem to suggest themselves immediately, viz.:

Severance, without creating power vacuums, of the colonial umbilical cord as a necessary condition for independence.

Individuation as a prerequisite of integration.

Resoluteness of purpose and flexibility of means.

Severance of the umbilical cord

It has been said that without colonialism most African states, as they exist today, would not be there or would have assumed completely different forms, geographically, politically and economically. Indeed, this has been said of African nationalism itself. It is European imperialism and colonialism, the geographical boundaries of which have become accepted by African states, which in no small measure have established the economic and political foundations and institutions—constructive and destructive alike—which in time led to national identities, even national idiosyncrasies. This is controversial, but it is not, of course, the same thing as saying that there are no inherent constructive forces on which African states and nationalism itself rest. Different African cultures, the pre-colonial social and political institutions such as the chieftainship, linguistic entities, inter-family links, tribal or clan affiliations, group forces deriving from common historical and cultural experiences which identify a people as a people, and in some cases even natural geographical boundaries such as rivers or mountains—these stand in their own right outside the pale of the first group of forces. Nations or states could have been born of these. And, of course, nations will grow—or grew—from family units coming together as a clan, clans joining together as tribes, tribes coming together to form larger units or nations, so that the rise of the nation state is dictated by the imperatives of co-operation in order to exploit fully the powers and the resources of smaller units which, left to themselves, could not meet the challenge of survival and defence, commerce and industry. Left to herself, without the patronising interference of colonialism, Africa too—as one or two of her countries actually did—would have arrived in time at the stage of the nation state. However, the process has at least been hastened, if not created, by colonial and imperialistic forces, and Africa has accepted the geographical confines, even the political definition, as well as the symbols and institutions, of the nation state. Disengagement must begin and had to begin here, with the cutting of the umbilical cord.

In doing so, complete isolation is impossible, and if it were possible, impracticable and undesirable, just as national absorption is suicidal. Thus a simultaneous process of breaking-up the old ties and building new relations and links, from a position of independence and self-respect, is the essence of constructive disengagement.

The old and obvious political and economic ties are either already broken or relatively unimportant. But there are still others.

Divided into three major monetary zones: Franc, Sterling, and dollar —not to mention *escudo* and *peso*, which are in a real sense appendages of the major three—Africa is further divided into foreign-controlled trade areas or zones, roughly corresponding to the monetary zones. So it is that Africa's monetary systems are often little more than adjuncts of external systems. An international monetary system in a world of harmonized development and fair trade practices is, of course, quite another thing. The world is far from it. At any rate, Africa today is mortally divided.

Extra-Africa economic groupings further divide the African continent. Thus, the European Common Market system embraces large parts of Africa, as does also the Commonwealth, and there is the trade pull of the United States of America and Japan among others.

Predominantly primary-producing, Africa as a whole is also most vulnerably trade-dependent on the outside world, to the point of over 80 per cent of her total trade. Intra-African trade remains insignificant, being barely 10 per cent of the total, and has tended to make but an unimpressive rise over the last five years.

What this means in practice is for economists to examine and say, but the observer will not be guilty of oversimplification if he should be tempted to note that it is inevitable that, with these ties, Africa's monetary and financial policies as well as trade arrangements and agreements are in the main fashioned and controlled from outside the borders of the continent.

This problem and challenge is recognized and, in good measure, is being faced—witness the actions of African countries, in concert with other developing countries, in examining the related problems and in supporting the establishment of the United Nations Conference on Trade and Development. Significant within Africa itself, are the many efforts at national reconstruction and at regional economic organizations and co-operation.[1] There is the work of the United Nations Economic Commission for Africa in the fields of development planning and co-ordination, industry and transport, inventories of natural resources, to mention only a few. The establishment of the African Development Bank and the Institute of Economic Development and Planning (Dakar) gives further evidence. There is also the work of the Organization of African Unity, whatever the shortcomings. In brief, in diverse ways, African countries together with other developing countries are seeking to establish new forms and institutions of intra-Africa as well as extra-Africa relations and co-operation, to disengage and construct at the same time. Yet the basic problem still remains real and pregnant with possibilities for exploitation, for better or for worse.

There are other ties. Ideological differences continue to plague the newly independent continent. Not infrequently African countries continue, or are constrained, for a multiplicity of reasons, to fight only the ghosts of capitalism and socialism, and all the other -isms of European vintage. Yet the business of economic and political development is a hard-headed one; the -isms can give the framework and the orientation, but they cannot be the development itself. Needless to say, Europe and America have long recognized ideological issues for what they are, even if they are not infrequently invoked for overt and covert reasons alike.

Turning to another matter, Africa's development plans, though in many cases well formulated, remain precariously dependent for their implementation on the availability of outside resources. It would take little effort, if any, to line up development plans depending for their implementation to the level of 75 per cent or more on foreign aid or finances.

However incomplete the inventories, Africa's natural resources are known for their abundance. Thus, for instance, in terms of trade Africa supplies almost 100 per cent of the world's lithium ores, 80 per cent of the world's diamonds, 75 per cent cobalt, 65 per cent cocoa beans, 60 per cent phosphates, 35 per cent copper, etc.[2] However unsatisfactory these random examples—and they refer only to trade—they are nonetheless indicative of real potentialities. The point of emphasis is that not only do the mineral and agricultural resources of Africa remain for the most part untapped, but also that, when they are tapped, they are utilized significantly more for the benefit of the outside world.

Intra-Africa communications remain minimal, in terms of rail, road and air as well as telecommunications. Many African states are most closely connected with and easier of reach from Europe, than with or from other parts of Africa. A telegram or cable from Nairobi to Accra goes via London. It takes a shorter time to fly from, say, Nairobi to London than from Nairobi to Conakry. Existing communications were constructed at a very different age and, to put it mildly, not always in the interest of Africa. Indeed, as Alioune Diop once pointedly put it: Africa goes to heaven through Europe! Greater intra-African trade, the very industrialization of Africa geared to African markets, necessarily requires more intra-Africa transport facilities and communication links. As long as these do not exist, the response to the challenge of intra-Africa trade and unity remains at the verbal level and devoid of substance. To that extent also Africa *remains engaged*, and *non-alignment* a largely *unfulfilled doctrine* and policy.

And what of cultural and linguistic differences which potentially give Africa the wealth which lies in diversity? Yet, in a real sense, English-speaking Africa tends to be closer to England and America and French-speaking Africa to France. Between the fraternal twins lies the divide of the age within the same maternal embrace.

The umbilical cord must be cut. This is a necessary condition of true independence. At the same time, however, there is the imperative and desideratum of international co-operation. In any case, independence is disastrous if it creates power vacuums which are the ideal situations for cold war and continued foreign exploitation.

Individuate to Integrate

The ties of African unity are many. They derive from the generic similarity, if not identity, of Africa's situations in respect of the historical and geographical setting, and in particular the common bitter experiences of the colonial past. They also derive from sociological and psychological factors of racial unity or feelings, despite Gabrieal Rokoungou's cry: '*Il n'y a pas de nègritude: il y a le Nègre!*' The sources of unity lie also in poverty amidst so much wealth in natural resources and the great potential African markets for African products. But unity cannot be forced, let alone brought about by the stroke of a magic wand. At any rate, there must be units before unity. In other words, it is necessary to individuate in order to integrate, or '*distinguer pour unir*', which may be rendered as 'analyse in order to synthesize'.

The two processes are, or should be, complementary, mutually self-supporting, being as it were two strands of the same process. To individuate without integrating in the African context must mean atomization and Balkanization of the continent. To integrate, without having individuated must, in the context of Africa's present problems, in particular in the absence of effective intra-African communications and in view of the persisting links and ties with the outside world, seem rather sterile. One builds with the bricks which one has, or as the Latin saying goes, *Nemo dat quod non habet*. In the process, the turning point must be reached when individuation necessarily leads to integration. It seems logical and realistic for one thing, to reckon with the facts of geography and the political and economic institutions, as established or bequeathed by colonialism, in order to individuate the nation states which have been left behind. It is necessary to cut in the first place the colonial umbilical cord, to forge new ties and evolve new institutions more immediately appropriate to each country: to give individuality and personality and an ethos, so that the people of the country concerned achieve a sense of identity, respect themselves and think and act as themselves for themselves. This is more unlikely to be achieved if they are suddenly plunged into a challenge, or challenges on a continental basis, greater than they can face or if in responding to the challenge they should feel they are being totally absorbed. This is not to say African continental unity is impossible, rather it is to say individual African states, however they may have come into existence, require in the first place to be accepted and themselves to be self-respecting and to stand in their own right. It may be said with reason that one cannot be outward-looking in a healthy sense unless one is also inward-looking. Africa's true conditions must in large measure determine the formulation of institutions which respond to those conditions within the framework of broadly accepted principles. If, for instance, the assumption is human respect and the principle equality of individuals, it does not follow that these, although of accepted universality, can only be given substance and meaning by institutions which are based on the concepts of private enterprise, liberal democracy or the two-party system, or parliamentary democracy; it is possible that the same assumption and principle can be enshrined in and vitalized by other processes and institutions. Many institutions which Africa today holds dear were thought out, formulated and fashioned in the completely different historical and social circumstances of Europe. They were imported into this continent either by the colonial masters or by African students and scholars. In the rush of events, leaving hardly any time for reflexion and experiment, Africa has for the larger part tended to accept them as if they were god-given and not man-made.

In spite of what has been said about 'individuation' and about accepting the existing African countries as building units, the very concept of the nation state itself, for instance, must be questioned. The socio-economic institutions which Africa has inherited must be examined. If upon examination and thorough analysis it is found that these institutions fit African conditions, well and good. If they do not, they should not be retained.

It is absolutely important in breaking the ties with the historical and colonial past that Africa's own history be unearthed and its culture reinstated. This is a vital part of individuation. Yet this must be within the context of modern conditions and demands. African socialism may derive from traditional family/tribal institutions and cultural values. Yet in the context of modern demands and practices, such as statutory title deeds in respect of land, trade unionism, cash economy processes and institutions, capital-intensive methods of production and the like, African socialism could never resemble the village activities and the family/tribal affiliations of old. Traditional African practices of voluntary co-operation and sharing must be preserved in their essential quality, but they must also be fitted within the modern context of organized production for economic surplus, commerce and trade, and expectations by individuals for tangible *personal* rewards and advancement.

In the process, different African countries are bound to react differently and to follow different paths. This again is a necessary aspect of individuation.

As a result of the forces of history and the relentless pressure of external forces, the continent is already a mosaic of a multiplicity of states, large and small. The process of individuation is bound to tend to aggravate this situation. That is inevitable. Yet, together but disunited, African states do not and could not constitute any force to reckon with internationally. To that extent also, there could be no real strength in non-alignment. Equally, Africa's potential economic strength will not be exploited in a situation where individuation is not married to integration. The question is not immediately one of a union, or united states of Africa. Rather it is one of African countries seeking to disengage, to break pernicious and undesirable ties with former masters, while at the same time forging new ones, based on Africa's new needs and the realization that such new ties, while inevitable, must not render impossible African independence and unity. It also must mean that positive efforts at integration have to be made on the practical basis of respect for *national* differences.

In breaking with the colonial past and in trying to individuate themselves, African states must inevitably realize that isolation could be their greatest enemy, considering the relentless forces of international economic relations and trade and the imperatives of international co-operation. There is no safety, perhaps no development, in the fastnesses of narrow nationalism and/or Africanism. For one thing, for a long time to come, Africa will require overseas aid. The risk which must be avoided here is financial or economic dependency. For another, there are the contingencies of geography which will make many African countries remain precariously dependent. Consider, for instance, the position of Lesotho, Botswana and Swaziland. These countries depend and will continue to depend largely on South Africa, although that country is the arch-enemy of Africa. Nay, Africa herself as a whole tolerates that arch-enemy on purely realistic grounds, for it is impossible at this stage to make an African assault on that racialist southern citadel. Realism then is important. Pan-Africanism must be embraced and it must act as a unifying and directing force. Yet it must never be doctrinaire; it must understand special circumstances.

In the field of international co-operation at large, the operative word is not independence but inter-dependence. The latter perhaps more than the former, calls for greater compromise and pragmatic actions. At any rate, 'disengagement', because 'constructive', calls for an outward-looking attitude on the part of all in these days of peace and progress through international co-operation. All this means practical and realistic actions. African countries having individuated themselves while integrating themselves, must at the same time be outward-looking so that they can bring their own weight to bear on international trade relations, international monetary arrangements and international political organizations. In this respect, it may be observed that it is easier to complain, denigrate and even destroy. It is quite another thing, and more difficult, to contribute in a positive manner. World organizations and institutions, such as the United Nations and the specialized agencies, were fashioned in a world which did not know Africa as it exists today. Thus, though their ideals and objectives remain valid, their structure and membership and *modus operandi* are matters which Africa can justly question and endeavour to alter or at least to revitalise. To disengage constructively must also mean to contribute positively.

The world today takes Africa on the basis of what she has been in the past more than on the basis of what she is or can be. The point must be reached when the world must take Africa on the basis of respect and equality; but the concepts of respect and equality have meaning only when the individual or the nation has substance or is truly an individual. It is not out of context to recall, *a propos* of this, the theory or policy of 'negotiating from a position of strength'. At any event, individuation must, if the disengagement is to be constructive, serve the larger purpose of international co-operation and integration.

Resoluteness

If the Republic of Guinea took the decision it did in 1958 to break clean with France, the political and historical justification and the relevant measure of success lay clearly in the preparedness of the new State to face all the consequences and to live, if necessary, in poverty in order to construct a new order and to underpin human respect and dignity. It also meant preparedness to experiment with new economic and social institutions. Whatever the consequences, once the decision was taken, honour and self-respect required that it be pursued. What the world outside Africa derides most, not without satisfaction, is hasty decisions taken without commensurate determination, and which only a few, if any, mean to carry out. The OAU decision in 1966 about Rhodesia and severance of diplomatic relations with the United Kingdom is but an isolated reminder. The cynic might be tempted, no doubt wrongly, to write a dithyramb on *Palaver: the Malady of the Struggling Giant*. However he might handle his prickly subject, he would probably remain at least within the penumbra of truth were he to add that the multiplicity of meetings and resolutions was inversely proportional to their effect, perhaps more than anywhere on this continent.

Resoluteness connotes deliberateness. It also necessarily implies an appreciation of the need to consolidate the ground gained, however limited, before further action is taken. The rash or unduly critical might be inclined to dismiss this as ineffective non-revolutionary pragmatism. Be that as it may. Consider the decision by the people of the Congo (Kinshasa) to break with their colonial masters. The decision was right and justified. Yet, realizing the formidable factors deriving from the huge geographical expanse of the country, its tribal divisions and the all-pervasive and pernicious foreign and imperialistic influences operating in that country, it was imperative to hasten slowly, even at the risk of not appearing to be truly independent, in order to consolidate stage by stage the ground gained before confronting fully the deeply entrenched forces at work. In other words, the decision had to be taken, yet in doing so there possibly was a temporary tactical *modus vivendi* somewhere which should have been adopted until inner strength had been mustered. The golden mean may not exist in fact; but certainly steadfastness and resoluteness, tempered with flexibility as to means and timing, must exist.

Like gold, Africa has to be refined through the furnace of tribulation and the diverse and perplexing circumstances and environmental difficulties which confront her today constitute her golden challenge and opportunity. These many challenges constitute the stimulus which must evoke in Africa the best she can yield. Her measure of success lies in the readiness, intensity, content and constructiveness of her response.

What is disastrous is the tendency to make hasty decisions which may be correct but which no one intends to implement. Fear of positive confrontation is as perilous as cutting the Gordian knot in too cavalier a fashion. The process of cutting the umbilical cord in order to be independent, and of individuating in order to integrate, demands resoluteness of purpose tempered with realism and flexibility of means. One is tempted to borrow Horace's words: *Fortiter in re, suaviter in mode.*

In fine it may be said, even at the risk of seeming unduly categorical, that the African situation demands the obvious but difficult and sustained exercise of constructructive disengagement: the continuous process of breaking clean in order to build anew and more firmly, of individuating in order to integrate, while balancing resoluteness with flexibility, not as to principles, as to means and timing.

Clearly, constructive disengagement is not a fixed policy and certainly not an ideology. Rather it is a question of strategy and attitude of mind.

REFERENCES

1 For example, the East Africa Common Services Organization (EACSO) which is soon to become the East African Economic Community, the Organization Afro-Malgache de Co-operation Economique (OAMCE), the Maghreb (Economic Co-operation), the Union Douaniere et Economique de l'Afrique Centrale(UDEAC). The first mentioned makes an extremely interesting study of the theory of constructive disengagement, from the colonial East African High Commission to the present arrangement which is still in the process of transformation in response to entirely new political and economic conditions following attainment of independence by all three East African countries.

2 UN Economic Commission for Africa, document E/CN.14 STC 20.

AFRICA AND THE HISTORY OF TO-MORROW

by

BASIL DAVIDSON

Anyone entrusted with the task, as I am here, of discussing what manner of relations may now evolve between Africa and the rest of the world must obviously take his courage in both hands. Yet if it is true, as I think it is, that 'history acquires meaning and objectivity only when it establishes a coherent relation between past and future'[1] then this is after all a task which has now become, even if within broad limits, at least partially possible. For it follows that the tracing of the future can depend on a proper understanding of the past, and in this respect, at any rate, we live in hopeful times. We live in times when the history of the Africans has acquired a shape and meaning, a conceptual momentum, that derive from a far better understanding of the past than any previous generation has ever had. For a number of years now, after all, we have in many ways been learning to understand 'where Africa has come from'. We have watched Africa in the process and travail of profound internal change. We can at least glimpse some of the probable routes along which Africa may now travel into a future that will be notably different from the past. So I make no apology for attempting to tread on ground that is yet to be fully revealed. If the experience can in no sense be conclusive, at least it may be interesting. With that possibility in mind I shall try to be as realistic as possible.

There are of course still those amongst us who continue to deny that the history of the Africans has yielded a dynamic, a movement, a process of its own, and for whom that history continues to resemble, as was lately said by an historian of Western Europe, 'the unrewarding gyrations of barbarous tribes in picturesque but irrelevant corners of the globe'.[2] Viewed in that light, no doubt, the African past can suggest nothing useful about the African future: one shapeless chaos could be expected to follow upon another. Perhaps the best answer to such outbursts of Eurocentrism—certainly the most courteous answer—was offered by Maurice Delafosse as many as thirty five years ago, when they were the common coin of the time. '*Certaines personnes,*' he observed, '*affirment volontiers que les peuples indigenes de l'Afrique occidentale*'—but, of course, he might have said this of almost any region of Africa—'*n'ont point d'histoire. Elles feraient preuve de plus de modestie et d'un souci plus grand de la vérité en se contentant d'avouer qu'elles ne connaissent pas l'histoire de ces peuples'*.[3] Even that today, would be a significantly generous rejoinder, since if it was undoubtedly the case, thirty-five years ago, that scholars had a large excuse for not knowing or even being able to know anything much of African history, there can be no such defence today. The past dozen years have been especially rich in scholarly research and publication bearing on the history not only of great and long-enduring kingdoms such as the one whose hospitality we enjoy at this meeting, nor of those ancient but vanished states to which Arab and Berber historians gave their attention in the time of the European Middle Ages, but also of nearly every region of this vast continent and perhaps a majority of its peoples. In many centres of learning in many parts of the world there is a clear recognition not only of the fact of African history—of its validity as a field of study on a level with any other large subject of historical research—but also of its bearing on the history of the rest of the world, and, if I may say so, on the future of the whole of humanity.

Where, then, has Africa 'come from'? What are the starting points for any sound speculation on the trajectory that Africa will now take in relation to the trajectory of other major regions of the world? How are these trajectories likely to meet and interact? Especially in this year of 1966, when so much of Africa seems to bear a puzzling and indeed disconcerting appearance, these are questions which call for serious discussion.

Historical Africa has trodden a path very much of its own. If the Neolithic and Bronze Age cultures of the north flowered five thousand years ago in the greatest of the civilizations of antiquity, in one which deeply imprinted its mark on the later cultures of the greater part of Europe and Western Asia, this Egyptian achievement had relatively little impact on the countries which lay south of the Sudanese grasslands: on all those countries, that is to say, which Europeans have generally subsumed under the convenient though often misleading label of 'tribal Africa'. These were left to work out their own destiny in an isolation from the rest of the world that was never complete but was always—or at any rate from times which are now exceedingly remote—a principal factor in their situation. Their separateness, the distinctiveness of their cultures, can of course be over-stated. It often has been. Anthropological inquiry has repeatedly shown that many aspects of their social, religious and political cultures possessed features that were comparable, sometimes closely comparable, with those of other 'tribal peoples' in other lands. Yet these comparable features—whether of belief, kinship organization, or the interweaving of the obligations of the individual with the duties of the community—took in Africa, as elsewhere, concrete forms and patterns that were shaped to ecological imperatives: in the African case, to the wilderness that the Africans were called to overcome and dominate; and they varied, accordingly, greatly in form and sometimes in content. Hence the specific nature of so much of traditional African culture.

The present state of African history in relation to these 'tribal peoples' suggests most strongly that the nexus of development, influence and invention, from which their cultural forms and patterns took their rise, was connected, persistently if no doubt indirectly, with the mastery of the use of iron. Although the data is still far from satisfactory, most of our evidence suggests that populations to the south of the Sahara, or at any rate to the south of the Sudan, were few and widely scattered before their iron age began. They appear to have consisted of rare groups which relied on hunting, fishing and the gathering of natural fruits and vegetables. Perhaps we shall never know much of their history of change and growth, or of lack of change and growth. What we do know, however, is that some of them began to use iron for tools and weapons rather more than two thousand years ago; that this departure led to, or at any rate contributed to, a notable improvement in food supplies and hence to an elementary division of labour; that populations began to settle, and, in settling, to multiply at a rate which the archaeological evidence suggests was fairly rapid. This was the period in the central and southern regions, for example, of what has been called 'the Bantu spread': of the movement and cultural diversification during the first millenium AD of populations, probably indigenous to the grassland-forest verges of the northern Congo-Niger basins and of the eastern highlands, which afterwards came to occupy the greater part of the central-southern continent.

Thanks to scientific archaeology, relying on such techniques as the dating of carbonaceous samples, we are likely during the next few years to learn a great deal more about this long epic of migration, settlement, and multiplication. As things stand today, one may broadly say that it set in motion a process of socio-political change which had led, at any rate by AD 1000, to the emergence of social and political organizations which were directly ancestral to the states and empires, as well as to the 'stateless societies', of later times. How far the critical inventions were the product of local genius or were borrowed from the Sudan, from North Africa, from the Nile Valley, may remain an open question. But whatever view one prefers to take on that point, there is no doubt that by about AD 1000 the pattern of Iron Age growth south of the Sahara had become both self-moving and original in many of its features.

It may be that the initial spur to Iron Age development came from the north. Yet there must in any case have been a great deal of local adaptation and invention. So much is clearly indicated by the comparison of a few of the better established datings. We know, for example, that the use of iron became fairly common in the lands to the north of the Sahara only in the last centuries BC: examinations of Egyptian, Berber and Meroitic grave-goods leaves little doubt on this score. But we also know that a Stone Age people in central Nigeria began smelting iron as early as the third century BC, and that other peoples, far distant in the south on the plateau lands of Zambia and Rhodesia, were doing the same only a few hundred years later. This rate of 'technological shift' over enormous and harsh geographical distances must seem extraordinarily rapid, unless one supposes that local initiative and invention were also at work. All in all, then, it seems reasonable to conclude that the history of most of the peoples of continental Africa, of inner Africa, begins as a coherent and dynamic process, having its own laws of growth, its own points of reference, its own limitations, with the outset of their Iron Age about two thousand years ago.

This Iron Age, viewed as the great central span of years in which the Africans peopled and dominated the whole of their continent, gives way to another in the late nineteenth century. Then it is that the world of science, mechanical technology, and cash production breaks violently in upon them with the consequences that we know. Between these two developments—between the initial movement and multiplication of Iron Age peoples and the invasion of the Europeans—there lies a long and complex period in which the potentialities of Iron Age culture, of a culture resting essentially on production, for subsistence and not for cash, are worked out to their greatest possible extension. This is what is really meant by the movement of history in Iron Age Africa: the continuous and expansive development of socio-political and economic processes which yet remained within the limits of production for subsistence modified only marginally by the influences of production for markets near or far. Of course there were exceptions. There were thrusting trading polities whose major effort lay in their function as middlemen between the producers of ivory and gold—Africa's most important items of export until the Atlantic slave trade of the seventeenth century—and buyers from outside Africa. There was Axum, parent of the later kingdom and empire of Ethiopia. There were ancient Ghana and its successors in the Western Sudan. There were the flourishing commercial states of the eastern and northern seaboard. Yet all of these, despite their often remarkable achievements, were in some degree peripheral to the life of the majority of Africans; and even they were largely built, in their countrysides if not in their cities, on economies of subsistence.

Herein lies the great equivocation of the African past. The picture that we can form has two sides. To anyone who has wrestled with the racist myths of African inferiority which have long bedevilled the intellectual scene of Europe, Asia and America, myths which reached their European climax in the imperialism of the late nineteenth and early twentieth centuries, and who has meditated on the nature of the African evidence, it must be perfectly clear that the cultures of Iron Age Africa represent, in their great majority, a memorable human triumph over one problem of collective survival after another. Cut off though they largely were from fruitful contact with the rest of the world, these peoples were neither dismayed nor defeated. They mastered their continent. They peopled it with expanding societies whose average standards of living would appear, for the most part, to have been perfectly adequate to their growing needs in material, moral and political equipment, and to have compared quite well, and sometimes very well, with average living standards in other continents. They invented techniques which ranged across the whole field and fury of life from the growing of food to the administration of justice; and the more we learn of these techniques the more we may respect them. Some of us, and certainly myself, have been accused of 'chanting hosannas' to this achievement: though I dislike the term, I accept the accusation with equanimity. If much of African socio-political and moral culture remains to be grasped and explained, enough is known and understood to show that its successes may indeed be regarded as a major chapter in the general history of human growth.

Yet there is another side to the picture. The Victorian engineers of European imperialism, men such as Sir Samuel Baker, had at least a part of truth on their side when they spoke so freely of 'primitive Africa'. This Africa 'of the tribes'—and even of the kingdoms—was technologically a handicraft society, materially a backward society, a society without any exact science, and consequently a society incapable of catching up with a more advanced world, much less of keeping pace with it. By the nineteenth century this was formidably clear. Almost from the time of earliest European contact with Africans south of the Sahara, back in the fifteenth century, the technological gap had been widening with every decade. If this backwardness, this developmental limitation, spared many African peoples a vast deal of the stress and suffering that were visited on their contemporaries in Europe, it also deprived the Africans of effective means of self-defence, and it placed a narrow frontier round their possibilities of productive expansion. While the leading powers of Europe pressed forward on their violent march towards hegemony across the world, the Africans (and not only the Africans) were still enclasped within organizations and attitudes which belonged to a dying past. One result of this was the ease which so many African peoples were delivered over—or delivered themselves over—to the miseries of the Atlantic slave trade. Another, still greater in its consequences, was the speed with which the European invaders of the nineteenth century were able, almost everywhere, to achieve their imperialist designs.

No doubt the detailed picture is far more complex than this. Traditional societies in Africa—tribal societies, to use the familiar term—were not incapable of self-adjustment to changing circumstances. The very nature of their history ensured as much. They were the product, after all, of a repeated adaptation to the circumstances of peopling and settling the continent in which they were formed. The records are full of examples of purposeful self-adjustment and of socio-political techniques for performing it. One needs only to think of the skill with which the trading settlements of the Swahili coast in medieval times exploited their intermediary position between the producers of the interior and the sea-merchants of the Indian Ocean, and of the directly comparable skill with which the fishing peoples of the Niger Delta did the same with regard to the Atlantic trade. Or one may point at one end of the political scale to the way in which patriarchal forms of rule in the Western Sudan gave way to bureaucratic forms of rule, and, at the other end of the scale, to the methods by which 'stateless societies' permitted kinship units to break away and form new societies. Fuller knowledge will confirm, I think, that traditional African society was never stagnant within given forms, but always changing, adapting, throwing out new initiatives into a different future. Behind their primitive technological equipments, these were cultures of persistent flexibility and inner transformation.

Yet the technological equipments, judged mechanically, productively, were undoubtedly primitive when compared with those of much of Europe and Asia. Not only that: built into traditional society, and stronger than its capacity for change and self-adjustment, there was also an innate conservatism which was itself the guarantee of survival. If most African peoples had succeeded in working out an effective balance between themselves and the lands in which they lived, this was a balance which depended on keeping to its rules. Any breaking with the rules might bring disaster. Hence the capacity for self-adjustment, which often gave these societies within themselves a remarkable ability to shift and change, was always countered by a conservatism which tended, still more persistently, to hold back the new in favour of the old.

These various achievements and limitations have been reflected in the differing relationships, whether political, economic, or ideological, that have evolved between Africa and the rest of the world. The Europeans who launched or participated in voyages of exploration after the middle of the fifteenth century had few or no preconceptions about African inferiority. If strange tales were told about 'the land of the Negroes', so were they also told of almost every other distant land. If Africans had begun to appear in medieval Europe as slaves, it was not therefore concluded (as it would be in later times) that Africans were somehow designed by Providence for servile labour. Countless Europeans likewise laboured as slaves or were exported as slaves: Europeans in this respect were manifestly on a level with Africans and Asians. Between ruling powers and potentates in Europe and Africa, moreover, the general sentiment was one of rivalry in power, authority and respect; and the records of the fifteenth and sixteenth centuries are full of proofs that this was so. For a long time, in other words, the effective relations between Africa and the rest of the world were relations of equality. Atlantic Europeans, like Indian Ocean Asians before them, might have the upper hand in maritime skill and naval technology: on land, the Africans remained the masters of their fate. Even where Europeans were able to establish footholds by assault and battery, as the Portuguese succeeded in doing along the east coast after 1500, their power was never more than strictly local, and was always fragile.

These relations of equality began to change before the sixteenth century was over. Not by any sudden shift or revolution, but gradually, persistently, as the leading peoples of Western Europe moved into new forms of productive and military powers, and, in doing so, excluded new attitudes. While much more research into these matters is required before any firm conclusions can be reached, it appears that the dominant ideology of Europe had begun to accept notions of African inferiority by at any rate the seventeenth century. Thereafter the influences of the Atlantic slave trade worked steadily towards the fostering of racist beliefs based on 'white superiority'; meanwhile, the real gap in productive power, in organizational power, gave a plausible basis for the Eurocentrism which was to dominate the nineteenth century and the colonial period. Africa became the 'Dark Continent', and its peoples the 'adult children' who were seemingly 'unable to grow up' in the eyes of colonizers whose technological supremacy was now so great as to appear, and sometimes not only to themselves, an almost inherent attribute. Slaves abroad, the Africans were now enslaved at home, and Nature, it was said, had given her consent.

But now, in our own day? Many of the racist myths are in retreat. If colour prejudice amounting to hysteria still remains powerful in the minds of many peoples, and crudely violent among certain white minorities, it is at least widely condemned. Politically, ideologically, the renaissance of Africa has had its profound and healing effect on a world distorted by old wars and superstitions. Much of Africa stands today in the same resolute posture of independence as in earlier times. The voice of its leaders and its governments is listened to attentively, whether at the United Nations or in other great councils of world opinion. The nature of African history and humanity is increasingly studied and given its rightful position in the ranks of human existence and endeavour. Even in a period suspicious of the word, and no doubt with good reason, all this can unquestionably be regarded as progress. After an absence, the Africans are restored to their place in the family of mankind: the great island of the 'Dark Continent' is once more part of the main.

Yet the central equivocation is still there. Though politically independent, the states of Africa remain dangerously vulnerable to upset from within or indirect domination from without. They do not enjoy the kind of independence which can give them the inherent equality of power and influence towards which their peoples understandably aspire. And they cannot enjoy this influence, achieve a new stability, readjust successfully to the modern world and fight off the dangers of a new subservience that threaten them, until they overcome the technological backwardness which they inherit from the past. It is here that we reach the essential question. Under what conditions of structural change can Africa—can the states of Africa, whether singly or collectively—complete this political independence, this often quite nominal independence, by the real independence which, in the last analysis, deals only in terms of productive power?

Historically, a choice is now imposed. Either to rest content with a political independence whose reality, given the forces now at work in the world, is likely to become increasingly frail or merely formal; or else to buttress and constantly reinforce this political independence by structural changes which can yield an ever-growing socio-economic capacity for self-development and thus for self-defence. Either a satellite Africa aping its 'betters', in other words, or a sovereign Africa striking out on new paths which can only be revolutionary in content, no matter what they may seem to be in form. This of course is the choice imposed on the whole of the so-called 'developing world'; and its constructive resolution may represent the greatest problem now facing humanity. Hazardously difficult in any case, this resolution is rendered more so by the ideological condition of the world today. Africa regains her political independence at a time when the most powerful nations of the globe are locked in what may yet prove to be a mortal combat between the poor countries and the rich countries. No previous 'world problem' has ever possessed such explosive force. From every side there come shouts of militant advice, threats of reprisal, warnings of doom, invitations to suicide; and the screaming of the bombs in Vietnam today is only another indication of the perils that lie ahead. At the very moment when Africans must undertake their structural revolution—or accept another period of tutelage—the conditions for undertaking it are rendered more difficult than ever.

But the central fact remains clear. However persistently the actions of the rest of the world may bear on Africa—and we have lately had some grim examples in the Congo, in the Portuguese colonies, in southern Africa—it is the actions of the Africans that will be decisive. The kind of relations which will now grow up between Africa and the rest of the world will depend, in other words, for better or for worse on the actions which the Africans take, or fail to take, in attempting their necessary transition from traditional society, subsistence-based society, to the modern society of cash exchange, mechanical production, scientific growth, and wide popular involvement in purposive national effort. Over what critical period of time? Within what kind of span of years will the issue be decided? One may well pose the question, however doubtful the answer. Personally, it seems to me that the next ten years or so are going to be of crucial importance in settling whether or not the Africans, in their great majority, will or will not achieve the genuine sovereignty they desire. A wider measure of the basic problem of structural change was lately offered by Mr. Surendra Patel of the UN Economic Commission. Reviewing comparative rates of production in the world's industrialized countries and in Africa, he suggested that 'a *per capita* growth rate of five per cent, maintained for 40 or 50 years, or only an adult's lifetime', could raise African productive levels to those which the advanced countries have achieved today.[4] The problem would then be to apply such policies of productive change as can, within a single lifetime, give Africa the socio-economic power base—the power base of large masses of men and women working coherently in new directions, at new skills, within relations of co-operation and common effort—on which international relations of genuine equality and mutual respect may be built between this continent and the rest of the world.

If this could be achieved, perhaps by AD 2020, that would indeed be a brilliant success; and the health of much more than Africa would have changed radically for the better. It is around a challenge of this order, it seems to me, that flint-hard meditation and agitation are now required. In one sense, the very strength of traditional Africa, its safeguarding conservatism, now becomes its greatest weakness. In another sense, the very circumstances of decolonization have added to the difficulties of constructive change. They have imposed, for example, the liberative concept of the nation-state, creative of many values such as those of collective identity, corporate solidarity within familiar frontiers, and to some extent a framework for cultural self-expression, but yet, at the same time, destructive of many other values which may now prove more important to the progress of the Africans: destructive of rational planning among many peoples faced with identical problems, destructive of common action in a continent desperately in need of common action, destructive of the wider solidarity which so many Africans—as the enterprise of the OAU most clearly shows—now ardently desire. The concept of the nation-state has greatly helped to liberate Africa, but can it go on doing so?

One may ask the same question in other fields. One may ask it of the concept of rule by an élite. It is extremely difficult to see how the African independence struggle could have been carried to success without the leadership of Africa's educated minorities, privileged minorities. They it was who raised the flag of national liberation and carried it forward, often at bitter cost to themselves; who studied the colonial situation and learned how to make their cause prevail; who spoke for the non-literate millions and found ways of drawing them to action. Yet given the lessons of the past half-dozen years in most African countries—and in this great continent there will always be exceptions—it is no less difficult to see how the necessary structural transitions, democratic transitions, can now be carried through while élites remain in postures of automatic power and privilege over against the millions whom they have led. For the root problem of achieving relations of genuine equality with the rest of the world lies inescapably in modernizing, industrializing, mechanizing, re-educating—in a word, culturally revolutionizing—not only *the urban minorities* of Africa but also and above all *the rural multitudes*. Only an heroic leadership, willing to throw everything into the scales, will achieve an impact of that order.

Even so, by what particular means? The rest of the world, as we well know, is not short with its advice. Yet the advice, even if disinterested, which is much to say, seems hard to follow. As generally presented, the alternative solutions are not exactly helpful. The Russians and the Chinese, for example, have solved or are tackling their problems of technological backwardness by forms of socialist reorganization. Yet these have had to pass through long years of adaptation to the actual conditions of those countries. What are the adaptations which Africa must require? Remarkably little thought appears to have been given to this basic question.

Meanwhile the offerings from the other side seem patently discouraging. The brilliance of capitalist achievement in some Western European countries and the United States of America comes only after long decades of bitter internal conflict and sectional warfare, by no means altogether ended. Are the Africans now expected to pass through a similar period of minority dictatorship, of acute social stratification ? And, if so, does anyone seriously believe that the structures of African society, a society without social stratification, will allow this to happen willingly ?

I have dwelt on the difficulties of transition. Yet to conclude on a defeatist note would not only be unpalatable: it would also, I suggest, be false to the totality of facts and possibilities which have comprised, and continue to comprise, the African renaissance of the twentieth century. Over the past few decades the Africans have enormously influenced the course of their relationships with the rest of the world, and they have done this, repeatedly, out of the resources of their own thought and courage, self-confidence and capacity for original action. Through the years of decolonization their best leaders have persistently found ways of buttressing Africa's claim to a destiny of her own. None of the ideological turmoil and political upheaval which now beset so many of her countries can be a surprise or even a discouragement to anyone prepared to look with the eye of understanding. What would be truly discouraging, on the contrary, would be a position in which newly independent countries followed meekly along conventional paths chosen by others: then indeed one might fear that the dismal fate of certain Latin-American countries, unfolded over the past hundred years, might be reserved for Africa as well. As it is, the very dimensions of Africa's current crisis of social structures, of political institutions, of priorities and aims, are themselves some measure of the search that is now going on, however variously and confusedly, for new and indigenous solutions. And even today, at this early phase of post-colonial transformation, several pointers seem to emerge. One is that rule by a class-stratified élite within the frontiers of a nation-state has probably exhausted its possibilities of progress and even of a minimal stability. Another is that the traditional socio-economic structures of the industrialized, capitalist West cannot now be successfully transplanted to the greater part of Africa. New and more democratic structures are required for further growth. To devise these structures is the greatest task lying before Africa's peoples today.

Equality of status can follow only upon equality of power; and equality of power can arise only from far-reaching transformations in every field of life. These transformations, in the minds and attitudes of men as well as in the works of men, can be effected only in the measure that Africans prove able to achieve and conserve a sufficient freedom of action—a sufficient neutrality, a sufficient refusal to follow without question—so as to allow them to penetrate the hard reality of their own situation, so as to reach their own conclusions, about what may best be done. Africa needs her own revolution, her own releasing of the energies of her millions.

Without it, she will remain a pawn. With it, she will fulfil the hopes of all those, who, yesterday and today, have looked and still look for a new continent tomorrow.

REFERENCES

1 E. H. Carr, *What is History*, London, 1961.

2 H. Trevor-Roper, 'The Rise of Christian Europe,' *The Listener* London Nov. 28, 1963, p. 871.

3 M. Delafosse, *Histoire de l'Afrique Occidentale Francaise etc.* London, 1931.

4 S. J. Patel, 'Economic Transition in Africa', *The Journal of Modern African Studies*, Cambridge, vol. 2, number 3, esp. pp. 336-8.

THE GROWTH OF AFRICA'S FOREIGN POLICY: FROM ILLUSION TO REALITY

by

COLIN LEGUM

The time for purring is past: for Africa purring with pleasure at the speed with which new States have been erupting all over the continent; for the Western Powers purring with satisfaction at the British, French and Belgian policies of liquidating their colonial empires, and at the goodwill this has earned for their side; and for the Communist countries purring happily at the prospect of friendships with peoples previously kept from their ken. All this purring was pleasant while it lasted; but it disguised the hard realities of the real nature of power in international politics. Today, nobody should any longer doubt that Africa's standing in the eyes of the world is lower than it was in 1960 or even in 1963—the year that witnessed the birth of the Organization of African Unity. More important, Africa's standing in its own eyes is much lower.

Africa has been fed, and has fed itself, on illusions for almost a decade: a decade in which optimism was often a substitute for policy; in which resolutions and conferences were too often a substitute for decision-making; in which attacks on external enemies were not infrequently an excuse for not facing up to unpalatable home truths.

Africa imagined itself to be strong because it liked to think of itself as being strong. It enjoyed being courted by the West and by the East. But it confused the extent to which its *influence* on international affairs could be converted into actual *power* at the points where its desires and interests conflicted with those of the major Power blocs. Africa's 'one-man-one-vote' at the United Nations enabled resolutions to be carried; yet not even a two-third majority of the General Assembly could successfully force international action against the wishes of the two super-Powers.

The road from a world of illusions to a world of reality has been deeply rutted by disappointments, setbacks and frustrations: of military coups and counter-coups, plots and counter-plots; of unfulfilled economic targets, mounting national indebtedness, disappointing results from aid programmes, growing imbalances of trade; of schools without enough qualified teachers, and children without schools; of land with too many peasants, and towns with too many landless peasants; and of *white supremacy* regimes still firmly embedded in vital areas on the continent.

The negative tally is dismally long even when set against the not inconsiderable positive achievements: but there is no value in trying to strike a balance between positive achievements and unfulfilled aspirations; for whichever way the balance is struck the inescapable reality is that Africa is very far still from achieving the kind of progress necessary to make an economic reality of its independence, to fulfil the essential needs of its peoples, and to exercise power in international affairs commensurate with its resources and importance. *Importance* is of course a relative term. In international politics a country, an alliance or a continent is only as important as its capacity to convert its influence and resources into effective power.

The weakness of African power cannot be denied; it is as obvious to the big powers and to the *white supremacies* in Africa as it is to Africans themselves. Today, when people in important places are asked to consider the possible repercussions of a planned course of action on African opinion, they tend to flick their fingers in contemptuous dismissal of the question. It may be an unpleasant fact to record; but it is as well to face it.

Over the last decade or so Africa has evolved a distinctive foreign policy of its own; it is now engaged in the much more difficult task of discovering how to make this policy effective. Realism dictates a policy which accepts, for the foreseeable future, that the strength of Africa's power will not be sufficient, on its own, to defend or achieve all its essential interests. Africa will therefore have to decide how it can increase its effective power to achieve particular objectives. This it can do through alliances of interests, or of convenience. Thus, on particular questions, it might link up with one or more of the Western Powers, or with one or more of the Communist Powers; on broad principles it might find added strength through alliances within the Third World complex. But the success of such temporary alliances will inevitably be affected by the actual strength of Africa itself, and this will largely be determined by the measure of unity or disunity within the continent.

The purpose of this essay is to examine in the field of foreign policy what Africa's experience has been, thus far, in trying to place itself firmly in the modern world. For Africa and the world this has been an entirely novel experience; never before has Africa, as a collective entity, played a significant role on the world stage. Two of its politico-cultural groups—the Egyptians and the Moors—did of course make their impact on the world scene at widely different periods, and Ethiopia has for centuries stood as a bastion against foreign foes; but for the rest, whenever Africa was engaged on the world scene, it was always as the victim and never as the agent of international forces. Its role was that of the world's underdog. Down the centuries coloured people everywhere—and especially black people—have been looked down upon and treated as inferiors. It is no surprise therefore that a major determinant in forming Africa's foreign policy has been a fierce desire to abolish completely the age-old international relationship between superior and inferior by redressing the balance between Africa and its former dominators.

Africa's demand to be accepted as an equal by other peoples of the world is not just an emotional urge, a begging for favours to be conferred by others: it is a positive assertion by Africans of their belief in their own capacities. Others may still think Africans incapable of making real their claims to equality: Africans have no such doubts. This crucial element in Africa's foreign policy expresses itself in practice as an assertion of the right to untrammelled political independence. But the difficulty has been now to defend this right in conditions of economic non-independence—the general fate of the continent—more especially in view of the close integration of African economic systems into the Western economy. To stand up to the West would weaken or destroy Africa's hopes for development; not to do so could injure its political independence. This dilemma has produced tension at the centre of Africa's foreign policy; it often inhibits freedom to act independently, even tough individual African states have tried to do so on a number of occasions. It also poses a sharp challenge to Africa to find ways of cutting the umbilical cord attaching it to Europe without damaging its own belly.

Africa's foreign policy has evolved as a direct response to three sets of challenges: its internal circumstances at the time of independence; its external relations with the former colonial powers; and the impact on itself of a divided world engaged in a nuclear race. It was Africa's fate that it was required to find its feet in the international community at one of the most dangerous and complicated periods in all history.

In the 1950's Western colonialism was heavily on the retreat, but not yet fully so: its off-shoots in Southern Africa were in no mood to move with the times. Two super-powers—the United States and Russia—were engaged in a highly dangerous Cold War, with nuclear weapons as the pawns in play. China was waiting in the wings to assert its own independent role: Peking's challenge, when it came, not only polarized the Communist world; it added a third dimension to international divisions, thereby immensely complicating the already difficult task of maintaining world stability, while adding to the competitive forces operating on Africa. In the struggle for a new balance of world power between the West, the Russians and the Chinese, Africa came to assume a role of special importance—along with South-East Asia and Latin America. Africa was courted, flattered, tempted, and sometimes pressurized. Overt efforts to get African States to side with one or other of the three world forces put a heavy strain on their African allegiances. The counter-force to these external influences was provided by Pan-Africanism.

A further complicating international factor faced Africa: it came to independence at a time when the great industrial nations stood poised on the threshold of an era of unparalleled affluence. But Africa was debarred at the outset from participating in this affluence because—in common with other regions with a long colonial experience—it lacked three of the basic requirements for a scientific and technological revolution: industrialization, universal education, widespread university and technical training. Thus Africa found itself automatically placed on one side of the modern international division between rich and poor nations. Its foreign policy was in considerable measure influenced by this division, which was responsible for the birth of the nebulous Third World concept.

Paralleling this development of *have* and *have-not* nations, was the emergence from colonialism of an independent Asia just ahead of Africa. This produced a natural sense of Afro-Asian soldiarity, characterized by the 'Bandung spirit'; and this provided another determinant of Africa's foreign policy. Political writers, and some politicians, have frequently made the error of writing about the Afro-Asian group as a 'bloc' which it never was. But even those who did not confuse the Afro-Asian 'alliance of interests' with 'bloc' politics, often tended to overestimate the strength and durability of this alliance.

Although Africa's foreign policy favoured an association with Asia—in conformity with the Bandung Declaration—it did not give a very high priority to such an alliance, except in two spheres—the United Nations and the UN Conference on Trade and Developments (UNCTAD). The African group at the UN worked closely with the Asian group in mobilizing support behind policies of mutual interest such as the ending of colonialism, non-interference by the major powers in Africa and Asia, the ending of nuclear tests, problems of world trade and aid, etc. On these questions a large measure of agreement was possible, and collective pressure was useful on a number of occasions in checking the super-powers. Common interests however, were most strongly shared in UNCTAD where the 'Group of 77' formed at the Geneva conference in 1964, was decisive in getting the major powers to consider seriously demands for reforms in international trade and aid along lines advocated by the *have-nots*. It has since then grown both in size and effectiveness. However, the 'Bandung spirit' was itself sadly damaged by the Indo-China war, the Indo-Pakistani conflict, and by Indonesia's confrontation with Malaysia. These blew away some of the frothy illusions about the effective potentialities of the Afro-Asian group, especially when its internal politics became an active threat to Africa's foreign policy. This threat was felt particularly strongly in 1964 as a result of China's forcing techniques in developing its strategy for a Third World bloc of Afro-Asian-Latin American States in open rivalry to the two super-Powers. This Chinese policy intensified the tensions within the Afro-Asian group by injecting Sino-Soviet rivalries into its affairs. The calamitous failure of the 'second Bandung' conference, scheduled for Algiers at the end of 1964, did immense damage to effective Afro-Asian cooperation.

Africa's foreign policy, in fact, runs counter to China's ideas for a Third World bloc on two fundamental points—in its repudiation of an open conflict with either or both of the super-powers; and in its refusal to take sides in such international entanglements as are raised by Sino-Soviet rivalries. These attitudes flow directly from the importance attached by Africa's foreign policy to the value of non-alignment. At a time when a number of the Asian signatories to the Bandung Declaration were moving further away from the practice of non-alignment, Africa was moving steadily towards making it more real. Even though all African states do not equally rigidly apply non-alignment, the general tendency has nevertheless been towards a strengthening of its practice. Non-alignment meets the mood and interests of post-colonial Africa on almost every score: its thrust has been accordingly stronger than the countervailing tendencies of individual African states.

Non-alignment in an African context is not so much a policy as an approach to policy-making. It defines the spirit in which Africa approaches particular world problems requiring African decisions. Non-alignment is not a careful balancing-act; it is not concerned with striking a comfortable balance between international rivals. It is concerned with judging issues on their individual merits and in terms of Africa's own interests. As practised in Africa, non-alignment is neither particularly moral nor opportunistic. As one writer has described it, Africa adopted non-alignment 'as the result of cool calculations of the advantages and disadvantages, political, economic and psychological, of aligning with one of the major blocs compared with those of non-alignment.' Africa can claim a defensible interest in exploiting the existence of international rivalries to obtain benefits which otherwise it would be too weak to obtain by itself. This is neither cynicism nor opportunism; it is realism.

Africa's interests are, after all, not identical with those of the dominant powers, even if they do sometimes coincide on major issues such as the prevention of nuclear warfare or halting major conflicts. But in most cases its interests are either different from, or even in conflict with, those of the major powers. These can have no special desire to assist in Africa's rapid industrialization or technological development; they certainly have no interest in altering the balance in world trade to suit Africa's needs; and none of the major powers has given a high priority in their foreign policies to ridding Africa of its *white supremacy* regimes.

An essential feature of Africa's foreign policy has been to harness the rest of the world to its own objectives whenever possible. One of the effective ways of promoting these objectives has been to exploit to its own advantage the foreign rivalries for Africa's friendship—or what might be better described as the desire for 'special relationships' with Africa. The objectives of African policy are easily stated. Firstly, the liquidation of colonialism and alien rule, including *white supremacy*, in the continent. Secondly, the defence of the national sovereignty of every independent African state, as well as of the sovereignty of Africa as a whole. Thirdly, the promotion of the independent economies of Africa as rapidly as possible.

The fundamental reality facing Africa in pursuit of these objectives is the economic weakness and balkanized condition of the continent at the end of its colonial era. Balkanization is itself not the fault of colonialism; in fact, colonialism contributed directly, if not intentionally, towards reducing the hundreds of autonomous or semi-autonomous kingdoms, states and tribal units to approximately fifty. But even fifty is too large for a continent with a population of about 270 millions. The real extent of Africa's fragmentation is simply illustrated by a breakdown of its population distribution. Over one-third of the total population lives in Africa's three numerically largest countries (Nigeria, the United Arab Republic and Ethiopia). Thus fewer than 180 million peoples are divided among the other 47 States: an average of under four million to each country. But even this figure is misleading because another third of the population live in the eight second largest countries (Congo-Kinshasa, South Africa, the Sudan, Algeria, Morocco, Tanzania, Kenya and Ghana). This leaves fewer than 90 millions shared among the remaining 40 or so countries; of these only 14 possess populations ranging between three million and six million. The rest are all below a million. This set of figures is more important than any other in measuring the actual problems and needs of Africa. What chance is there of the continent producing real economic and industrial growth, or of developing a proper security system, when the great majority of new African states is no larger in population size than a single important city in a major industrial country? Moreover, the populations are often spread over areas as large as several industrial countries put together. The conditions produced by this degree of balkanization guarantee permanent poverty and insecurity.

Until Africa succeeds in establishing a new African order capable of promoting effective economic and political co-operation and of keeping intra-state disputes to manageable proportions its future is bleak. Yet, Africa cannot afford to wait until the continent one day produces either a a single political system (as envisaged by Nkrumahists) or a system of fully integrated economic and political institutions (as envisaged by Pan-African functionalists). Its battles for economic independence, for political stability, for peace along its internal frontiers and for the exclusion of alien forces cannot be postponed. If, in the meantime, it should lose too many of these battles the inevitable result will be to make its conditions of balkanization and dependency more permanent. It is vital, therefore, that Africa should promote the rapid formation of regional economic and political groups associated together within a transitional type of organization endowed with more policy-making and executive authority than the OAU now possesses. Against the argument that this is a second-best solution, one can only say that it is more realistic to suppose that an approach of this kind will produce a moderately effective Pan-African organization than an uncompromising demand for total economic or political unification. After all, the Nkrumahist approach to Pan-Africanism has not failed, so far, for want of passionate, informed and urgent advocacy.

Nevertheless Pan-Africanism must remain the real priority of Africa's foreign policy. Theoretically, at least, it has been given the priority by a majority of African governments; but in practice the commitment remains a nominal one. *Emotionally* the majority are for it; *logically* they are for it; *rhetorically* they are for it; *intellectually* they are for it, but in sum, their reservations are more important than their commitment. Acknowledging this fact is to come closer to reality than to foster illusions about the effectiveness of Pan-Africanism thus far.

The creation of the OAU at the historic conference in Addis Ababa in May 1963, was an event of outstanding significance. The immediate effect was to raise Africa's morale to its highest point yet, and to cause the outside world to take seriously the possibility of a united (if not unified) Africa. Since 1963 the success or failure of the OAU has been the major factor in determining the effectiveness of Africa's foreign policy. Though perhaps not the popular thing to say, it is nonetheless true that the OAU has not yet proved itself to be capable of effective action, or even of survival. It represents a start in the practical application of Pan-Africanism, but it has not advanced anywhere near as fast as the challenges to Africa's unity require it to do. That it exists at all is admittedly an important gain, not only symbolically but practically. It has proved its value as a vehicle for con-conciliation in intra-African conflicts, but not yet for solving them. It has given valuable help to some of the African liberation movements, especially in the Portuguese colonial territories. It has promoted the exploration, if not the implementation, of ideas for functional co-operation on a continental scale. It has contributed towards plans for regional economic co-operation largely in association with the Economic Commission for Africa. It has brought African leaders together and taught them about each other and about each other's problems in a way that would not otherwise have been possible. (Nigeria's greatly revered figure, the late Sir Abubakar Tafawa Balewa, once told me that this was the OAU's greatest contribution to date). It has also provided Africa with a single voice in world affairs. These are no mean achievements, and it would be wrong to minimize their value or their impact on African and world affairs; but it would be equally wrong to over-estimate the OAU's achievements, or its present capacity for effective action. It badly needs revitalizing if it is not simply to become a husk of its early promise or of its real potentialities. No useful service is performed by treating the OAU as a sacred cow: sacred cows often end up as expensive white elephants!

The remainder of this essay is devoted to considering in some detail Africa's experience in facing two challenges to its right to control the continent's destiny without foreign intervention. This right rests on the principle that the whole continent is a sphere of African interest in much the same way as the Monroe doctrine applied to the Americas, and Soviet policy to Eastern Europe; but there are crucial differences. Firstly, Africa's policy rests on voluntary and mutually accepted obligations by all the signatories to the OAU; neither the Latin American States nor those of Eastern Europe had any real choice about whether or not they wished to become part of their own security systems: the experiences of Cuba and the Dominican Republic are reminders of the dominant role which the US retains to itself in interpreting the Monroe Doctrine, as operated through the Organization of American States; while the experiences of Hungary and Yugoslavia illustrate Russia's wish to dominate developments within its own sphere of interest. These events also illustrate a second difference: the dominant role played by each of the super-Powers in maintaining collective security within its own sphere. This gives them the advantage of centralized decision-making when vital decisions are required—notwithstanding the treaty provisions of the OAS and Warsaw Pact. In Africa's case no single Power, or even nucleus of Powers, is capable of enforcing its own decisions; decision-making remains pluralistic, and power is diffuse. The third difference of course is that military and economic power in Africa does not measure up to its commitment to protect its sphere of interest against antagonistic elements. The fourth difference is that Africa contains within its sphere of interest five undefeated elements of the very alien Power to which it is committed to denying a foothold. These elements —the Portuguese presence in Mozambique, Angola and Portuguese Guinea; the Spanish element in North Africa and in West Africa; the British colony of Rhodesia; and South Africa with its appendage, the trusteeship territory of South West Africa—are hangovers from the colonial past: as such they represent 'the unfinished African revolution'.

Each of these alien elements present a different kind of challenge to Africa's foreign policy. The least important is that of Spain. Apart from Morocco and to a much smaller extent Nigeria, no African country has a special national interest which would justify priority being given to the elimination of the Spanish element.

The Portuguese—by maintaining the myth that its territories are part of the European motherland in the same way as the French once stubbornly insisted on the policy of '*Algerie Francaise*'—have invited an armed struggle to destroy its myth. This armed struggle is now in progress with varying degrees of success; but of the outcome there can be no doubt. Portugal has neither the resources nor the allies to avert defeat; it is only a question of time and of how much Portugal must bleed and destroy in defence of its myth. Africa's foreign policy towards the Portuguese element is expressed in four ways: open support for the liberation movements in the Portuguese colonies; active pressure against Portugal in the UN and through international organizations; suspension of African diplomatic links with Lisbon; and diplomatic pressure on Portugal's NATO allies to exercise their influence on the Salazar regime.

The third alien element is Rhodesia—Britain's last important colonial responsibility in Africa; here Britain and Africa are faced with a rebellion in support of the ideology of *white supremacy*. Africa's response to this challenge will be considered presently.

The fourth element is the Republic of South Africa, which is not only the strongest outpost of *white supremacy* on the continent but economically and militarily the most powerful state in Africa. In Africa's present circumstances, South Africa cannot be destroyed by the collective military and economic forces of the rest of the continent put together. This is the kernel of the racial crisis in Africa. For the foreseeable future, South Africa can only be weakened by an internal liberation movement capable of achieving the thrust developed by the FLN in Algeria; but such a struggle is impracticable as long as the apartheid Republic's neighbouring territories are controlled by elements hostile to Africa's foreign policy. This gives added urgency to the problems of liberating the Portuguese territories (especially Mozambique), Rhodesia and South West Africa. Their submission to the 'African revolution' is an essential requisite for the success of an effective liberation movement in South Africa. But a violent struggle is not the only method favoured by the OAU for the destruction of the apartheid regime: its preference is for collective international action in support of a blockade of South Africa. But this aim can be achieved only with the support of the major Western Powers. For reasons of national interest the Western powers—notably Britain and the US—are not willing to support international action against South Africa through the UN. This Western unwillingness to share the priorities of African foreign policy is the major source of tension between Africa and the West. These tensions are bound to increase the longer the crisis in relations between Africa, South Africa and the West lasts—and in direct proportion to the sense of frustration and importance felt by the concert of African States over their powerlessness to make real their aspiration to establish control over their own sphere of interest. In this crisis lies the greatest single source of danger to race relations in Africa, to the West's interests in Africa, and eventually, too, to international peace. It is not often that one can detect so clearly the origins of a major international conflict as one can over this triangular engagement.

A major obstacle to mobilizing full support for Africa's foreign policy is the difficulty of getting agreement between OAU members when confronted with acute crises involving one or more Western Powers. Disagreements mostly have less to do with objectives than with tactics: the reasons are varied—sometimes it's a case of protecting the side on which one's bread is buttered; often it's due to genuine differences about methods or timing. Whenever these divisions occur the immediate result is the temporary collapse of effective African unity; a resultant rise in intra-African tensions; and intensified suspicions of the West due largely to the externalization of these painful internal tensions.

The OAU's response to two major challenges to its authority—the 1964 Congo crisis and the 1965 Rhodesian rebellion—show its powerlessness as yet to make real its claim to protecting its sphere of interest in Africa.

Concern in the OAU about the Congo was caused by Mr Moise Tshombe's assumption of the premiership from Mr Cyrille Adulla in September 1964. Many saw this development as an attempt by certain foreign interests to intervene in the Congo's internal affairs. Their fears were increased by two developments. The first was Mr Tshombe's decision to rely on white mercenaries (many of them South Africans) to put down the rebellion—an action deeply insulting to African dignity and policy. The second was America's decision to supply transport aircraft and personnel to the Congolese forces, in addition to providing anti-Castro Cuban pilots (through a disguised agency) to fly the planes. Tshombe, relying heavily on Belgo-American support, turned to find allies in Africa. At the same time the rebels also sought African allies and foreign military support to offset Tshombe's Western aid: this they got first from China and later from Russia and from Cuba—the latter did so in revenge for the use of anti-Castro pilots; the Cuban reaction stirred the Americans to further action! African governments, which had been among the first to protest at American aid for the Kasavubu-Tshombe government, in their turn became the first to agree to facilitate the transport of Chinese and Russian arms and Cuban recruits to redress the balance in foreign military aid. In this way those leaders most strenuously committed to resisting foreign intervention in Africa's affairs, chose as a matter of deliberate policy to escalate foreign military aid on the ground that this was the only means available to them to increase their power to stop Mr Tshombe. The confrontation between Tshombe's supporters and his opponents reached its climax on November 24, 1964 with the Kisangani (Stanleyville) paratroop drop when American and Belgian forces, in defiance of strong African protests, carried out their humanitarian operation.

The controversy over this 'drop' was not so much over the issue of saving white lives, but over two points: whether the 'drop' was in fact designed primarily to save human lives or to facilitate the mercenaries' advance on Kisangani, the seat of the rebel government; and whether this priority should have been set for saving white rather than black lives. On these issues African attitudes diverged; but whatever the merits of this particular controversy, the Kisangani 'drop' left Africa's foreign policy transparently naked. There was nothing it could do to dissuade the West: and it was helpless to stop white paratroopers dropping on African soil. The 'Hands off Africa' policy took a heavy knock; so did African illusions about its influence and power.

In the short run Tshombe won; the rebellion disintegrated into a pathetic shambles; and Africa stood divided and ineffectual in preventing foreign intervention in an internal African conflict. But in the slightly longer run Tshombe lost—not because of external pressures but because he had upset the forces inside the Congo.

The Congo crisis of 1964 raised a number of important questions for Africa's foreign policy. First, how realistic is it for the OAU to challenge the domestic right of a member-state to change its leaders even though such changes may be unconstitutional, or even if assisted by foreign elements? Second, what can the OAU do to prevent changes which may involve interference in its sphere of interest? Third, what role can the OAU play when it fails to establish a sufficiently strong consensus in support of collective action? Fourth, what real sanctions does the OAU possess to deter or repel major powers from defying its wishes?

The African imbroglio in the 1964 Congo crisis does not provide simple answers to these questions. While it is true that Mr Tshombe's policies and methods were widely felt to imperil the objectives of the OAU, his assumption of the premiership was endorsed by President Kasavubu who was recognized by the OAU as the legitimate constitutional head of the Congo government. President Kasavubu and Mr Tshombe could therefore legitimately remind the OAU (as they did) of the principle in its Charter providing for non-intervention in the internal affairs of member-States. It was this issue which divided the OAU's membership at its first meeting called to discuss the Congo crisis. The chosen way out of this dilemma was to appoint a reconciliation committee under President Kenyatta. But with Mr Tshombe's failure to implement the terms of the agreement reached—notably over the withdrawal of white mercenaries—the Reconciliation Committee ceased to be effective, and the OAU members no longer pretended to be acting collectively. OCAM's decision to admit Tshombe's Congo to membership publicly set the seal on this division within the OAU.

The split contributed to, and facilitated, the process of enlarging foreign intervention in the Congo and in some of its neighbouring States—especially in Burundi and Congo—Brazzaville; the Sudan, too became affected by the lack of control over arms passing through Juba. The non-theoretical nature of the dangers of foreign intervention in Africa was demonstrated by the speed with which the situation deteriorated in and around the Congo: the large-scale shipment of weapons into uncontrolled hands produced risks to the security of several countries other than the Congo; the angry suspicions that sprang up even between normally well-disposed neighbouring states increased intra-African tensions; the political climate of paranoia enabled reports of plots and subversion to flourish alarmingly with detrimental effects on the political stability of the Congo and its neighbours, and on their international relations. Over a brief period of months a considerable part of East and Central Africa became politically inflamed and neurotically uncertain about problems of internal security. Within another few months, with the crumbling of the Congo rebel front, fresh problems were posed for those African States which had given the rebel leaders refuge because of the angry quarrels which broke out between them. Then, with Tshombe's overthrow by the military, an entirely new situation arose: the Belgians were forced heavily on the defensive, and

General Mobutu came to be accepted with warm friendliness by his former critics.

It is hardly necessary to point up the many lessons provided by this experience: its major effect was to inflict a serious wound on Africa's foreign policy by demonstrating two facts. First, that the doctrine of a 'Hands off Africa' policy is not yet enforceable; and second, that the risks of invoking one set of major powers to redress the balance against another are more hazardous than was commonly supposed in 1964. It provided a third lesson of a different kind by reminding Africa of its own patient teachings to outsiders: to rely on the ultimate good sense of the nationalist leadership and internal forces to deal with alien forces in their country in their own way: despite its nightmare experiences, the Congo today is less dominated by alien economic forces than it was in 1960.

Africa hardly had time to recover from its Congo experience when it was faced with a second and even more damaging challenge: the illegal declaration of independence in Rhodesia on November 11, 1965, almost exactly a year after the Kisangi paratroop drop.

Africa's role in the Rhodesian crisis has, up to now, been neither effective nor creditable. The OAU has been thrown off balance; it has failed to take any worthwhile initiative; and its actions have contributed towards lowering rather than raising African morale. This is a hard judgement: but is it a fair one? An approach to this question is to analyse the main elements involved in the Rhodesian challenge and to examine the OAU's response to it.

1 The Rhodesian rebellion is a manifestation of a desire for continuing *white supremacy* among certain European leaders in Southern Africa. It is not an isolated phenomenon.

2 The defeat of the rebellion can only be secured by treating Rhodesia as part of the wider complex of *white supremacy* in Southern Africa. Therefore, Rhodesia is to South Africa and Portuguese Africa what Spain was to Nazi Germany and Fascist Italy in the 1930's. It is a battleground of ideas and tactics; the outcome will greatly influence morale in the rival camps in precisely the same way as the triumph of Franco in Spain immeasurably strengthened the Fascist cause.

3 The defeat of the Rhodesian rebellion is essential to the eventual defeat of *white supremacy* in South Africa and in the Portuguese territories. As in the case of Hitler and Mussolini, Verwoerd and Salazar are bound to assist Smith to resist the forces threatening them all. Yet the chances of Smith's success were never rated very high either in Lisbon or Pretoria before the rebellion occurred: this explains why they counselled Smith against his rebellion. But once Smith had embarked on rebellion they had no option but to support him, so long as this did not directly threaten their own national interests.

4 A Smith victory would undoubtedly strengthen the Verwoerd-Salazar position temporarily; but there are serious limits to the extent to which

they can afford to become too deeply involved—just as there were limits to intervention in Spain. Hitler and Mussolini were not prepared in 1936 to take on France, Britain and Russia: they preferred to operate surreptitiously under the fictitious policy of non-intervention. In Rhodesia, too, South Africa and Portugal pretend to be following a policy of non-intervention by merely keeping up 'normal trade'. The limits imposed on South Africa's interventions in Rhodesia are strictly dictated by its own national interests. However, these interests are not easily reconciled. Thus, South Africa has a direct national interest to prevent the effective operation of economic sanctions in Rhodesia because this would strengthen the demand for sanctions against itself. (Although the Rhodesian economy is much more vulnerable than South Africa's, the psychological value of a successful international programme of sanctions would bear directly on the diplomatic campaign waged against South Africa). On the other hand, South Africa has a strong interest in avoiding open conflict with the Western nations—and especially with Britain and the USA—since this would finally isolate the Republic in the international community. Dr Verwoerd's problem all along, therefore, has been how to undermine the effectiveness of sanctions without coming into open conflict with Britain.

5 Britain, too, is unwilling to force an open confrontation with South Africa for economic and security reasons, and because she has no thought-out policy for dealing with such a challenge. This view is shared by the USA, France and West Germany. Verwoerd knows that just as he is inhibited from pushing his involvement in Rhodesia too far so, too, are Britain and the USA. But while Dr Verwoerd has not budged from his existing commitments to the Rhodesians, his officials make little secret of the fact that he was greatly shaken by Mr Wilson's decision to invoke Chapter 7 of the UN Charter. Up to then he was convinced that Britain would never go so far over Rhodesia.

6 From the outset, sanctions have been the only acceptable policy to Britain and the US for bringing down the Smith regime. Since Britain's national interests are deeply committed to this objective, its commitment to making sanctions work is strong—subject only to not producing an open clash with South Africa. Thus one finds a sharp contradiction between British and South African national interests over the application of sanctions in Rhodesia. Africa's interests lie in exploiting and sharpening this contradiction by a relentless demand for more stringent economic measures.

7 If sanctions are rejected, either on the grounds that they cannot work, or because it is felt that Britain has no serious intentions of making them work properly, it becomes necessary to suggest a practical alternative policy. What does Africa propose? One proposal has been for the use of military force; another is to rely on an armed struggle by African liberation fighters. How realistic is either of these alternatives?

8 In Rhodesia's case the use of military force was unrealistic for reasons which will be presently argued. An African liberation struggle was, and

remains, possible; but not as a short-term solution. It will require time and commitment to launch an effective struggle; also it requires Zambia's willingness to allow its territory to be used as the base for such a struggle, despite the economic and security dangers this would hold for President Kaunda's Republic.

9 In South Africa's case it is obviously unrealistic to suppose that the western powers will seek to bring down South Africa's apartheid regime by military force, either now or in the foreseeable future. Nor is it realistic to suppose that the military forces in Africa will be strong enough, even in the foreseeable future, to crush Dr Verwoerd's Republic. To rely on the development of an effective liberation struggle in South Africa is to postpone for a long time to come the defeat of apartheid. Besides, a liberation struggle depends on the prior liberation of, at least, Rhodesia and Mozambique.

10 If armed intervention by the major Powers against South Africa is ruled out, as it must be, only two alternatives remain: an effective African armed struggle or collective international action involving the use of non-military force, i.e. an economic blockade. These two alternatives are of course not exclusive. But Africa has to make up its mind whether it is willing to rest its policy entirely on the promotion of an armed struggle, or whether it attaches importance to promoting international collective action in the meantime. It has, in fact, already committed itself to both these courses of action. The OAU's official policy has for many years been to demand international economic sanctions. But it has failed in the past to get acceptance of this policy at the UN mainly through Anglo-American opposition: their switch of policy over the appropriateness of sanctions in Rhodesia's case, presented the OAU with an important precedent for action against South Africa. But the first necessity was to prove that an international programme of economic sanctions could work in Rhodesia.

11 However, if sanctions are to work at all they must be total, comprehensive and enforceable: this can only be ensured by mandatory sanctions under Articles 41 and 42 of Chapter 7 of the UN Charter. Africa's foreign policy has, in fact, based itself largely on the logic of this analysis: but its practice has not always measured up to this realistic approach.

On the one hand, the Africa group at the UN endorsed a policy for mandatory sanctions under Chapter 7 in November 1965, while on the other, it insisted that the primary responsibility for ending the Rhodesian rebellion was Britain's alone. It therefore endorsed the view that Rhodesia was a colonial rather than an international responsibility. This attitude can be justified pragmatically on two grounds: Britain having got Rhodesia into its present mess should be responsible for clearing it up; secondly, collective action by African states, involving direct military intervention in Rhodesia, was not feasible for several reasons: these ranged from Zambia's well-grounded fears of a race war being precipitated by a conflict between black and white armies, to a general unwillingness at a time of internal insecurity in various parts of Africa to mount a joint African military operation.

The next question to be considered is whether Africa committed a major error of policy by unnecessarily limiting its choice of options to either British or African responsibility—instead of making a third choice—that of international responsibility for Rhodesia. If this had been the policy from the start the demand should have been for a UN solution, and not just for mandatory sanctions. Such a policy would have opened the way for supervision of sanctions by a Special Committee of the UN on which African states and Britain could have shared responsibility for supervising the sanctions campaign. One immediate result would have been that the choice of the degree of sanctions to be applied would not have left to been to Britain alone; even if she were reluctant to do more, she would have been under constant pressure by the Special Committee to make sanctions mandatory. A standing committee of this kind would have kept the Rhodesian crisis under continuous review; it would not then have been left to the Security Council's periodic meetings to deal with the issue, whenever fresh pressures had to be considered. It would have been much more effective, too, than the Commonwealth Committee on Sanctions which is an *ad hoc* body of representatives, not particularly well briefed on the way sanctions are working. Since Britain had invited UN cooperation in making sanctions international, it could not sucessfully have refused a UN demand for a supervisory committee. A precedent for this type of operation was provided by the Congo Advisory Committee, which comprised only African members, set up to advise the UN Secretary-General. A UN Sanctions Committee would have left Britain with her portion of responsibility; but she would have had to share this responsibility with the international community, and especially with the African states which are most directly concerned with the outcome of the Rhodesian crisis.

A second major weakness in Africa's policy flowed from the first: insistence that British troops should be used to crush the rebellion. This persistent African demand is wrong on two grounds. First, it is unrealistic. Whether Africa likes it or not, it should have been obvious from the start that British troops would not be committed against Rhodesia (except *in extremis*) for reasons of British domestic politics. These reasons might displease Africa: but Africa's displeasure is a small matter in Mr Wilson's eyes compared with the survival or defeat of his own government. Faced with such a choice, which political leader would have behaved differently? The second reason for suggesting it was wrong for African leaders to place their reliance on the use of British troops in Rhodesia is that the presence of such troops would be likely to become a threat to the efforts of a nationalist movement challenging the temporary colonial authority established after the crushing of the Smith regime. In the end, the struggle for majority rule must be contested between the rival forces in Rhodesia: direct British military involvement would hinder rather than help an effective African nationalist movement from developing in Rhodesia. Yet, if Rhodesia is one day to have an effective majority government (and not just become another 'client' government of South Africa), it is essential to produce a strong nationalist movement before power is transferred. The absence of an effective nationalist movement (whatever the reasons) has all long been a critical weakness in the Rhodesian situation; its continued absence, after the Smith regime passes from the scene, would be the final tragedy.

One recognizes, of course, the special problems raised for Zambia in considering the right policies to be pursued in Rhodesia. It would be a major tragedy if Zambia were to be seriously damaged in the course of defeating Mr Smith. However, it should be recalled that the Zambian government's insistence on the use of British troops to crush the Rhodesian rebels became stronger only as its confidence in Britain's readiness to apply effective sanctions weakened, and as its fears of an eventual 'sell-out' to Mr Smith grew. But President Kaunda has never wilted before the dangers involved in applying economic sanctions provided only that he was satisfied they could be made effective, and that Mr Wilson's ultimate objective to establish conditions for effective majority rule was credible. Therefore Zambia is not, and never has been, a critic of a policy of sanctions, as such.

The failure, thus far, of the sanctions programme is the failure of African policy to secure the application of mandatory sanctions under Chapter 7, or to secure a UN Supervisory Committee as the first step towards making sanctions effective. Why is this Africa's failure and not Britain's? Because it is necessary that Africa should face up to the reality that no foreign Power (whatever its responsibilities or pretensions) will do for Africa what Africans want or need. Therefore, to blame Britain, or any other Power, for the things that go wrong is not only an evasion of the responsibility Africa has assumed for its sphere of interests, but an evasion of the weaknesses of its policies and power which prevent Africa from discharging this responsibility. Since Africa is serious about assuming responsibilities for its own affairs it must, at least, be prepared to examine its own weaknesses in order to determine how these can be reduced or repaired. It is in danger of assuming a slightly ridiculous posture by pinning its faith on British troops in Rhodesia. Surely, in terms of its own policy, it should be pinning more faith on the African liberation movements; and if these are inadequate then more effort and funds should be spent *in the right way* in making them more efficient. Yet one has heard much more in the last year about Mr Wilson's failure to produce British troops than about the OAU's failure to produce more effective African liberation fighters.

Let us turn now to examine how Africa lost its initiative in the Rhodesian crisis. When the first proposals for sanctions came before the Security Council in November 1965, the Africa group at the UN did try to have them made mandatory under Chapter 7; but they failed. This critical failure was due both to Western pressures and to African awareness of the urgent need at the time to respond to Smith's challenge with some measure of international agreement. Subsequently, however, the OAU failed to keep up a relentless pressure for action under Chapter 7; instead it quickly seemed to lose heart in sanctions altogether. Some of the OAU's outstanding leaders were saying, within a month of the application of sanctions, that they did not believe sanctions would work, and that they had, in fact, never worked. In that case, one wonders why the self-same leaders had relentlessly pressed, year after year, for sanctions—not against puny little Rhodesia—but against South Africa? What was one to make of this *volte face*? No one with the slightest knowledge of the inevitably slow process of sanctions could have supposed that their effects could be felt in a matter of weeks. Admittedly, Mr Wilson's performance did not inspire confidence within Africa: but was this an adequate explanation for abandonment of efforts to get mandatory sanctions—and without offering a credible alternative policy? It can be said in justification that Africa had lost confidence in the possibility of persuading the Western Powers to accept Chapter 7: but when Mr Wilson's government took the initiative to invoke Article 42 of Chapter 7 to halt the pirate oil tankers in the Mozambique Channel, he very nearly failed, because of African opposition. Yes, it will be said, but would he ever go the whole hog and invoke it against South Africa as well? Granted that the answer may well be 'no', this is no reason to halt the pressure. On the contrary, the correct response, surely, was to increase the weight of international pressures to compel Britain to go further. Only the African states acting with relentless, single-minded determination, could have produced this kind of pressure. This did not happen. In just one month after the beginning of sanctions on December 3, 1965 ,the OAU Foreign Ministers—with only two abstainers—committed themselves to breaking off diplomatic relations with Britain by December 15 unless, by then, she had crushed the Smith regime; in other words, the OAU had restricted itself to a single demand for the use of British troops. The adoption of this resolution by the OAU marks a high point in the frustrations felt by Africa over its powerlessness to defeat its enemies independently, and a low point in the application of its foreign policy.

The history of diplomacy is littered with damp squib ultimatums. Ultimatums seldom achieve their purpose—never unless their threats are credible and the demands they make are practical. Neither of these conditions were met by the OAU resolutions. It was not credible because Britain did not seriously expect that the African states would break off diplomatic relations; in fact only seven did—and these did not include many of those who had taken the lead at the Foreign Ministers' meeting in demanding a break with Britain. The second condition, too, was absent: nobody could seriously have supposed that Britain could have brought down the Smith regime within the two weeks set by the ultimatum. It was subsequently argued that the ultimatum's terms would have been met by evidence of Britain's willingness to use her military forces; but this was not what the resolution demanded.

The failure of the majority of African states to implement their almost unanimous resolution was to devalue Africa's standing in the eyes of the world; more important, it devalued its standing in its own eyes, thereby contributing to dangerous feelings of frustration and impotence.

The only useful result of this sadly miscalculated piece of diplomacy was that it contributed further towards stripping away illusions about the real nature of power. The debacle of the OAU's December 3 resolution was a direct consequence of Africa's reliance on a policy of pressures to compel Britain to take the initiative through military action in Rhodesia. If instead the OAU had pursued a policy of demanding mandatory sanctions its pressures would have been differently directed. A demarche on the UN at that time might well have produced a Chapter 7 resolution on sanctions. Several African Heads of State now know that the British Government was actively considering the need to accept further measures under Chapter 7 in the middle of December: but the condition for success was for enough pressure to be exercised within the Security Council to make Britain's position untenable at the time. By deflecting the pressure from the Security Council and by issuing instead a call for diffuse action by individual African States, the OAU resolution in fact eased the pressure within the Security Council. To be effective, power must be exercised at the point which is most vulnerable to pressure: this simple but crucial factor of power politics was ignored.

Africa's foreign policy-makers have learnt two bitterly expensive lessons from their unfortunate experiences in failing to meet the challenge of the 1964 Congo crisis and the 1965 Rhodesian crisis. Although Africa's power is still limited by lack of military and economic resources and by the absence of the necessary unity to ensure effective collective action, the continent is, nevertheless, by no means as weak as it has been made to appear as a result of some of its policies. But, until Africa does succeed in evolving policies that realistically take account of its own resources and are capable of mobilizing international support, it will remain vulnerable to external pressures and subversion, and it will be unable to destroy the alien islands of *white supremacy* which prevent the completion of the African revolution, and which keep some of Africa's finest sons prisoners on Robben Island and in scores of other prisons, or under house arrest, throughout the length and breadth of Southern Africa.

ETHIOPIA: A CASE STUDY IN INDEPENDENT DEVELOPMENT

by

RICHARD PANKHURST

Ethiopia, the sole country to maintain its age-old independence throughout the era of the Scramble for Africa, enjoys a unique position in African history. Its economic history is in many ways different from that of the rest of the African continent, being characterized on the one hand by isolation and resistance to change and on the other by development carried out by the rulers of the country independent of the European colonial powers. A review of certain aspects of its development history may therefore be of interest in the wider perspective of Africa and the world.

Any consideration of Ethiopian history must take into account the geographical difficulties of the land: its high mountains intersected by deep gorges, mountain streams and river valleys, often inhabited by mosquitoes, and the hot malarious lowlands which tended to intensify its isolation. Such obstacles to communication, which contributed largely to preserving Ethiopia's independence, were no less significant as a handicap to development.

The idea of development of one kind or another is by no means new in Ethiopia. Already in the Middle Ages the rulers of the country were aware that they could not live in isolation, but had to utilize objects and skills which had by then been developed in other lands. The innovating interests of these rulers were, however, largely confined to the military sector. The period was one of much fighting and it needed little imagination to see that what Ethiopia needed was fire-arms and men to teach the soldiers to use them. The country, it should be remembered, was then confronted by enemies many of whom had relatively abundant supplies of modern weapons. The import of foreign guns and skills was therefore a matter of life and death.

The preoccupation of the Emperors of the past was, however, by no means exclusively restricted to this question. On the contrary they often evinced an interest in other things, above all foreign medicine, new types of handicraft and the construction of improved buildings, particularly palaces and royal churches.

The attitude of the rulers of the time is clearly apparent from their correspondence with foreign sovereigns. As early as 1428 we find the Emperor Yeshaq appealing to King Alfonso of Aragon for skilled craftsmen, and almost a century later the Emperor Lebna Dengel (1508–1540) wrote to King Manoel I of Portugal in some detail, saying:

Send master who can make figures of gold and silver, copper, iron, tin, and lead, and send me lead for the churches; and masters of gilding with gold leaf, and of making gold leaf; and this soon, and let them come to remain in my favour. And when they may wish to return at their desire, I will not detain them and this I swear by Jesus Christ, Son of the Living God.

In a subsequent letter to Manoel's son, Joào III, he wrote:

Sir, brother, hear another word now, I want you to send me men, artificers to make images and printed books, and to make swords and arms of all sorts for fighting; and also masons and carpenters, and men who can make medicines and physicians, and surgeons to cure illnesses; also artificers to beat gold and place it, and goldsmiths and silversmiths, and men who know how to extract gold and silver and also copper from the veins, and men who can make sheet lead and earthenware; and masters of any trades which are necessary in these kingdoms, also gunsmiths. And he added: *Assist me in this, which I beg of you as a brother does to a brother, and God will assist you and save you from evil things.*

A couple of generations later we find the Emperor Sartsa Dengel (1563–1597) writing to King Felipe II of Spain asking him to send experienced workmen who knew how to make helmets and cannon and to prepare gunpowder and other war material; and not long afterwards the Emperor Za Dengel (1603–1604) wrote to King Felipe III, requesting him to send many artisans as well as soldiers quickly '*so that peace and love should take root between us who are united in the faith of Christ*'.

There can be no gainsaying the desire of such rulers to embark on a significant amount of technical innovation, albeit mainly in the military area. It must, however, be added that the mentality of the past, which of course still lingers on into the present, was by no means conducive to change. Thus when in the sixteenth century the Portuguese priest Alvares inquired of the people of Tigre, then suffering from a severe plague of locusts, why they did not try to kill these insects he received the reply: '*they had not the heart to resist the plague which God gave them for their sins*'.

The rulers of the past had no intention whatsoever of any slavish imitation of the west as is evident above all from their resolute opposition to foreign ideas in the religious field. The position of the Emperor Galawdewos (1540–1599) was a characteristic one. He had received significant assistance from the Portuguese in the defeat of the Muslim Ahmed Gragn, and employed European, Syrian, Armenian and Egyptian craftsmen to build his palace, but he would have no truck with the ideas of the Roman Catholics. The chronicler of the reign tells us that a Roman Catholic bishop came to Ethiopia '*to criticize the true faith . . . and to proclaim the false belief which issued from Rome*'. Describing the Emperor's reaction to this propaganda the scribe reports that Galawdewos held '*controversies with the Ferenje on the subject of their lack of faith*' and '*defeated them in argument and confounded their falsehoods*'.

Though the Emperors Za Dengel and Susneyos (1607–1632) both later espoused the Roman Catholic faith, largely it appears in the hope of obtaining Portuguese military aid, the population as a whole were steadfast in their rejection of the new religion. The seventeenth century German historian Ludolf relates that when Susneyos finally abandoned his efforts to convert the people to Roman Catholicism it was '*a thing almost impossible to be believed with what an Universal Joy the Emperor's Edict was received among the people. The whole Camp, as if they had some great Deliverance from the Enemy, rang with Shouts and Acclamations. The Monks and Clergy who had felt the greatest weight of the Father's Hatred lifted up their thankful voices to Heaven. The promiscuous Multitude of Men and Women danc'd and caper'd; the Soldiers wish'd all happiness to their Commandors, they broke their own and the Rosaries of all they met*'.

Traditional Ethiopia, confronted with the technical superiority of the West, thus refused to abandon its established beliefs, the rulers of the country being determined to accept innovation only in those sectors which they chose.

The policy of the nineteenth century rulers of Ethiopia was essentially similar to that of so many of their predecessors. King Sahle Selassie of Shoa (1813–1847) is a good example. One foreign eyewitness, Schroff, reported that this monarch's '*first intention seems to be directed to military reforms*', while another observer, Johnston, recalls that Sahle Selassie questioned him closely about the relative merits of gun-barrels, and adds: '*I had to describe how they were manufactured; what was the difference between plain and twisted; in what manner the grooves on the rifles were made; and whether long or short barrels were most economical for service*'. The King's interest in technical matters likewise impressed the Saint Simonians, Combes and Tamisier, who declared, doubtless with some exaggeration, that workmen were '*the most important men*' at Sahle Selassie's court, and that the sovereign '*found time to devote himself to the industrial arts in which he is passionately interested. He liked to see work carried out under his very eyes; his palace was full of weavers, carpenters, masons and other workers engaged in making gunpowder, repairing rifles or working in gold, silver and ivory*'.

Sahle Selassie employed a Greek craftsman, Demetrius, to build a palace at Angolala and also opened up diplomatic relations with the outside world. In a revealing letter of 1840 to the British India Company he declared: '*God has given me a good and large kingdom; but arts and sciences have not yet come to my country as they have to yours. May it therefore please you to assist me, particularly in sending guns, cannon, and other things which I have not in my country*'. The King's attitude was no less clearly formulated by the Protestant missionary Krapf who quotes him as declaring that '*he did not need spiritual teachers so much as doctors, masons, smiths, etc.*' That this was not a mere idle thought is evident from the fact that Sahle Selassie soon afterwards expelled Krapf and a fellow missionary and refused to allow them to return despite strong pressure from the British envoy Conwallis Harris, who quotes him as declaring: '*Isenberg and Krapf cannot come to my country again. . . . I have considered upon this subject a long time, and it is better that they should remain away*'.

Determination to innovate on the country's own terms sometimes in practice meant a refusal to innovate at all. The story of the country's first water mill is a case in point. Harris records that Sahle Sellassie wished to have such a mill erected near his capital at Ankober, but though the mill was set up by Demetrius and another Greek its use was prohibited by the clergy. '*Although it cost my people a year of hard labour to construct*', said the King, '*it was useless when finished, because the priests declared it to be the Devil's work and cursed the bread*'. A subsequent French traveller, Arnoux, confirmed the story, declaring that the King's confessor called the establishment the work of a demon, ordered it to be burnt down to destroy the evil spirit responsible, and excommunicated not only those who erected it, but also anyone who brought grain to it for milling or ate bread produced from its flour.

Innovation was greatly handicapped by the conservative, misoneistic attitude of the people. This may be illustrated, for example, by the popular opposition in the early nineteenth century to the introduction of the Maria Theresa dollar, for all practical purposes the country's first currency. 'Primitive money' such as bars of salt and pieces of cloth had long been used for purposes of exchange, but was extremely inconvenient. The society was, however, most reluctant to adopt the use of coins. The travellers of this time are unanimous in declaring that the public would only accept Maria Theresa dollars with suspicion and after the most minute scrutiny. Thus Johnston, writing of the Shoa of Sahle Selassie, says that the coin when offered in payment would be '*at first well scrubbed with the fingers, then spat upon, followed by a good rub in the hair, and very probably, after all, the coin is handed back with a sagacious shake of the head, as much as to say, "I am not going to be done in that way*".' Harris tells the amusing, but no less revealing story of a chieftain of Shoa who wished to sell a horse. The price agreed to was two hundred pieces of salt. So many pieces not being readily available, the purchaser sent the equivalent in dollars, whereupon the chief replied: '*I have kept your silver because you have sent it; but in future when I sell you a horse, I shall expect you to pay me in salt*'.

The rigidities of traditional life found expression also in the case of tobacco and coffee which, in certain areas of the country were forbidden by the priests. These commodities were rejected, as the modern scholar Caquot says, because they were regarded as belonging '*to the enemies of the monophysite church*'.

The reign of the Emperor Tewodros II (1855–1868) opens a new page in Ethiopian history. Tewodros, who was described by the British writer

Markham as the most remarkable man of the nineteenth century, was, above all, a great innovator, but his innovations, like those of previous rulers, were mainly of a military character, and included the reorganization of the army, the building of strategic roads and the making of cannon and mortars.

This Emperor's decision to manufacture fire-arms of his own is of some significance. It is symbolic both of Ethiopian rulers' overriding interest in military innovation and of the manner in which they utilized foreigners to serve the interests of the Ethiopian state. Tewodros was in contact early in his career with Protestant missionaries who were then bent on distributing the Bible in Ethiopia, but he acknowledged to his English friend John Bell that he '*would have been more pleased with a box of English gunpowder than, as he said, with the books he already possessed*'. Samuel Gobat, the Protestant bishop at Jerusalem, recognized the Emperor's desire of practical and technical, rather than spiritual aid and therefore arranged to send him a group of young German and Swiss missionaries who had received some technical training at the Chrischona Institute near Basle. On their arrival in Ethiopia these craftsmen were given land and settled at Gafat near the Emperor's capital at Debra Tabor. Dufton, an English traveller who met them a few years later, recalls: '*Things went smoothly for some time until one day orders came from His Majesty to the effect that he wished them to commence the construction of mortars and bombshells. The order came upon them like the bursting of a bomb itself, for none of them had ever had an idea that they would have been required to undertake a work of that description. They of course demurred, informing the King that, not having learnt the founding of cannon, they were totally unprepared to enter an engagement of that description*'. The Emperor nonetheless insisted, and, to emphasize his will, imprisoned the missionaries' servants until their masters consented to carry out his will. '*In their perplexity*', Dufton continues, '*they could not otherwise than promise to try. Only one of them, Herr Moritz, could be said to have the slightest acquaintance with the work at all, and his knowledge only extended to the formation of the mould; the clay to be used in the construction of the fire-bricks, the formation of the furnace; the proportion of the metals, and the making of the fuse being equally unknown to him as to the rest. However, by putting their heads together, and seeking information from books, they eventually managed to turn out something. What? A mass of vitreous matter formed by the melting of the fine sand of the bricks; the metal refused to flow. Their only resource was to try again; and away they went over the country to seek better fire-brick clay, and now another venture was made. The result was a flow of metal that came pouring out in a molten stream now, and all hearts are hopeful that at last the object is gained, but alas! the metal had stopped, and the mould was only half full. They tried again. To the inexpressible joy of these persevering men, and to the intense joy of the King himself, their wishes were accomplished, and Debra Tabor for the first time saw the balls soaring up into the air and bursting with a loud crash which made the hills resound with a hundred echoes*'.

Such attempts at cannon-building—which may almost be described as Ethiopia's first attempt at an Industrial Revolution—were extremely difficult, based as they were not on an industrialized state, but on an economy of primitive peasant agriculture. This is evident from the fact that the craftsmen used old-time bellows made of sheep skins and melted the metal required for each cannon in as many as thirty crucibles of traditional style.

The Emperor's determination nevertheless seemed capable of overcoming all obstacles, and is perhaps an object lesson of the need for such forcefulness in the process of development. Henry Blanc, one of the foreigners Tewodros later imprisoned, has left a record of the manner in which the Emperor built his roads. Writing of the latter's participation in the work the Englishman declares: '*From early dawn until late at night Theodore was himself at work; with his own hands he removed the stones, levelled the ground, or helped to fill up small ravines. No one could leave so long as he was there himself, no one would think of eating, drinking, or of rest while the Emperor showed the example and shared the hardships*'. Markham, who saw the finished road, called it '*a remarkable work, a monument of dogged and unconquerable resolution*'. Determination to overcome all obstacles never failed Emperor Tewodros. Well might the German missionary exclaim, '*He had indeed an iron perseverance*'.

Tewodros was, on any showing, a man of vision. In his desire to modernize his country he attempted to attract foreign craftsmen from abroad (and thus became involved in his famous dispute with the British Government) and also contemplated sending Ethiopian craftsmen for study in Europe.

Though this innovating genius will ever be reckoned as one of the greatest pioneers of present-day Ethiopia it was Menelik (King of Shoa, 1865–1889, Emperor of Ethiopia, 1889–1913) who laid the foundations of the modern Ethiopian State. The developments of his reign are of especial interest to the student of African history for they are a case study of how an African State could develop without either foreign tutelage or the relatively massive capital injections which in some cases—but by no means all—were effected as a result of colonial rule.

Menelik appears early in his reign to have realized the importance of utilizing foreign skills for the modernization of his country. As early as 1874 we find him writing to the Khedive of Egypt, a country with which Ethiopia had long had strained relations, requesting his assistance in finding persons with a knowledge of the arts and crafts. This appeal seems to have been fruitless, but a few years later in 1877 Menelik sent a message to a Swiss trader at Aden with whom he had business contacts, asking him to send him some Europeans skilled in various crafts. The trader informed some of his compatriots of the sovereign's desire, with the result that three young Swiss technicians arrived in the following year. They were Appenzeller, a specialist in ironwork, Zimmermann, a specialist in woodwork, and

Ilg, a young graduate of the Zurich Polytechnic. Menelik also made good use of other foreigners, including a number of Armenians who settled in his country some years later, as well as craftsmen and technicians of other nationalities, including Italians, Greeks, Indians and Arabs. Such foreigners inevitably contributed much to the process of development, but never attained the prestige or influence acquired by Europeans in many other African territories where, as a result of colonialism, they exercised political power. In Ethiopia, on the contrary, foreigners tended to be regarded quite simply as employees or servants of the sovereign, their status being further depressed by their participation in manual work and trade, two occupations which were traditionally considered of low repute.

Menelik's early preoccupations, like those of so many sovereigns of earlier reigns, were largely of a military order, and he displayed great skill in obtaining fire-arms, partly from French and other traders, and partly from the Italian Government. Fire-arms in the 1880's became so widely diffused that when the Ethiopians found the need to coin a word for the screw-driver they called it *yetab manja mafcha*, *i.e.* an implement for use with a gun, a term used to the present day. A generation or so later the British ambassador reporting on the visit of an Ethiopian delegation to Hamburg in 1907 noted that they were shown the latest military equipment. '*Their hosts*', he reported, '*were much astonished at the knowledge displayed by them in handling the weapons, and at their announcement that they themselves were in possession of most of the models shown*'.

Early in his reign Menelik also turned his attention to various kinds of innovation. In 1886 he arranged for the construction of the country's first bridge, over the Awash River, which was built by his Swiss craftsman, Ilg, assisted by an Italian, Capucci, and an Indian, Haji Kawas. The Swiss in a humorous yet significant letter which once again reveals the difficulties inherent in the first stages of development, observes: '*Shoa has advanced a step forward . . . the beams had to be carried 15 kilometres on human shoulders. For the bridge-heads I had to square up the stones on the spot. I even had to burn charcoal in order to forge the nails, rivets, screws and bolts required—add to this a tropical sun with all its dangers, heavy rains with resultant dysentery, intermittent fever, and cyclones which almost pulled out my beard and carried the tent in all directions. At night the hyenas almost stole our leather pillows from under our heads, jackals and other rabble plundered the kitchen and obliged me to obtain respect with strychnine*'.

Other innovations followed. In 1887 Menelik established a new capital, Addis Ababa, and in 1892 he reorganised the system of taxation. Two years later he granted Ilg a concession to build a railway inland from the port of Jibuti, and, in the same year, established the country's first national coins which were struck in France and issued, as the official proclamation declared, '*in order that our country may increase in honour and our commerce prosper*'. The country's postal system was set up by French and Swiss experts at about the same time, postage stamps printed in France being put on sale at the end of 1893, and Ethiopia in due course joined the International Postage Union in 1908. Two telegraph systems, set up and operated by French and Italian engineers respectively, had likewise come into existence by the end of the century.

Menelik's success in importing fire-arms—and a handful of military specialists—from France and Russia led in 1896 to his famous victory over the Italians at the battle of Adowa, perhaps the first triumph of an African over a European army since the time of Hannibal, and opened a new era in which foreign diplomats flocked to Addis Ababa. Several powers, including Britain, France, Italy and Russia, established legations there, and worked hard to gain influence in Ethiopia, but never succeeded in gaining undue influence there. Harrington, the British envoy, noted in 1902: *'I have not yet seen that any of us have what I would really call influence, i.e. influence that would make Menelik do what he did not want to do. Influence to the detriment of others is plentiful here, but to one's own advantage is decidedly infinitesimal'.*

Early in the twentieth century the first modern roads were constructed in the capital, between Addis Ababa and Addis Alem, and between Harar and Dire Dawa, the latter roads being made with the assistance of Italian and French engineers respectively. A few years later the Emperor began to establish the country's most important modern institutions. The Bank of Abyssinia was founded in 1905, as an affiliate of the British-run National Bank of Egypt, the Menelik School, which was staffed by Egyptian Copts, in 1908, the first modern hospital, which had doctors of several nationalities, in 1910, and a State printing press in 1911.

A significant feature of the developments of the Menelik period, and one which was to continue until our own day, was that Ethiopia in this way utilised the capital and skill of a number of different industrialized countries rather than a single such state. In this manner she succeeded in grafting modern institutions on the living organism of an independent African state without endangering its age-old independence.

Ethiopia, it may be concluded, has long displayed an interest in innovation. She succeeded, until Mussolini's poison-gas invasion of 1935, in her basic objective of utilizing the military technology of the Europeans to withstand all threats to her independence. By basing her development on a multiplicity of foreign powers and avoiding reliance on any one she likewise set an example which must perforce be followed by all self-respecting African states in our own era of the Cold War. The resistances to innovation outside the military sphere, which she displayed are, however, no less significant, pointing as they do to the need for resolute determination and sacrifice as essential prerequisite for change.

REFERENCES

C.F. Beckingham and G.W.B. Huntingford, *The Prester John of the Indies*, Cambridge, 1961.

H. Blanc, *A Narrative of Captivity in Abyssinia*, London, 1868.

E. Combes and M. Tamisier, *Voyage en Abyssinie*, Paris, 1838.

W.E. Conzelman, *Chronique de Galawdewos (Claudius), roid' Ethiopie*, Paris, 1895.

H. Dufton, *Narrative of a Journey through Abyssinia*, London, 1867.

W.C. Harris, *The Highlands of Aethiopia*, London, 1844.

C. Johnston, *Travels in Southern Abyssinia*, London, 1844.

C. Keller, *Alfred Ilg*, Frauenfeld, 1918.

J. Ludolf, *A New History of Ethiopia*, London, 1682.

C.R. Markham, *A History of the Abyssinian Expedition*, London 1869.

M. Morgan,(Continuties and Traditions in Ethiopian History), *Ethiopia Observer*, 1969, XII, No. 4.

R. Pankhurst, *An Introduction to the Economic History of Ethiopia*, London, 1961.

R. Pankhurst, (Misoneism and Innovation in Ethiopian History,) *Ethiopia Observer*, VII, No. 4.

R. Pankhurst, *Economic History of Ethiopia*, 1800 - 1935, Addis Ababa, 1968.

REPORT ON THE HISTORICAL AND POLITICAL SITUATION

COMMISSION A

The general trend of discussion on historical and political questions touched on the many successes scored in the interests of African liberation, but agreed that Africa as a whole now faced a major crisis of social structure, of political institutions; and that the further progress of Africans towards independence must depend on the constructive and resolute solving of this crisis. Several speakers drew attention to the fact, which was generally accepted, that this was essentially a crisis of historical transition from the relative isolation of the pre-colonial and colonial past to the full participation of Africa in the evolution of the modern world.

In discussions on the detailed nature of this crisis there was much, though varied, emphasis from many sides on the harmful and wasteful values now current in the world, some of which have been transmitted to Africa under and by the colonial system and by other external influences, and then carried over into the newly independent states. There was emphasis on the fact that Africans have adopted modes of behaviour and values which constitute serious deterrents to the solving of Africa's problems. The élites of independent Africa showed themselves particularly vulnerable to the corrupting influence of such values.

It was argued by many speakers that only a drastic and deep remoulding, rethinking and reshaping of values, attitudes, aims, habits of life, could now free Africa from the heritage of colonialism and enable her to confront the problems of the continent. In this regard, the new generations should be helped to acquire and appreciate a new set of values, to develop a sense of sacrifice, responsibility and solidarity. Such a process could close the widening gap between leaders and the masses of the people. Only thus could the creative energies of Africa's millions be harnessed to the tasks of reconstruction.

It was emphasized that the heritage of pre-colonial Africa, with its richly various cultural patterns and political, social, economic and artistic achievements, must be called on to play a fuller part in the work of continental reconstruction.

A number of contributors stressed that recognition should be accorded to the many achievements which recent years had shown: in raising the national and cultural consciousness of Africa's people; in forming all-African organs; in asserting the identity of Africa among the major groupings of the world; and in forging firm ties of friendship with peoples all over the world.

Yet at the same time attention was repeatedly drawn to the serious instabilities now developing within many national units; to the grave setbacks which now appeared to obstruct the further growth of African integration; and to the many weaknesses which still prevented Africa's full influence from being felt in the councils of the world.

The Conference was generally of the opinion that, for her future foreign policy, Africa must increasingly resort to constructive disengagement from systems and practices relied upon before independence and from obligations or agreements which could threaten Africa's peace, development and freedom. In this connection the tragedy of racialism in South Africa, Rhodesia and the Portuguese colonies was carefully examined. It was agreed that these racialist regimes existing in Africa represent a problem not only for Africa but for mankind as a whole, and deserve far stronger measures by the international community. It was strongly expressed that the failure of Britain to end the rebellion in Rhodesia and of certain countries to implement a boycott, was a serious setback to the liberation of Africa. It was emphasized that all countries have an obligation to take action to rid Africa of the inhuman regimes of South Africa, Rhodesia and the Portuguese territories. At the same time it was powerfully argued that a primary responsibility rests upon Africans to put themselves in a position from which they can play an effective role in the solutions of the problems on the continent.

Policies of constructive disengagement or non-alignment, it was further recommended, must go hand in hand with constructive co-operation: a co-operation which, to be fruitful, must be two-sided, so that Africa can make her own contribution to the civilization of the rest of the world.

The Conference recognized that the Organization of African Unity (OAU) can be the most effective channel through which such constructive disengagement and co-operation can be achieved.

Africa must develop out of her own experience in the context of world experience. Comparative studies to evaluate this experience must always be welcomed. It goes without saying that African studies in all fields will contribute to the progress and welfare of the continent.

COMMISSION B

ECONOMIC SITUATION

SOME ASPECTS OF TRADE AND DEVELOPMENT[1]

by

BELAI ABBAI

THE TRADE GAP

There has, in recent years, been a growing recognition of the importance of foreign exchange scarcity as a strategic constraint on the economic growth of the less developed regions of the world. In this respect, important contributions have lately been made by the UN[2] and others[3] bringing new ideas to bear on the practical and urgent trade problems facing developing countries today. In its study of the trade needs of developing countries, and in its long-term projections, the UN secretariat demonstrates quite clearly that if the growth trends of the 1950's were to continue during the current decade, then the developing countries as a group should expect a substantial increase in their trade gap by 1970; and foreign exchange scarcity is likely to be the dominant constraint[4] on their economic growth for the foreseeable future. This conclusion would apply with more force if the developing countries were to grow at higher rates than in the 1950's.

The statistical evidence upon which the UN conclusions are based has now been fully set out. According to the UN data the exports of developing countries as a whole declined from 12.1 per cent of their combined GDP in 1950 to 11.6 per cent in 1960. Meanwhile imports increased from 12.1 to 13.3 per cent between 1953 and 1960, leaving a commodity trade gap of 1.7 per cent of GDP by the end of the decade. The developing countries also experienced an increasing net deficit on account of investment income and service payments. The increase in the net deficit on services during this period showed a close relation to the increase in the volume of imports; and all in all the overall trade gap of developing countries had deteriorated significantly by the end of the decade. From the point of view of economic growth therefore great significance attaches to the relative trends in import and export ratios.

This is because—beginning from a position of deficit—an increase in the average import ratio, combined with a decline in the average export ratio, opens up the trade gap and consequently creates foreign exchange scarcity. The observed tendency for the exports of the developing countries to lag behind the growth of their imports has been due to the slow growth of primary exports, combined with the high income elasticity of import demand for manufacturers on the part of the developing countries themselves.

Thus one aspect of the problem has to do with the nature and characteristics of the exports of developing countries, which have put definite limits on their import capacity. This is so because the bulk of their exportable supplies has hitherto consisted of primary products, namely food and raw materials, whose growth has been impeded partly by the low income elasticity for food and partly by the continuous application of modern technology in the advanced countries, resulting in cost-reducing innovations, e.g. cheaper substitutes, synthetics, etc., and in great economies in the use of raw materials. Policy impediments, such as protective tariffs and internal taxes, have also been invoked to account for the slow growth of primary exports, but they probably do not form a basic element in the explanation. This, however, is an area where generalizations are hard to make and the factors governing the demand for each commodity need to be analysed separately. For instance, countries which possess large reserves of oil—with its high income elasticity of demand in the advanced countries—are important cases to the contrary.

With regard to imports, it is evident that despite the efforts of developing countries to replace imports, not only does their aggregate import coefficient remain high, but also, if the experience of the 1950's is a sufficient guide, their income elasticity for imported supplies is significantly greater than unity. This tendency for the growth of domestic output to lag behind imports has been taken as evidence of the structural rigidity inhibiting developing countries in the production of essential domestic supplies, both for consumption and investment requirements. This generalization would however require qualification, since a number of developing countries that have attained a higher rate of industrial growth have been in a better position to reduce the import content of domestic consumption and to a lesser extent their investment requirements. But for the majority of developing countries that are still at a low level of development, there is strong evidence that their marginal propensity to import continues to be higher[5] than the average, which clearly points to the persistence of internal structural rigidities (e.g. lack of large markets, capital and entrepreneurial ability, and a whole range of other skills) inhibiting an increase in domestic supplies of manufactures.

The grave implications of this prognosis for developing countries is now widely appreciated, for it means that, should the international community fail to take active and concerted measures designed to increase the import capacity of developing countries and/or to reduce the import content of their gross domestic expenditure, even the modest growth performance of the 1950's might not be repeated in the 1960's. Therefore, developing countries must reduce the projected trade gap by increasing exportable supplies and/or increasing the domestic supply to substitute for imported supplies, if they are to maintain even their current growth rates. Alternatively, an increase in the net inflow of external financial resources would be necessary. Thus either to maintain or to increase the rates of growth would require policy measures which are bound to entail a substantial change in the composition of domestic output of developing countries.

So far as the African region is concerned, however, the movement in the foreign trade ratios has been somewhat different from the average for developing countries. While during the 1950's, the same tendencies towards widening the trade gap could be observed, the position was reversed during the early sixties when there was a big rise in exports. At the same time imports began to slow down and in consequence the big commodity trade gap, which Africa experienced in the early fifties, had vanished by 1964. It would be dangerous, however, to infer from these trends that trade did not, or is not likely to, have a constraining influence on African development. As discussed in the latter part of this paper, a breakdown of the aggregate trade figures by country and commodity reveals that only a limited number of countries produce export commodities which experienced high rates of growth.

EXPORT EARNINGS

During the past decade and a half, the value[6] of African exports increased faster than that of the developing countries as a whole. Between 1950 and 1960, the value of African[7] commodity exports achieved a growth rate of 4.6 per cent, while the growth rate of total commodity exports of all the developing market economies was probably not greater than 4.0 per cent. The difference between the rate of growth of African exports and that of exports from all developing countries was even greater in the first half of the 1960's. During this period African exports increased at 7.8 per cent per annum. As a result of these developments the share of Africa in the exports of the developing countries has increased.

Table I
Trends in Foreign Trade

	Per Cent of GDP			Growth Rate	
	1950	1960	1964	1960/1950	1964/1960
Africa					
Exports	18.3	20.5	23.9	4.6	7.8
Imports	21.1 (1953)	25.2	23.4	5.2	1.9
Developing Market Economies					
Exports	12.1	11.6	—	4.0	—
Imports	12.1	13.3	—	5.9	—

Sources: (1) Based on the UN Monthly Bulletin of Statistics and data compiled by ECA Statistics Division.
(2) 'UN Studies in Long-Term Economic Projections for the World Economy,' Tables 3-3, 3-6 and 3-7.

Africa's trading partners (see Table 2) still continue to be the developed market economies, Western Europe being by far the largest market for its primary exports. In 1960, Western Europe provided 65 per cent of the market for the exports of African countries. Of this the European Common Market alone accounted for 45 per cent, while the share of the EFTA countries was 18 per cent. At the same time, North America accounted for 10 per cent. The share of the EEC market is not only large but has been expanding rapidly in recent years. Between 1960 and 1964, the proportion of African exports going to the EEC increased from 45.2 per cent to 48.4 per cent. African exports to the centrally planned economies still continue to be very small, amounting to only 7.3 per cent of total exports in 1960.

Table 2

Direction of African Trade and Growth Rates at 1960 Prices

	Total	North America	West Europe Total	West Europe EEC	West Europe EFTA	Other[a] Devel-oped	Devel-oping[b]	Centrally Planned
Percentage Share								
Imports 1960	100.0	7.8	67.6	46.9	19.5	11.0	9.2	4.3
1964	100.0	11.6	58.8	38.1	18.9	9.6	12.8	7.2
Exports 1960	100.0	10.3	65.2	45.2	17.9	3.3	14.0	7.3
1964	100.0	10.5	66.8	48.4	15.7	3.9	12.9	6.0
Growth Rate in Per Cent								
Imports 1964-60	1.9	12.6	-1.6	-3.2	1.1	-1.5	10.7	15.9
Exports 1964-60	7.8	8.4	8.5	9.7	4.3	12.0	5.7	2.7

Sources: See Table 1.
Notes: [a] South Africa, Australia, New Zealand and Japan.
[b] Including Africa.

The composition of Africa's exports (see Table 3) has changed radically in one important respect: the exports of petroleum and natural gas which were negligible in the fifties now occupy first rank in the region's commodity exports. Throughout the 1950's, fuel exports of the developing market economies increased very rapidly. Africa began to produce large quantities of petroleum and natural gas mainly during the first half of the present decade. As a result, the share of these commodities in total exports grew from 3 per cent in 1960 to 19.0 per cent of the region's total exports in 1964. Nonetheless, the bulk of Africa's exports still consists of foodstuffs and raw materials, amounting to about three-fourths of total exports other than fuels. So far as the export of manufactures is concerned, Africa is well behind the other developing regions. For instance, Africa's exports of manufactures amounted to only 8 per cent of total commodity exports in

1960, while the corresponding figure for the developing market economies as a whole was as high as 13 per cent.[8]

Table 3

African Trade by SITC Groups, and Growth Rate at 1960 Prices

	Total	Food Beverages & Tobacco	Raw Materials	Mineral Fuels	Chemicals	Machinery & Transport Equipment	Other Manufactures & Metals
Percentage Share							
Imports 1960	100.0	15.0	4.8	8.0	7.0	30.9	34.4
1964	100.0	13.7	5.0	6.8	7.4	35.0	32.1
Exports 1960	100.0	39.1	50.0	3.0	—	8.0	—
1964	100.0	34.7	38.7	19.0	—	7.6	—
Growth Rate in Per Cent							
Imports 1964-60	1.9	-0.3	3.0	-2.1	3.4	5.2	0.3
Exports 1964-60	7.8	4.7	1.1	71.4	—	6.5	—

Sources: See Table 1.

A major exception to the slow growth of primary exports, particularly of African exports, has been the dramatic rise of crude petroleum exports in recent years. This has tended in Africa to raise the total value of exports and to conceal the overall decline. It ought not to be forgotten, however, that petroleum resources are unevenly distributed in the developing world and it is only a minority of countries that are fortunate enough to possess this vital resource. Because of its high income elasticity, together with its concentration in a limited number of countries, doubts have been raised as to whether the inclusion of foreign exchange receipts from petroleum might not exaggerate the import capacity of developing countries.[9] As is evident, projections of export earnings with and without petroleum will lead to widely differing expectations about the growth prospects of developing countries as a group. There is, of course, no reason why petroleum should be excluded from a global assessment of the import capacity of developing countries while other primary products, such as cocoa, say, or for that matter any product with low income elasticity, should be included.

The problem is a real one, however, and is of a rather general character. If, for instance, the exports of developing countries were ranked according to their income elasticities, and if it could be assumed that the export structure of each individual country were a microcosm of the total export spectrum, then the question of inclusion or exclusion could not arise. However, the fact of the matter is that developing countries widely differ in their resource endowments and, in consequence, the export structure of each developing country represents, more often than not, a very small cluster of the total export spectrum. It is this fact that gives rise to differences in expected future export earnings among developing countries. The exports of African countries provide a good example of the uneven distribution and limited range of resources among countries which, quite apart from the issues arising due to price fluctuations, do seem to enjoy differing future demand prospects in the markets of the advanced countries. Largely for this reason, not all developing countries—even in cases where the rates of investment and savings are reasonably high so that the internal constraints are regarded as not unduly restrictive—can be expected to develop a trade deficit.

Any substantial trade surpluses of a few developing countries would, however, provide no comfort for the majority with substantial trade deficits, because the foreign exchange reserves of surplus countries cannot readily be used to enhance the import capacity of the deficit countries. It may be argued, of course, that the surpluses of petroleum and other products could be put to good use within the framework of payments arrangements. This, however, raises a whole set of complex issues concerning the scope and feasibility of economic integration among developing countries in which trade and payments arrangements are only one aspect of the problem. So far as the African region is concerned, Libya, Algeria and Nigeria are at present the countries which export large amounts of crude petroleum. While Nigeria, at present a trade deficit country, could not be expected to accumulate large reserves for the benefit of the West African sub-region in the immediate future, there is no doubt that the North African sub-region could immensely benefit from a regional payments arrangements that would transfer present surpluses from within the sub-region to countries such as Tunisia and the UAR that have suffered from chronic foreign exchange shortages. Whether or not such arrangements would materialize is of course another matter.

With regard to the majority of developing countries which at present rely on the exports of foodstuffs and raw materials, the long-term prospect of the improvement in their import capacity through trade lies in their ability to effect a substantial increase in the share of manufactures and other processed and semi-processed raw materials in their total exports. This proposition is at any rate true, if the import capacity of the developing countries as a whole is to improve, since, on present evidence, the growth of foodstuffs and raw material exports has seriously lagged behind the growth in the export of manufactures. Looked at from the standpoint of an individual developing country, however, the capacity to export manufactures depends on the degree to which manufacturing capacity is already developed, or can be developed internally, because of the need to achieve scale economies and thereby reduce internal unit costs to levels commensurate with external (international) prices.

At present only a minority of developing countries have reached such an advanced state. For the majority of developing countries—including most African countries—whose manufacturing capacity is as yet small, the time dimension needed to effect such a structural change to develop a capacity for the export of manufactures should not be underestimated. During this intermediate phase it might be necessary for many of these countries to strive to improve their export performance in the primary field, including the export of processed raw materials. It is conceivable, for instance, that many African countries which are still marginal producers of traditional primary commodities could improve their relative position quite rapidly, and no doubt many African producers benefitted from this process during the post-war period. But the benefits accruing from this process must, sooner or later, come to a halt. Specific commodity agreements might thus benefit large producers of traditional export commodities on which they have come to depend for a significant part of their export earnings. While commodity agreements may stabilize export earnings of large producers they need not raise import capacity to a level required to sustain a reasonable rate of economic growth. It is for this reason that countries depending on one or two traditional commodities for their export, as many African countries do, have often been advised to diversify their exports.

In this regard, of the proposals for tariff reductions on the exports of developing countries that have been discussed at the UNCTAD, tariff reductions on processed raw materials such as palm oil, groundnut oil and cocoa, butter would seem to be of special relevance to Africa, especially for the West African countries. It is significant, for example, that the accelerated reductions in internal tariffs granted by the Common Market to their African associates do not cover processed products such as the ones mentioned above.

Moreover the tariff reductions as they are granted by the Common Market countries to their African associates may not entail benefits that are quantitatively significant, since the common external tariffs on these products in relation to the level of internal taxes and duties prevailing among the countries of the European Common Market are very small. Other things remaining the same, what has to be compared is the level of the external tariff on these products with the differences in unit costs as between associate and non-associate supplies. In any case the development of commodity agreements such as coffee and cocoa which stipulate supply targets for producers may nullify the alleged advantages.

The main criticism against association of African countries with external economic groupings of advanced countries is based on two grounds: that the import capacity of the African countries (primary producers) is found to deteriorate in the long run in relation to their import needs; and that the development of significant manufacturing capacity for import replacement in these countries cannot be achieved without protection, particularly as most of them are not large viable economies.[9] This argument is now generalized for the trade relations between developing and developed countries and is the basis of the proposed UNCTAD recommendations for a unilateral reduction of tariffs by the developed countries on their imports from developing countries. If the principle of non-reciprocity in trade relations is accepted, however, it is clear that the interest of the least developed countries, as for the majority of the African countries, lies in the universal application of this principle. It is not enough that unilateral reductions of tariffs are granted by the developed countries alone; it is also necessary that similar tariff reductions be granted by the more advanced developing countries to the less developed ones.

IMPORT SUBSTITUTION

Africa's dependence on foreign supplies is very high indeed in relation to the average for the developing market economies. A rough idea of this dependence is obtained when the average import ratio of Africa is compared with the corresponding average for the developing market economies. In 1960 the average import co-efficient[10] for Africa was about 0.252, while the corresponding average for developing countries as a whole, was only 0.116. Thus the fact that imported commodity supplies are twice as high as the average for developing market economies as a whole together, with the fact that the average per capita income for Africa was not markedly different from the average for all the developing countries, means that Africa is less diversified as between manufactured and primary production in its economic structure than the other developing regions. When, given a low level of per capita income of roughly US$110, a quarter of gross domestic expenditure is spent on imported supplies of food, essential materials and capital equipment, there is hardly much scope left for domestic manufactures. This inference is substantiated by the currently low level of manufacturing output which, according to rather incomplete data that is available, is probably not significantly different from 8 per cent of GDP. Of course, it does not follow from this fact alone that there is greater scope for import substitution in Africa than in the other developing regions. What does follow is that the impact of a given percentage decline in the terms of trade in primary products is bound to have a much more pronounced effect in Africa than perhaps in the other developing regions.

In Africa, not only is the import content of domestic expenditure excessively high but also the marginal propensity to import has for the most part been greater than the average import ratio. As Table 1 shows, total commodity imports grew much faster than the combined GDP of the African region, with the result that the average import ratio increased from 21.1 per cent to 25.2 per cent between 1953 and 1960. The rapid increase in imports was made possible by the increase in import capacity which was mainly due to the favourable export prices that prevailed in the early fifties. In contrast to the fifties, the growth of total imports was severely curtailed during the first half of the 1960's which may be attributed to two principal causes. The first had to do with the nature of expatriate response to African political independence which entailed adverse economic consequences particularly in countries of former European settlement where expatriate capital and skill had been of crucial importance. The most dramatic examples of this response were shown in the case of Algeria and the Congo, where a combination of the cessation of private investment and large-scale departure of expatriates resulted in a temporary decline in output and imports. Secondly, a number of countries continued to suffer from a severe decline in the prices of their principal exports, and as a result, their capacity to import became inadequate to sustain their normal import requirements. For instance Ghana and Senegal experienced continued stagnation in their capacity to import owing to the fall in cocoa and ground-nut prices.

In any case the recent stagnation in the growth of Africa's commodity imports cannot be attributed to import substitution.[11] As a matter of fact, even in those countries that have embarked on a course of planned development, such as UAR, Nigeria, Sudan, etc., the increase in imported supplies far outstripped the respective increases in their output. It is nonetheless true that the efforts of African countries, especially those with published development plans, have been largely oriented to reducing import needs, partly because the exports of manufactures depend to a great extent on the prior expansion of domestic manufacturing[12] capacity, which is currently low, but, perhaps, mainly because of the greater range of policy instruments at their disposal.[13] Accordingly, many of the development plans envisaged a rapid growth of manufacturing output. The evidence so far available, although by no means conclusive, shows quite clearly that actual industrial growth has fallen markedly below planned targets and at the same time actual imports have been greater than planned targets.

The argument for import replacement must not be carried too far, however, since the limited resources at the disposal of African countries need to be allocated efficiently. In other words, a rational programme of import substitution should ensure that unit costs of domestic substitutes are not seriously out of line with external (i.e. international) prices of equivalent imported supplies. The experience of developing countries provides ample proof of the conflict between the conditions of growth derived from the consideration of foreign exchange scarcity on the one hand and the requirement for an efficient allocation of scarce resources on the other. The conflict is most clearly revealed when developing countries allocate scarce resources to new projects. Normally attempts are made to adhere to the efficiency criterion and in this respect the external price (c.i.f.) of the product is an important element in estimating the benefits accruing to new projects. However, this criterion is somewhat modified by invoking the infant industry argument which states that a tariff which bridges the gap between the external price and internal cost of the product is justified so long as the long run unit costs of the industry can be brought down to the level of the external price.

In addition to this long established practice there has, in recent years, been an explicit tendency to invoke another criterion: industrial projects are increasingly being appraised by the contribution they make to the saving of foreign exchange. Clearly this criterion is derived from the notion that economic growth is constrained by foreign exchange scarcity. Hence criteria of efficiency, the infant industry argument and foreign exchange scarcity have all become essential elements in making decisions on the allocation of scarce resources. The saving of foreign exchange as a criterion depend, however, on whether in each specific case foreign exchange scarcity can be shown—presently or potentially—to be the dominant constraint to development.

The factors responsible for the inflexibility in domestic supplies of essential commodities and which militate against a rapid industrialization programme of African countries are fairly well known. These problems are daily encountered by development officials and private businessmen when appraising the cost and benefit sides of industrial projects. Costs are high—either because factor prices deviate from their true opportunity costs and/or because transport costs are unduly high. Transport costs have become excessive, either because the traditional infrastructure was largely irrelevant to the growth of internal trade and development, or because of the great population dispersion in many countries which makes for excess capacity and high unit costs.

These aside, the main limitations to import-substituting development in Africa derive from consideration of the benefit side of projects; because the size of the internal markets for individual manufactured items is small in the majority of African countries, large-scale production is not readily feasible. Scale economies are of special relevance in the production of intermediate materials like steel and fertilizers as well as producers' goods. Estimates of the minimum size of plants economically required for production of intermediate and capital goods for which Africa has a favourable resource base clearly show that, unless some form of economic integration could be assumed among neighbouring countries, many of these projects are clearly out of the reach of the average African country. It is thus in respect of small national size and the consequent absence of scale that the majority of African countries are so handicapped in confronting the task of economic development.

Moreover, the pattern of income distribution and the nature of consumption functions in these countries could not have failed to reinforce the tendency for a high import coefficient. In all these countries the distribution of personal incomes is highly uneven, being more pronounced in those countries of former European settlement. Quite naturally the upper income groups command a pattern of consumption (e.g. durable consumer goods and other luxury items) corresponding to their *per capita* income levels and since, by and large, the market (i.e. the size of this class) is small, the bulk of disposable incomes of the upper income groups is spent, except for services, on imported items. Account must also be taken of the spatial dispersion of major population centres and the consequent lack of unified national markets. Small national markets and the polarization of the markets due to uneven distribution of incomes, the corresponding difference in consumption patterns and their spatial dispersion, all combine to whittle down the demand for domestic manufactures. Hence the high import content of gross domestic expenditure in African countries.

A factor of considerable significance has also been the role played by the export sector which, even though the contribution of the export sector to domestic incomes has been very large, did not generate significant demand for, or supply of, intermediate material inputs. It is true that the development of mining and cash crops for export had induced an increase in service inputs (transport, electricity) which by their nature cannot be transported, but their requirements of material inputs were largely imported.

There is no doubt that the principal obstacles which stand in the way of significant economic advance of the African countries—industrialization in particular—can only be removed through the co-operation or integration of neighbouring countries, because the enlargement of the domestic markets and the creation of an integrated transport system is a necessary precondition for economic viability of the majority of African countries.[14] To argue that the creation of viable economic units is an indispensible condition for African industrial development is not to minimize the difficulties involved in achieving the task of economic co-operation or integration. The experience of other developing countries in this respect does not as yet provide many brilliant examples of successful co-operation. If economic co-operation assumes the form of a Customs Union or Common Market, for instance, there is ample evidence to suggest that such a solution would in most cases lead to a cumulative process of unequal development among member countries. This may be due to initial disparities either in levels of development or in resource endowments or both.

The difficulties that the three East African countries are facing today may be attributed to this factor: Uganda and Tanzania have claimed that the operation of the East African Common Market worked against them and in favour of Kenya's processing industries. The unequal economic development of the component parts of the Federal Common Market contributed significantly to the breakdown of the former federation of Rhodesia and Nyasaland. As is well known, this process was aggravated by the operation of the Federal fiscal mechanism which, in effect, was designed to transfer funds from Zambia to Rhodesia. The root cause of these difficulties has been the application of reciprocity in economic relations between the strong and the weak, which tends to aggravate the initial disparities. So far the Central African Customs Union appears to be the most successful experiment in economic co-operation in Africa. It is interesting to note, however, that the Congo is still not a member of the Central African Customs Union, primarily because of its superior productive capacity.

Another complicating factor to integration is the close economic ties of African countries with external economic groupings. For instance, the Francophone countries are associate members of the EEC and have in principle reciprocal tariff arrangements with escape clauses. These countries, however, benefit from the EEC Development Fund for the purpose of diversification of their economies. If sub-regional co-operation among associates and non-associates is to be achieved, it is imperative that careful thought should be given on all sides to the problem of reconciling the commitments and benefits which African countries derive from association with the need for African sub-regional co-operation or integration.

EXTERNAL AND INTERNAL CONSTRAINTS

In the first part of this paper brief reference was made to the recent trends in the African trade gap. It was observed that, although the commodity trade gap of the African region had opened up quite widely by the end of the fifties, it had disappeared again by the middle of the sixties. All in all, this means that the overall deficit on current account of the African region reflects the extent of the net deficit on account of services and investment income.

It is, however, unfortunate that the magnitude of the current trade deficit cannot be fully ascertained because balance of payments data are notoriously incomplete for Africa. For instance, the manner in which the trade and payments statistics are compiled by the Francophone countries are not suitable for this purpose. The great majority of countries for which adequate balance of payments statistics exist reveal, however, consistently large deficits on account of services, reflecting the well-known fact that the African countries are almost entirely dependent on foreign shipping and insurance services. Net transfers abroad on account of dividend and interest payments show considerable variations among countries. These outflows have been typically large in mining and petroleum-producing countries where the greatest part of expatriate capital had been invested, but of course these countries have usually enjoyed a favourable balance on commodity trade.

Apart from the statistical difficulties involved in measuring the deficit, there are obvious dangers in trying to establish the trade gap for the region as a whole. For one thing an aggregate view of the external deficit of the African countries is bound to hide the plurality of causes and special circumstances affecting different economies. For instance, the phenomenal increase in total African commodity exports in recent years showed little relation to the trends in aggregate imports, which have almost stagnated since the beginning of the present decade. But the lack of relationship between the growth of import capacity and actual import purchases becomes readily apparent when one realizes that nearly half of the recent increase in foreign exchange earnings was derived from petroleum exports which accrued to a few countries (mainly Libya), while import purchases fell only in some countries—either because of the decline in investment and output that accompanied independence (Algeria, Congo) or because of the decline in export earnings (Ghana, Senegal). Much is also lost in judging the adequacy of external reserves for the region as a whole by adding country totals, in a situation where the foreign exchange reserves of some countries have been steadily rising, while in others they have been steadily declining; furthermore, no arrangements for pooling these reserves exist except for the East African countries. Thus it would be wrong to generalize from aggregate figures about the position of individual countries.

It seems therefore much more meaningful to look at the trade gap of each country separately. In this respect, it is gratifying to see that the work of UNCTAD has tended to move in that direction. UNCTAD has recently initiated a programme of country studies in which several African countries have been included where the extent of the trade deficits and the respective dominance of external and internal constraints will be fully examined. Meanwhile it would be of interest to record here some provisional results regarding the dominance of the external and internal constraints of selected African countries using certain partial indicators. For the purpose of this exercise trends in import capacity and changes as well as the level of reserves have been taken to identify the relevant constraints, the result of which are summarized in Table 4.

Table 4

Some Indicators of Import Capacity and Growth

	Annual Compound Rates of Growth		Increase (+) Decrease (—) in Reserves
	Exports[a] 1964/1950	Imports[a] 1964/1950	1960-1964
I. Libya	35.6	21.6	(+)
Gabon			
Ethiopia	10.3	10.7	(+)
Ivory Coast	10.1	10.2	(+)
Former Federation of Rhodesia & Nyasaland	7.9	3.6	(+)
Tanzania-Tanganyika	8.1	4.4	(+)
Kenya	7.6	6.5	(+)
Uganda	6.1	5.6	(+)
Cameroon	7.0	4.8	(+)
II. Nigeria	6.4	10.6	(—)
Sudan	5.3	9.4	(—)
Morocco	6.0	2.4	(—)
Senegal	4.0	1.4	(—)
Ghana	3.0	6.8	(—)
Madagascar	1.9	3.3	(—)
Congo (Dem. Rep.)	1.8	3.0	(—)
Tunisia	0.8	3.7	(—)
UAR	0.5	3.7	(—)

[a] Current value of visible trade.

The best single indicator of import capacity is the long-term trends in export earnings. Country data on the rate of growth in export earnings for selected African countries covering the period 1950–1964 are presented in Table 4. Earnings from services are a small proportion of commodity exports and their exclusion need not invalidate such inferences as may be made from the analysis of trends in commodity exports. It is evident from these figures that export performance has been very uneven among African countries. For some countries such as Gabon, Libya and Ivory Coast, the rate of growth has been exceptionally high and for others, including several East African countries, their export performance throughout the period has been satisfactory. In contrast to these, there are a number of countries in North and West Africa such as UAR, Tunisia, Ghana, Senegal whose export earnings throughout the 15-year period have hardly increased. The long-term growth rates do not, however, reveal the fluctuations in export earnings during intervening years which have implications for the level of external reserves. Receipts from traditional commodities did in fact fluctuate during this period. Generally export earnings were high during the early fifties (Korean boom) and began to decline since the middle fifties (post-Korean recession) although they began to edge up again during the first half of the sixties.

With these qualifications, it would be fair to assume that those countries which, over the whole period of a decade and half, attained growth rates in export earnings above 6 per cent, could have maintained a capacity to import which would sustain adequate rates of investment and economic growth. The countries whose export performance has been satisfactory are listed in the upper half of Table 4. In contrast, the countries listed in the lower half of the table have had a poor export performance and for some, like Tunisia and UAR[15], there has hardly been any increase in foreign exchange receipts from commodity exports throughout the period. It is obvious that in these cases, unless there is a substantial increase in net capital inflows and or import substitution, growth will have to be seriously curtailed.

The growth trends in imports did not in all cases parallel the growth in exports. In a few cases, including the Ivory Coast, Libya, Gabon and Ethiopia, imports increased almost as fast as the growth in export earnings. In the case of Libya the situation had changed from a balance of payment deficit to a surplus because of the exceptionally high growth of petroleum exports. While the growth in export earnings was relatively high in many of the East African countries (including the countries of the former Federation of Rhodesia and Nyasaland), the growth in imports failed to catch up with the growth in export earnings. There were thus many African countries whose foreign exchange earnings were satisfactory in relation to their important purchases. So far as the other countries listed in the second half of Table 4 are concerned, where the growth in import capacity has been modest or low, the growth in imports was also very low, but on the whole they increased somewhat faster than exports.

As a result of these developments the second group of countries were carrying large balance of payments deficits, especially in the sixties, which were financed through a substantial inflow of public aid and to some extent private foreign capital. During 1960–1964 the largest recipient of public aid in absolute terms was the UAR. Ghana and Nigeria also received large sums of public aid during this period. So far as foreign private resources are concerned, Nigeria was by far the largest recipient during this period. Tunisia and Ghana also obtained substantially large amounts of private funds.

The inflow of foreign financial resources was, however, inadequate to finance the trade gap of several of these countries. The result was that most of them began to draw on their international reserves. Between 1960 and 1964 the foreign exchange reserves of several countries were drawn down to dangerously low levels. For instance, Nigeria's reserves went down from 74.1 per cent to 36.0 per cent of total imports between 1960 and 1964; Sudan from 91 per cent to 26.5 per cent; and Ghana from 106.8 per cent to 37.7 per cent. These were the countries with initially high reserves. The others, including Morocco, UAR, and Tunisia, whose reserve ratios in 1960 were not even as high as 50 per cent, came down in 1964 to 11.5 per cent, 13.5 per cent and 14.6 per cent respectively. This is the dangerous situation in which several African countries find themselves. As can be seen from Table 4, all the countries in group II experienced declining reserves, whereas the opposite seems to have taken place in group I countries. The evidence is therefore strong that the trade constraint has been dominant for group II countries. So far as the rest are concerned (group I), it is the domestic constraints that have played a much important role in recent years.

REFERENCES

1 This paper was written when the Author was a staff member of ECA and the opinions expressed here do not represent those of the Imperial Ethiopian Government. Its order of presentation has been revised since it was first submitted at the Haile Selassie I Prize Trust Meeting. I am grateful to my ECA colleagues Messrs. T. Gedamu and J. Pickett, for their extensive and useful comments.

2 See United Nations, Economic and Social Affairs, *World Economic Survey*, New York, 1963, Part One.

3 See Hollis B. Chenery and Allan, M. Strout, Agency for International Development, *Foreign Assistance and Economic Development;* AID Discussion Paper, Washington, 1964.

4 See United Nations, Department of Economic and Social Affairs, *Studies in Long-Term Projections of the World Economy*, New York, 1964, Chapter 3, pp. 49-70.

5 Alternatively the income elasticity for import demand is greater than unity. However, this condition alone is not a sufficient indicator of domestic inflexibility, for if two economies reveal elasticities greater than unity and one grows at twice the rate of the other, clearly the structural transformation taking place in the latter is more significant than the former.

6 Unless otherwise stated, data relating to foreign trade, GDP and investments are valued in 1960 prices and exchange rates.

7 Africa in this context excludes South Africa which, by UN Convention, is treated as a developed country.

8 Ragnar Nurske, *Trends in World Trade* in Kyklos Vol. XII-1959-FASC. 1. page 13.

9 This criticism assumes that association would *per se* increase the rate of growth of imports into African countries and that non-reciprocal rights could be more easily obtained from developed countries as a group in the absence of association.

10 This refers to the ratio Commodity Imports GDP.

11 Import substitution implies the replacement of particular import commodities by domestically produced goods. It should be realised that in certain circumstances—*e.g.* in highly agricultural economies—such import substitution may paradoxically increase for a time the total import bill.

12 See Nicholas Kaldor, 'International Trade and Economic Development', *Journal of Modern African Studies*, Vol. II, No. 4, Cambridge, December 1964.

13 These include protective duties, reduction of customs duties on the imports of essential materials and capital goods, special tax reliefs for new industries, etc.

14 A further aspect of integration which perhaps needs to be emphasized is that the creation of viable economic units is bound to cause a greater inflow of international financial resources. This is readily apparent when it is realized that a considerable part of international funds are geared to a few large developing countries whose absorptive capacity is high. So long as the absorptive capacity criterion is adhered to—and there is hardly any alternative that can be put in its place—a large part of international aid may well by-pass the African countries unless they organize themselves into viable economic units.

15 In the case of U.A.R. however, earnings on invisibles (Suez Canal) were substantial.

SHIFTING PERSPECTIVES OF AFRICAN AGRICULTURE

by

JOHN DALTON

Introduction

Perhaps there is little need for yet another brief and general treatment of African agriculture. But to judge from the apparent impasse which development policy and planning in most African countries have reached—that is to say, to judge from the disappointing results, from the performance of agriculture in the past decade—maybe a conference on Africa and the world can hear yet another attempt to set forth a view of where we stand with respect both to what we know about the problem of African agriculture and to what should be the direction of policy.

The relative importance which African governments assign to agriculture may be reflected in the proportionate attention paid formally to agriculture by this conference—one general paper in a week of papers. In both cases it may well be that this represents not so much oversight or failure to appreciate agriculture's significance, but rather a growing frustration or near despair as to what to do with agriculture in Africa. We continue to hear that the pace of change in African agriculture is almost glacially slow, at least compared with construction, transport, education, and even the modest steps of industrialization. The list of failures of important large-scale projects and of disappointments in programmes of extension and credit, grows with each country's report. The subsistence share seems tenaciously to maintain itself, and the old practices still completely dominate. Rising imports of food and other agricultural products are still typical, and what information we have on urban food prices always shows an increase. Admittedly both population and food production statistics are notoriously poor, but from all sides we continue to hear that they show that food production has fallen behind population growth or has barely kept pace. Further, the expected increases in population growth rates are compared pessimistically with estimates of recent rates of increase of food production. And, to conclude the indictment, in the context of the United Nations Development Decade, which calls for a five per cent annual rate of growth in GDP, agriculture is charged as the sector of the economy responsible for the failure of the whole economy to attain such a rate, because agriculture comprises say two-thirds or nine-tenths of GDP, and its slow pace puts an intolerable burden on the non-agricultural sector to pull up the average rate for the whole economy.

One detects a good deal of impatience, not to say irritation, on the part of observers, planners, economists, and UN officers, who are outside of agriculture, with respect to those responsible for improving agriculture—officials and specialists of ministries and departments of agriculture, FAO officers, extension and agricultural schools' staff and students and writers on agricultural development in Africa. Why does agriculture remain so backward? What is wrong with those responsible for agriculture that they have so little to show to their credit?

Full answers cannot be given here to all these questions, but an attempt follows to indicate certain of the problems in their complexity and to put the problems in a historical setting in one of a succession of shifting and different recognitions on the part of European observers and leading figures in the conduct of agricultural administration and research in Africa. There follows an all-too-brief recapitulation of what might be called the colonial approach to African agriculture and its consequences. This in turn is followed by a brief discussion of the key roles of research and training, the trend of food production and population, and some suggestions on the orientation of policy. Many significant topics, such as land tenure and commodity trade, are not discussed. It should be clearly understood at the outset that it is only inter-tropical Africa which is being discussed.

CHANGING ATTITUDES ON AFRICAN AGRICULTURAL POTENTIALITIES

Until the 1930's, or possibly even the 1940's, the European attitude to African agricultural possibilities might be best described in the following terms. The tropics were regarded as a veritable storehouse of nature's riches. The low material levels of existence seen there were attributed to the backwardness of the indigenous people and their alleged isolation from civilizing influences. Rational management and control by Europeans would unlock this storehouse, to the simultaneous advantage of Europeans and Africans alike (the 'dual mandate'). To those who have witnessed how fast weeds can grow in the rainy season in the African tropics, such an outlook has a certain credibility. Further credibility was lent to this view by early success with sugar, coffee, rubber, bananas, cocoa, and other tropical crops which became the classic exports of the tropics to the developing and industrialized countries of the West. (Possibly we should use 'North'.)

There followed an almost wholesale reassessment which virtually turned previous assumptions on their heads. The reappraisal had three sources: the development of pedology, soil science, as an organized and separate field; the failure to obtain anything like the same results with the staple food crops, notwithstanding the application of 'Western' methods;

and a slowly dawning general recognition that the tropics would have to be studied and comprehended largely on their own terms.[1]

It should be noted first that the original 'successes' with the classic export crops should be understood with certain qualifications. These involved, for the most part, tree crops, not field crops; they were with crops peculiar to the tropics and for which no ready comparison could be made to the staple foods of the temperate zone; they were on choice lands; they benefited from cheap labour under colonial political control; and finally, in some cases, plantations were found not really to be competitive with relatively small scale peasant production—as in the case of cacao in West Africa.

The reassessment of the fertility and potentialities of most African soils dates from the 1930's and 1940's. In addition to a general downward revision, there was increasing allowance for the relatively greater vulnerability of tropical African soils to both leaching and erosion, and recognition of the higher production and operating costs attendant on operating in the African environment. We all should know, though some seem to forget, that almost any plant can be grown anywhere—but at what cost? Time does not permit dealing with the many facts of this shift in assessment. It was not a complete shift. Many today, unfortunately including some Africans, still assume that all that tropical agriculture needs is the application of 'modern methods'—that is, methods proven in temperate zone practice. Unhappily this is not always or even usually the case. Many thorny technical and even scientific problems remain to plague Africa: for instance, the failure of legumes in rotations to show the same beneficial effects of nitrogen fixing as they have done in temperate zone agriculture. To simplify, a generally pessimistic view came to prevail—and it may be that in some of the colonial administrations this pessimism helped in the acceptance of modest programmes both in research and in attempts at development.

It is not intended here to exaggerate this pessimism. To be sure, on a conscious level it may have been more a matter of observers outside of Africa who promoted the revision of scholarly opinion—Pendleton and Gourou, for example. But there was a gradual recognition during the '30's and '40's that the special characteristics of tropical agriculture in Africa implied that development and transformation, or even conservation and the maintenance of low levels of productivity, promised not only to be very much harder than elsewhere, but also to be exacting, gradual, costly and problematic. One conceivable positive response to such a recognition would have been that far more attention and resources then should be devoted to research and to attempts to overcome the special difficulties of these environments. This indeed was the response of individual scientists and even some research institutions, such as the *Institut national pour l'etude agronomique du Congo belge* (*INEAC*). But it was hardly characteristic of colonial governments in their budgeting and policy. There were some notable exceptions here, of course, in the years immediately following World War II. But these exceptions were usually not in the ordinary budgets. Some ventures, including some foolhardy ones, such as the Groundnut scheme in Tanganyika, and the Niger scheme in Nigeria, the Gambia Egg scheme, the Richard Toll Irrigation project in Senegal, may appear to contradict the contention that colonial governments showed little heart for facing up to the challenge of transforming tropical agricultural practices. But these schemes were somewhat freakish in character, often adopted on the instigation of outside forces. (United Africa Company of Unilever, ironically, was largely responsible for the identification of the Groundnut scheme, for persuading its adoption, and for its installation and operation during the critical first year and a half). In no instance were such projects an indication of a genuine new approach to peasant agriculture. They were, rather, often isolated projects which promised little toward the problem of what might supplant the systems of peasant agriculture given the exacting features of the environment. But substantially new attempts and approaches finally were made, late in the colonial period, most notably, in the late 40's in the Belgian Congo and in the 50's in areas of French and British control. Even so, the classic export crops still received disproportionate attention compared with food crops. In the Belgian Congo a series of whole-hearted attempts to devise new systems of peasant farming was begun from the mid '40's, *the paysannats indigenes*, undertaken by local administration and the *service d'agriculture*, often with the close association of INEAC. Such experience promised much in the search for practical alternatives to traditional shifting cultivation. Unfortunately there was little attempt, virtually none, to associate the Congolese with the direction of such programmes, so that the practical results have been almost totally absent since the disruptions following independence.

In Kenya, largely as a by-product of the Mau Mau emergency, another prominent new departure was the Swynnerton plan of field consolidation and village settlement in the Kikuyu highlands. But the point is still advanced that serious and comprehensive research began virtually only yesterday on alternative systems of farming, and that important experience relating to such problems in the peasant environment only then began to become prominent. Agricultural research, and the gaining of knowledge by experience in the actual peasant environment, are inherently slow processes. These are instances in which 'time' cannot be bought with money. We must face the fact that if all research budgets were multiplied, coordinated, and focused on the outstanding bottleneck problems it would still be many years before African agriculture as a whole could be transformed, even assuming a great compression of the lag between research and field adoption. Certainly more could and should be done. If it is to be a long hard row to hoe, then there is all the more reason to get started and to devote more resources. But I want to add, in emphasis, that this does not mean I favour some prior, more basic, heavier emphasis on agriculture in development strategy. As a matter of fact I think one can hardly expect much progress in agriculture unless there is a big push in the other sectors which will provide the needed demand. Such stimulus is certainly not a sufficient condition by itself, but it is necessary.

Since about the mid-'50's the generalized pessimistic evaluation of tropical, and specifically African, potentialities has largely ceased to be as prominent as before, and a more measured formulation now tends to hold, in which potentialities are assumed to be sufficient, given sufficient study and effort on all the questions facing research.[2]

RESEARCH AND DEVELOPMENT

Current policies and attitudes to research of government, and apparently of many research institutions, however, seem still to be deficient in in certain important respects. There is too little attention paid to farming systems, as compared to that given to specific plants and varieties. There is virtually no micro-economic analysis of suggested innovations. There is grossly inadequate recognition given to the implications of innovations with respect to use and availability of peasant labour. There is too little attention paid to social factors which may be decisive in determining whether proposed innovations will be accepted.

It is accepted that primary research attention should be on cash crops, but there are at least two reasons why a relative shift in attention must be made in favour of the staple food crops. First, the subsistence food crops must increasingly become cash crops as well; and secondly, there remains a tremendous backlog of research which was not done on staple foods while disproportionate attention was paid to the classic export crops of compelling importance to commercial interests of the metropolitan powers. For many years we have heard that 'simply' by adherence to the proper early planting schedule, cotton yields of two or three times the average could be assured. But from Mali to Ubangi there has been continued difficulty in getting adherence to the early planting regime. It is now gradually becoming recognized that the problem is not well-posed as one of peasant resistance to sensible advice; it is now apparent that early planting of cotton usually sharply conflicts with the establishment of the traditional food crops. There has been inadequate research on the food crops, inadequate attention to the whole complex of the peasants' operations and how best cotton could have been integrated with staple food crops cultivation. In general it can certainly be said that the usual starting point for research has not been the existing traditional systems of cultivation. Yet only full understanding of existing systems, including their economic characteristics, can indicate how given innovations may be introduced. Virtually no research institutions associated rural sociology or agricultural economics with their programmes until the last decade. It is still not standard procedure. On these issues it is heartening that an authoritative study of selected African agricultural schemes, undertaken by the International Bank, and scheduled for publication in 1967, has stressed the need to integrate social and economic analysis with technical research.[3]

To say that applied research has lagged is neither to disparage basic research nor to suggest that there are not critically important basic research questions unanswered which in fact need concentrated attention. But applied research—technical, economic, and social—has been too seldom specifically related to critical bottle-necks or to economic problems such as the relative high cost of fodder, the difficulty of pasture improvement, the smoothing of seasonal labour peaks, etc. For all practical purposes it is only in the last few years that we have, thanks to a great extent to the FAO Freedom from Hunger Campaign Fertilizer Trials Programme, any extensive work under appropriate field conditions on the economics of fertilizer use in West Africa. Typically, fertilizer experiments have been expressed in terms of physical responses. Even put in terms of net value—cost ratios—the analysis of the trials have seldom included certain costs typical of peasant conditions. In particular, costs of the last stages of transport, those borne directly by the peasants, are often neglected, and certainly most imputed labour costs are usually ignored.

To compress (and inevitably and necessarily to distort to a degree) agricultural research in Africa needed to take the existing situations of the peasants as starting points. Thorough understanding of traditional agriculture would have helped indicate the priorities and would have improved the design of research programmes. Without such basis and orientation much research has inevitably been less effective and certainly less efficient in economic terms. To a great degree I shall venture that this is still an important criticism. These considerations were much less applicable to the practice of the Belgians in the 1950's and in recent years to that of the French. A newly-planned Institute of Tropical Agriculture sponsored by the Ford and Rockefeller foundations, to be located in Western Nigeria, is a hopeful sign in this connection as it promises to focus on food crops, to stress systems of farming, and to integrate economic analysis with technical considerations. But as Prof. Dumont has emphasized, agronomy is a science of localities, and in addition to the important local natural features and economic characteristics, localities have social systems which must be understood, as a precondition to prescribing new patterns.

With respect to research, three additional points must be made. First, extension work, or what activity in Africa has gone by this name, has not been closely integrated with research. Rarely have extension staff been trained in ways that make them effectively familiar with the research programmes. Even more rarely have research programmes been influenced by the experience of extension workers. Secondly, research effectiveness depends also on the determination of what the appropriate shape and size of the unit of production is to be and what type of management it should have.

If basic scientific research and applied research can be said to have lagged, this is even more true of economic research. It is even much more the case as far as the kind of social research which might inform us of what kinds and shapes of social organization are socially and politically feasible and could fit the technical and economic requirements. On such questions we are even further behind. Until more is systematically known on this point it will often prove to be difficult to decide one of the all-important overall policy questions: to what extent should policy emphasize the modification of traditional practice and forms, on the one hand, and, on the other hand, to what extent should reliance be placed on the initiation of totally different, large-scale, 'modern' production units, by-passing the difficult task of reaching and changing the multitude of small peasants and small communities?

It should be noted that the implications of all the above discussion of research are that more elaborate research programmes will require very much larger staffs. Yet it must be recognized that, on the technical side, the supply of such staff is diminishing. We approach the end of a phase of drawing upon colonial-trained staff. These may have had their faults or deficiencies, but we must recognize that what we know of African agriculture can fairly be said to have been found out by and resides primarily in ex-colonial agricultural officers. The assumption that the equivalent of Belgian, British and French tropical agriculturists can be found among Americans, Russians and Israelis seems to me to be foolish whatever their goodwill, energies and competence at home. Such expatriate officers are being produced at a far slower rate now. African replacements, to be sure are being trained at a faster rate, but there is and will be a gap—not only quantitatively, but qualitatively in terms of experience. This is apt to be so even if we make the unfortunately shaky assumption that African governments will decide to quicken the rate of training of technical and related staff at all levels. Of course there are shortages not only at the higher levels. All proposals for improvement—seed distribution, provision of insecticides, co-operative marketing, improvement of storage—depend on field staff at middle and lower levels as well as at higher, if the proposals are to be implemented. I have no solution here—agriculture needs more of the budget than it typically receives; and recruitment of people to these occupations has to be organized; and better salaries must be offered. In other words, agriculture needs much more attention and more resources than it gets. (But this is not to state any falsely-posed opposition of agriculture to industry.)

An idea of the magnitude of skilled manpower requirements may be had from a recent study by Makerere College of the University of East Africa.[4] Rounding the figures, we find the following prospects (including the private sector) for the next ten years for the three countries of Kenya, Tanzania and Uganda:

Diploma and degree level posts,	1966	700
Posts filled	1966	—500
Vacancies		200
Replacements at 5% a year		500
New posts, 1966–1975		1000
Total demand, 1966–75		1700

The present graduation rate, at home and abroad is about 40 per year. If this can be doubled and can average 70 per year over the ten years, there will be 700 new recruits, to be compared to an overall demand for 1700, leaving a deficit of 1000.

It should be noted that the deficit for the decade is precisely equal to the estimated new posts needed. At present roughly 500 out of 700 posts are filled. In 1975 there would be 700 filled out of 1700, even supposing a doubling of the graduation rate. (A further implication of the study is that it will require until 1984 to 1989 to be able to supply 100 per cent of the public sector and 80 per cent of the private sector from local graduates).

It should not be thought that these demand projections are fanciful. They are made on the assumption that the projects in the countries' respective development plans will be implemented, but that after 1970 the increase in demand for such skills will taper off. The implications are quite clear: a continued need for overseas recruitment, a lowered level of effective implementation, or a postponement of plans. There will likely be a combination of all of these. The essential point, of course, is that these shortages simply cannot be made good. It takes too many years for minimum training. The supply on the international market is shrinking. The adjustment will mostly be made by reducing the number of projects unless a way is found of using assistants, volunteers and the like in ways which can multiply the effectiveness of the men with the higher skills. I must stress this last point. We simply must hope that there can be found some qualitatively new approaches to this training and manpower problem. Simple quantitative expansion of the numbers indicated for all practical purposes cannot be achieved. Can some new way not be devised?

SOME INDICATIONS OF THE RECENT QUANTITATIVE RECORD IN PRODUCTION

The factors already discussed—policy attitudes, research orientation, staff deficiencies—may go some way to account for the disappointing performance so often asserted today. The disappointing performance must be clearly recognized and kept in mind when projections of possible growth rates for the economy as a whole are under consideration. Yet some qualification of the usually rough assertions as to the level of performance might be made. In this we are certainly plagued by almost hopelessly bad data. Outside of a few special export crops we know next to nothing with any confidence as to what have been the trends and levels of production. It is safe to say that it will be years before this situation is changed. FAO publishes estimates, from official country submissions, of the production of main crops. When these are assembled by countries, we are left with bad guesses which in many cases do not cover even all the important food products.

FAO also constructs weighted indices of total agricultural production and of total food production, but for virtually all the countries of tropical

Africa these are not released. (From an organizational point of view they may have reason. The figures would be difficult to believe, and so the organization is spared some embarrassment. From FAO sources, e.g. at ECA we have recently calculated country indices of production of just the staple foodcrops. Some of the results I fear simply cannot be right.) The Economic Research Services of the US Department of Agriculture, making its own adjustments, without explanation of method, of FAO and other official estimates of production, constructs its own weighted indices for most of the countries of Africa. But they wisely try to restrict these to internal distribution. This is not the place to present in any detail the data of either of these efforts. But for what it is worth (very little) it should be said that when North Africa (and the Republic of South Africa) is excluded, the picture may not be as dark as it is usually painted. Derived from the USDA estimates, the following indices and rates of growth with respect to food production are given for the listed countries and sub-regions, for the nine year period, 1953–62, that is, from a base period of a three-year average of the crop-years 1952/53–1954/55 to an average of the recent three crop-years, 1961/62–1963/64.

Table 1

Indices of Estimated Food Production in Selected African Countries (Base Period 1952/3–1954/5 = 100)

	Country	Index 1961/62—1963/64	Implied Annual Rate of Increase %	Approximate Average Annual Rate of Population Increase 1953-1963 %
1	Niger	181	6.8	3.0
2	Ivory Coast	176	6.5	2.2
3	Kenya	164	5.7	3.0
4	Senegal	148	4.5	2.3
5	Malawi—Zambia—Rhodesia	146	4.3	3.0
6	Sudan	144	4.1	3.0
7	Tanganyika	143	4.1	1.8
8	Ghana	138	3.6	3.0
9	Malagasy	137	3.6	2.8
	East African Average[a]	135	3.3	2.3
10	Nigeria	134	3.3	3.1
	East and West African Average[b]	130	2.9	2.5
11	Guinea	129	2.9	3.2
12	Uganda	128	2.8	2.5
	West African Average[c]	126	2.6	2.7
	All African Average[d]	126	2.6	2.5
13	Mali	119	2.0	2.0

(Table 1 Cont.)

14	Upper Volta	119	2.0	2.2
15	Dahomey	119	2.0	3.;
16	Ethiopia	119	2.0	1.8
17	Sierra Leone	114	1.5	2.0
18	Cameroun	114	1.5	1.9
	North African Average[e]	112	1.3	2.5
19	Togo	103	0.3	2.2
20	Liberia	097	—0.3	1.1
21	Rwanda and Burundi	90	—1.0	2.9
22	Congo (Kinshasa)	78	—2.2	2.1

- Adapted from USDA *Indices of Agricultural Production in 28 African Countries,* December 1965. Average country price weights are used. 'Food' does not include cocoa and coffee (ECA adjustment). [a]Includes Sudan; excludes Somalia. [b]Includes Sudan, Cameroun and Congo (K). [c]Includes Congo (K) and Cameroun; excludes Mauritania and Gambia. [d]Excludes Mauritania, Somalia, Gambia, South Africa, Chad, Congo (B), UAR, Gabon and all dependent territories except Rhodesia. [e]Excludes Sudan. [f]From UN Demographic Yearbooks, and UN, *World Population Prospects as Evaluated in mid-1963*, adjustments made by ECA, 1966.

The picture presented in Table 1 is of extremely limited worth and should be used only with the greatest care. The population estimates are not very reliable, the food production estimates even less so, and in many cases the production estimates are partially derived from the population estimates.[1] For what they are worth the estimates seem to indicate that North Africa (as defined excluding Sudan) pulls down the average for the rest of the continent. The East African average rate, including Sudan, is 3.3 per cent per year against an estimated rate of population increase of 2.3 per cent per year. For West Africa the figures include those for Congo (K). If the extremely low rate of this much-disrupted country were omitted, the estimates would change as follows:

Table 2

Significance of Congo (K) in Averages of Rates of Increases of Food Production in Africa

	Average annual per cent increases in food production		*Average annual percent increase in population*
	Including Congo (K)	*Excluding Congo (K)*	
East plus West Africa-	2.9	3.3	2.4
West Africa-	2.6	3.2	2.7
All Africa-	2.6	2.8	2.5

- As defined in notes to Table 1.

North Africa, particularly the Maghreb, and the ex-Belgian areas, pull the averages down for the region and for their sub-regions in which they are included.[6] Perhaps the following shaky and tentative assertions may be made:

1 Generally in inter-tropical Africa, except for the poorer countries among those of the Guinea Coast, and for the gravely disrupted former Belgian areas, total food production is estimated to be growing slightly faster than the population.

2 The pattern shown however, must be interpreted within a context of diets clearly deficient in proteins, especially of animal origin, and while generally perhaps average caloric levels are not too low, they mask important discrepancies among groups of the societies: for example, women and children and lower income groups receive an appreciably inferior diet.

3 The apparent tendency for food production to increase at or near the rate of population increase is of course partially due to methods of estimating each of these. But given the high weight of subsistence production in the total, it would be idle to expect food production to increase much faster than population except in unusual circumstances. Subsistence producers 'plan' to produce what they can or what they want, allowing for bad years. They will, in my opinion, if they can, given labour and land availability, try to expand output *only if markets are growing sharply and seemingly assuredly*. Instead of the assertion that the 2 or 3 per cent annual increase in the agricultural sector, particularly the food production sector, 'holds down' the growth rates for the whole economy, it might in many cases be more appropriate to say that the rates of growth outside of agriculture, whatever they may be in annual percentage rates, are too small and too slow or too uneven to induce farmers to exert much more effort or take much risk. I want to emphasize these last remarks in the hope someone will try to convince me otherwise if I am mistaken. Obviously the peasant must become more 'market-oriented' and must also be better provided with productive aids, including credit. But it must be clear to him that extra effort and risk will be remunerative, and this depends upon the growth of the market.

4 The appropriate dimensions of the development problems in agriculture are not, it seems, to be comparisons of estimated annual rates of increase of total production or total food production with population rates, but the comparison of rates of increase in the production of *those products the demand for which is rising* and in the areas where the demand is. In other words, the maintenance or the lowering of consumer food prices, in the areas of growing industrial populations, and the reduction of food imports, are the appropriate measures of success. But increases in production for such markets also require to an important degree changes in the composition of output, and changes in the structural units of production. The urban demand pattern increasingly is for wheat, rice, meat, fish, milk. To a great degree the failure in agriculture has been a failure to make structural

changes in marketing, in transport facilities, and in the adoption of new products, not a failure of production or capacity to produce.[7]

In much of tropical Africa population density seems to be still fairly weak, and though there are those who will argue the point strongly and well, it may be probable that considerable population increases will be provided for by an extension of the traditional systems of food production. Experience seems also to indicate that intensification of food production methods can be expected when population densities reach critical levels. But such methods are not spontaneously initiated when population density is below such a level. This has been strongly and persuasively contended by Mrs Ester Boserup in her stimulating essay.[8] Unfortunately, this sort of intensification of production usually does not improve the real income per capita. For the more general case, there are three points, some of which may be hard to accept, but which I present for discussion.

1 Urbanization and industrialization, of a sort, have been enough to raise food prices in the towns and to induce increased food imports but not enough to bring about a transformation of agriculture; we need some careful studies of the supply responses in agriculture to the rising monetary demand in the cities. There have been few empirical studies of this.

2 Unfortunately, as things stand, we must realize that economically the old ways may often be best. That is, the new ways often simply do not pay.

3 Surprisingly, it is possible that total agriculture and even food production can be rising at rates higher than the rate of population increase, while at the same time food prices in the towns are rising sharply and so are food imports. The Ivory Coast situation is a good case in point. Wheat and beef and milk are not local products nor are the many packaged foods. But production for local processing, and the local processing industries themselves may well not yet be profitable under present circumstances, including those relating to scale of production. Food imports can be a very small fraction of total food consumption, but nevertheless a very significant fraction of total imports or total export earnings.

At least in the context of the next two decades, it would appear to be more helpful not to pose the key questions of development strategy explicitly in terms of population and food supply trends. Even if African agriculture could show annual growth rates appreciably higher, the key problems would remain, which are not so much ones of overall rates and quantities, but ones of sufficient responses to the specific challenges of development—the transformation of traditional practices and organization; the raising of per capita productivity; the provisioning of urban and other developing centres (with their new tastes); the responsiveness of supply to changes in demand; the improvement of diets; the substitution for imported foods; the supply of new industries with adequate new materials; and the general improvement of the rural environment.

The concept of annual growth rates needs to be considered carefully. Historically there are few instances in which rates of four per cent per year have been sustained for several years. It is universally conceded that only Japan in the period 1870–1920 showed an impressive record extending over decades of sustained high growth rates, and this record is one of about 4 per cent per year. Israel is probably another claimant to fame on this score, but it is debatable whether either of these cases are of much relevance to tropical Africa. Mexico has sustained rates of growth of total crop output of over 5 per cent per year for well over a decade. More significantly, Mexico has been able to reduce agricultural imports sharply, increase earnings from agricultural exports, and roughly maintain urban food prices while undergoing almost 20 years of industrialization. But history shows very few instances of the rapid and sustained transformation of traditional agriculture. We must have some respect for a problem so universally difficult. The inference is clear that there are no obvious or easy solutions. Targets must be realistic.[10] On the one hand tropical Africa for the most part starts from extremely low productivity levels and has a potentially large extensive margin of resources as well. In such circumstances it is quite possible to achieve and maintain at the outset high percentage rates of growth. But the many unsolved technical questions, the shortage of cadres, and the low priority which has in effect often been assigned to agriculture make the sustaining of annual growth rates of over 5 per cent unlikely. In this context the case of Mexico is probably instructive. Mexico has concentrated research, extension, investment, credit, and attention only on the most critical areas, most receptive farmers, most economically rewarding projects. As a result there has been virtually no change in technique or productivity or prosperity in most areas or for most of the peasantry. There are indications that this phase is finishing and that Mexico must start to deal with the much more difficult tasks of general agricultural improvement, for rural elements begin to reassert their interests, and the economy will need to bring them along as consumers.

But there may be lessons from Mexico to be applied to the strategy and tactics of agricultural development in many African countries. The essential elements of the Mexican approach have included the following:

A dense concentration of all relevant resources in critically important areas and sub-sectors of agriculture which constitute perhaps as little as ten per cent of the whole sector;

A holding operation for the vast remainder of the sector, sufficient to keep the bulk of the peasantry in a sort of political ice box, having met their minimum demands in terms of land tenure. (The cooperative *ejidos* of the village communities were not stressed as instruments of development and have played a passive role in development);

A focus on the all-important tasks of holding the line on urban food prices and reducing imports of agricultural goods; and

Maintaining a high rate of growth of industry, and thus of demand for agricultural products.

It is not necessary to approve all aspects of the Mexican experience to infer its relevance to Africa today. The most significant is the effective concentration of very scarce resources: skilled staff at all levels, from planning to field execution. In fact it may be said that one of the key policy issues—the degree of concentration or dispersion of effort and resources—might be more easily settled in African conditions precisely because of the extreme shortage of skilled staff.

CONCLUSION

To conclude, first there is a condition which most African countries have failed to fulfil or create, that of at least a minimum political link between the peasantry and the government. Most African governments do not have their political bases in the rural sectors. Whatever the understandable historical reasons for this, the result has been a lack of enthusiasm and responsiveness to proposals coming from the centre. All too often farmers feel that governments do not have rural interests at heart. So long as there is this lack of identification it will be difficult to effect the radical changes necessary to transform agriculture. It should be noted that almost all the indicated changes in methods will involve more and better work. Such work must be made worthwhile to the farmers and allowance must be made for risks.

Finally it is idle to suppose that most of the relevant skills in policy-making, research, and implementation can continue for long to be provided from abroad. The proper appreciation of the natural and social environment must ultimately be made by those in that environment. Is it unrealistic to infer that the appropriate means of unlocking the potentialities of the African tropics will have to be found by Africans? It is imperative for Africa to try to discover means of speeding up the creation of the needed army of African scientists and technicians.

REFERENCES

1 Pierre Gourou's *Les Pays Tropicaux*, Paris, 1948, is generally credited with the most effective presentation of this revision. Jean Paul Harroy's *L'Afrique: terre qui meurt*, Brussels, 1946 is perhaps an even better reference, because of its greater detail on specifically African conditions. Marston Bates, in *Where Winter Never Comes*, termed the older approach, certainly still to be found, as 'mid-latitude thinking'.

2 See W. Allen, *The African Husbandman*, London, 1965, for a thoughtful overall consideration of the character and patterns of traditional African agricultural systems.

3 John de Wilde and associates, for the International Bank, *Experiences with African Agricultural Development*, Baltimore, 1967.

4 Handbook 1966, Faculty of Agriculture, Kampala, 1966; pp. 65-69.

5 Perhaps some extra scepticism might be appropriate for the figures for Niger, Ghana, Malagasy, Ivory Coast and Kenya, which would seem to be too high.

6 The regions used here correspond to those of the UN—ECA except for the inclusion of Sudan in East Africa instead of North and Congo (K) and Cameroun in West Africa instead of Central. There are no data for the rest of Central Africa.

7 There are obviously many different patterns to be found. In Ghana in the last three years there were special circumstances in marketing and transport which caused marked shortages of traditional staples in urban areas. There appears to have been not only a failure of produce to move to markets, but a significant drop in production for the market.

8 *The Conditions of Agricultural Growth: The Economics of Agrarian Change under Population Pressure*, London, 1965.

9 Etienne N'Dongala, at IRES, Universite de Lovanium, Kinshasa, and Thomas Poleman in *Stanford Food Research Institute Studies*, May 1961, have been among the few to treat the subject at all, (Kinshasa and Accra, respectively).

10 Prof. Rene Dumont stresses this again in his recent study for the UN Economic Commission for Africa: *Developpement agricole africain*, (*Tiers-Monde* series of University of Paris, Nov. 1965) and English version, *African Agricultural Development*, ECA, 1966.

INDUSTRIAL DEVELOPMENT IN AFRICA : THE RESPECTIVE ROLES OF AFRICAN COUNTRIES AND EXTERNAL ASSISTANCE

by

ARTHUR F. EWING

Much of the discussion on development in recent years, in Africa and elsewhere, turns on industry. Yet in Africa, especially, thinking in most countries is based on the need for massive external assistance in finance, in entrepreneurship and management, in project preparation, in technology and in skilled personnel. Almost all governments have drawn up national development plans and with varying emphasis favour a mixed economy. Yet there is a common thread through most of them—the need to attract resources from outside. In this paper, an attempt is made to look at the problem in a broader perspective and to show that while external assistance is essential for many years to come, much more can be done by the African countries themselves, and indeed must be, if real industrialization is to be contemplated.

After a brief examination of the kind of industrial strategy which would seem to be essential, and of the industrial perspectives which have been opened up, the emphasis is placed on three problems: financing, the prerequisites of industrial development and the instruments of industrial development. In each case, the respective roles of African countries themselves and of external assistance are examined.[1]

The case for industrialization is now fairly well established. In the initial stages of economic development the generator is the export of raw materials. Export markets for raw material, with limited exceptions, grow rather slowly owing to the relatively low income elasticity of demand. It has been estimated that one per cent rise in the *per capita* income of an industrialized country increases the demand for food and raw materials by only 0.6% but that the same increase in *per capita* income in a country importing manufactures corresponds to an increase of 1.8% in the demand for imports.[2] There is no reason of principle or experience to suggest that the future prospects for the export of agricultural raw materials are likely to be better than in the past, although a more optimistic view may be taken so far as petroleum and some mineral products are concerned. Furthermore, in some raw materials, e.g. coffee, iron ore and copper, Africa would seem to have a comparative advantage and should therefore look warily at unduly restrictive commodity control schemes. Yet the major conclusion remains that without a basic structural transformation of African economies, adequate rates of growth will not be obtained, not least because the necessary foreign exchange for development purposes cannot be earned.

If, as will be argued, industry is the key to development, it is essential first to dispose of a false antithesis between agriculture and industry. The out-and-out protagonists of industry rather than agriculture have, on the face of it, much to be said on their side, since it is a characteristic of under-developed countries that 80% or more of the population are employed in agriculture and a very small fraction in industry, down to less than 5% in Africa. In its simplest terms, economic development is nothing more than a reversal of these proportions. Yet Africa remains a heavy importer of food and agricultural raw materials. The growth of industry requires increasing markets in the agricultural sector for capital goods such as agricultural implements and machinery and for intermediate goods such as fertilizers and pesticides, as well as for consumer goods. Agricultural production has to increase to meet not only the growing needs of the agricultural sector itself, but also an increased demand for food and raw materials in the industrial sector. Without this, as has been seen all too frequently in developing economics, the demand for imports increases rapidly and balance of payment problems intervene. Furthermore, for a considerable time to come industrialization is a means of increasing incomes and productivity but makes a relatively insignificant contribution toward employment. Much of the increase in employment has to come from the modernization of the rural sector, including physical infrastructure.

The stimulus of growing markets in the industrial sector is a necessary condition for the growth and modernization of agricultural production. Structural change in an under-developed economy means, in fact, both industrial development and the modernization of agriculture.

In considering the strategy of industrial development, the starting point is that international specialization in a free-world economy does not automatically give rise to equilibrium. On the contrary the gap between rich and poor nations tends to widen. Hence the need for under-developed countries to move away from dependence on export earnings from a limited range of primary products, to structural change, import substitution, industrialization under protection and export of manufactures.[3] Although there is still considerable scope for import substitution in Africa, experience elsewhere, particularly in Latin America, shows that the limits of what has been called 'easy' import substitution are soon reached. Even in Africa import substitution is an imperfect guide to an industrial development policy, partly because it lays too much emphasis on present demand—rather than demand as it can or will be in the future as a result of development—and structural change; and partly because mechanical reliance on substitution of consumer goods can divert scarce resources from those industries making intermediate and capital goods, which are the basis of structural change.

When the limits of import substitution are reached on a national basis, it becomes clear that export markets for manufactures have to be found, and this was a major theme of the Geneva World Trade Conference in 1964: the campaign by developing countries to force open the doors of the markets of the advanced countries. For most African countries, it will be a good many years before they can hope to compete in world markets in exporting manufactures, but there is an alternative approach: export of manufactures to each other. This is the underlying argument for the grouping of markets of African nations and co-ordinated industrial development, the approach of much of the work of the Economic Commission for Africa.[4] Most African markets are limited partly as a result of the small population of many countries and partly because of the low income per head. Many industries cannot hope to be economic without a sizeable market, owing to the influence of economies of scale. The advantages of international specialization are clear. External economies plus linkage effects cannot be realized within the boundaries of most individual African countries.

The appropriate pattern of industrial development is clear from the past experience of other countries now industrialized, even though countries at present under-developed need not follow slavishly the exact experience of others. It has been shown that as industrial development proceeds there is a fairly sharp fall in the relative importance of food processing and textiles in the early stages of growth, with a continued though reduced rate of decline subsequently. Metals and engineering products show the reverse movement with a declining rate of growth relative to the total when the later stages of development are reached. Chemical production shows a continuous rise, while the miscellaneous group first rises and then tends to fall in relative importance.[5] The essential point is that industry helps to raise the productivity of the economy and the increasing productivity in turn determines the pattern of industrialization. The process depends partly on the linkage effects already referred to and therefore on the establishment of a range of basic industries; partly on the transmission and creation of new technologies; and partly on the development of skills at all levels. The real issue therefore, if serious development is intended, is to launch a programme for the production of capital and intermediate goods, 'the production of machines which produce machines' to change the structure of the economy. Furthermore, much of the strength of the case for production of iron and steel and chemicals in Africa lies in the need to produce the inputs of agriculture in Africa: tools, implements, agricultural machinery, fertilizers and insecticides.[6]

In classifying industries from the point of view of development, the real distinction is between the production of capital, intermediate and consumer goods, with the emphasis on the first two. This does not mean that there is no scope for pressing on with production of consumer goods, particularly those based on agricultural raw materials, where value added is high. Nor does this strategy mean that most industries are necessarily large-scale. In all the three major branches of industry production is often economic at a relatively small scale and notably in the essential metal manufactures sector.

There is a growing literature on the detailed perspectives for rapid industrialization in Africa.[7] It has been suggested that Africa could be brought up to the present levels of economic development of Western Europe if it were to double its present *per capita* industrial output. The implication of such a structural change would be that the share of agricultural production would fall from 35 to 20 per cent and that of industry would rise from 20 to 40 per cent. Total industrial output would have to rise at about 8% per annum to 1980 and thereafter at 9% with a rate of growth of mining somewhat lower and of manufacturing somewhat higher. Within the manufacturing group, heavy industry would have to expand significantly faster than light industry, in line with historical experience. Such perspectives are not unduly optimistic in the light of experiences in other countries.

Some time has been spent on the strategy of industrial development, in addition to showing the perspectives, since this is highly relevant to the kind of policies which need to be devised and followed by African countries and without which the perspectives remain so much fantasy on paper. They cannot be realized by relying primarily on the outside world.

Any discussion on the financing of industrial development must necessarily be examined with the whole problem of capital formation, from both domestic and foreign sources, in view. It has already been suggested that current discussion has placed too much emphasis on external aid and not enough on possibilities of mobilizing and employing domestic savings. Nevertheless, in order to establish the orders of magnitude of the capital required, it is convenient to start from the quantitative estimates which have been made in the discussions on aid policy.

The quantitative case for capital aid has been put in its sharpest terms by the United Nations Secretariat.[8] A projected 4.8% average growth in GDP in the under-developed countries as a whole would give rise to annual import requirements which would be 95% more in 1970 than in 1959. Export receipts from a sale of primary products at constant prices are expected to rise by only 40%. Accordingly, the current trade gap with developed countries, after taking into account some increase in the export of manufactures, would rise by US$11 milliard and the balance of payments gap on current account, on the assumption that the net adverse balance on invisible account increased by US$4 milliards, would rise by US$14 milliards. Thus the total gap would be of the order of US$20 milliard without making allowance for amortization of past debts. By 1980 the figure would be US$57 milliard.

A calculation has been made of a hypothetical character attempting to put into perspective the whole problem of how the current balance of payments of the under-developed countries might move in the next 40 years. It is assumed that imports increase by 6% a year, a necessary consequence of a growth rate in GDP of 5%. It is further assumed that exports of primary products to the developed countries would increase by 3% and those to Eastern Europe by 9% and that exports of manufactures would increase by 10%. It is also assumed that the terms of trade remain constant and that the average interest charged is 3%. It will already be apparent that these assumptions, as far as Africa is concerned, are distinctly optimistic. Nevertheless, using them as a basis, the trade gap expressed as a percentage of imports does not begin to diminish until after 1980 and the balance of payments gap until after 1990. The cumulative deficit in the balance of payments gap up to the year 2000 is US$1,366 milliard, an almost inconceivable sum but no more than 1.5% of the GDP of the developed countries over the period, assuming a growth rate of 4%. More than 40% of the total deficit is accounted for by additional interest payments. If the aid were in gifts or interest-free loans the cumulative deficit would fall to US$7.5 milliard, or only 0.8% of the cumulative GDP of the developed countries.[9]

These figures should suffice to show the need for much higher rates of saving in Africa or in other words of financing domestically a far larger proportion of the higher rates of investment required. The net domestic product in Africa could rise from US$32 milliard in 1960 to US$100 milliard in 1980 on the basis of a growth rate of 5.9% (necessarily of course, implying considerable structural change). The present level of capital investment in Africa has been calculated at from US$4 to 4.5 milliard in 1960 prices. To achieve the growth rates indicated would mean raising capital formation to about US$20 milliard in 1980, i.e. from 14% of output in 1960 to 20% in 1980. These figures are large but it should be borne in mind that the periods of rapid development of the present advanced countries were not normally preceded by a considerable rise in capital formation. On the contrary, an acceleration of growth led to an increase in the level of capital formation. Furthermore, these calculations are based on a capital output ratio of 31, which could well be too high. Japan and Israel, to cite two examples of successful development, show capital output ratios closer to 21.

There is much more scope for domestic saving than has hitherto been realized and this despite the low *per capita* African income. There is a simple general principle which is not sufficiently understood. In the static economy of the text book, it is argued that investment, which in a static economy is necessarily equal to saving, can increase only if consumption falls and that this is difficult when the economy is at or near subsistence level. But investment generates income, which in turn makes possible increased saving. If the economy is growing fast enough, investment and consumption can both increase. A look at what has already been achieved in the way of saving in

Africa is far from discouraging. In the West African sub-region the level of gross capital formation increased from 8.9% of GDP in the early 1950s to 16% by about 1960. It has been calculated that to achieve a growth rate in GDP of 6% in North Africa over the next 20 years, the increase in investment outlays required could be reached if 50% of the yearly per capita increment in national income were to be saved in addition to the present 11.5% of GDP. This implies a high marginal rate of saving but not an impossible one, given present levels of development. As far back as 1961 the rates of saving as a percentage of GDP in some African countries were relatively high; 10% in the U.A.R. (and higher still more recently), 12.5% in Ghana, 14% in the Democratic Republic of Congo, 13.9% in the former Federation of Rhodesia and Nyasaland and 32.2% in Gabon. In a considerable number of other African countries, the rates were low but this is no more than evidence that they might have been much higher.

Thus far, all that has been shown is a good *prima facie* case for much higher rates of saving in most African countries. The problem is, of course, to make suitable arrangements to ensure that these higher rates are achieved. Small-scale savings can be mobilized in a variety of different ways. Equally important is the identification of opportunities for domestic investment in small-scale enterprise, this, in turn, promoting savings. Perhaps still more important is the need to attract small-scale investment into industry rather than into land or construction unrelated either to industry or agriculture. Diversion of savings into non-productive investment is a notorious vice in under-developed countries and African countries appear to have developed this practice too easily.

There is now need for institutions to mobilize domestic savings for local investment, such as co-operative banks, unit trusts and life insurance organizations. The industrial development bank is gradually gaining ground but has still a long way to go in West African countries and here the World Bank can help both through IDA and IFC. Within the same context, domestic institutions for industrial promotion can also play a part in assisting small-scale industrialists in obtaining capital equipment, loans at reasonable interest rates and foreign exchange for imported raw materials and equipment; an example is the recently established organization in Gabon, known as Promogabon. The industrial development corporation is more than a means of financing industry and is generally concerned with the development of the state or mixed sector. African experience of this device has not so far been particularly encouraging, but there is an important exception: the Uganda Development Corporation.

There remains what is perhaps the most important instrument: fiscal policy as a means of generating savings for all forms of development and thus also for industry. It is common knowledge that there is scope for better taxation systems in most African countries, in the double sense of the range of taxation and efficiency of collection. Some countries such as the United Arab Republic and Guinea have made marked efforts, but they are the exception rather than the rule. There is scope for more progressive taxation of personal incomes and for reaching down into the income-earning population. The efficiency of taxation of business incomes can be greatly improved through better and more honest accounting and record keeping. Looking to the future, and since the problem is as much one of administration and collection as of devising effective systems, there is a need to break down the traditional dichotomy between taxation departments, the treasury and the national planning authorities. There is also scope for devising new taxes on internal production, land, property, wealth and capital gains.[10]

Emphasis has deliberately been placed on the need and scope for more domestic saving in order to increase the proportion of industrial development financed from local sources. Furthermore, a better domestic performance in this respect is one of the keys to attracting more foreign aid. It is not intended here to devote much attention to the latter. It is obvious that even if domestic resources are much more fully drawn upon there will still be a need for large external funds. There has been much debate in recent years, not only on the volume of external aid required, but also on ways and means of improving its distribution. So far as the volume is concerned, the testimony of the President of the International Bank would seem to be sufficient when he stated recently that 'the preliminary study by the World Bank's staff, utilizing available data and their own experienced judgment, suggests that the developing countries could put to constructive use, over the next five years, some US$3 to 4 billion more each year than is currently being made available to them'.[11] In the long run, the right course is to develop a concept of international taxation leading to automatic availability of sufficient quantities of aid on a continuing basis.[12] In the short run, action has to be concentrated on some much-needed practical reforms with greater multilateralization as a general objective. Thus aid should progressively be more on a national development plan than on a project basis. It should be based on total costs including domestic costs. It should become steadily less tied. Grace periods before repayments start should be lengthened as well as the period of the loan, and rates of interest lowered. The suppliers' credit should disappear as quickly as possible. Grants for the poorer countries are preferable to loans. The period of planning aid should be lengthened. Aid should be provided, in Africa in particular, more and more in terms of groups of countries, and in this context, consortia or consultative groups are a useful device. Contrary to some current thinking, the case for concentrating a higher proportion of aid on the weaker countries of Africa is a strong one. Finally, it has to be recognized that much potential aid has been lost through inadequate project preparation on the part of African countries.

The next few years are bound to see important reforms in the practices of aid-giving countries and this process will be facilitated as it is increasingly recognized that external aid is a contribution to development, but not the major factor. There is one further point of importance. Developing countries, perhaps most of all African countries, have to realize that whatever reforms may be introduced, the developed countries are bound to remain not wholly disinterested. These have shown themselves ready to promote the financing of infrastructure—human and physical. There are foreign investors who are interested in promoting the creation of profitable new industries, generally on a national scale and concentrated to a considerable extent on consumer goods. There are fewer signs of a willingness to finance basic industries, intermediate and capital goods. This has to be recognized in a spirit of realism and can therefore be a guide to policy in the distribution of sources of finance. In other words, efforts can be made to attract external resources in directions of interest to the aid-givers and yet also of interest to Africa and in this context there are prospects of obtaining more in two key areas: human infrastructure and agriculture. The counterpart is for the African countries, by the grouping of their efforts, to finance basic industry largely from their own funds, this necessarily requiring a substantial public sector.

The pre-requisites of industrial development have to be dealt with briefly here. These are: science and technology and the application thereof; education; manpower planning; the discovery of natural resources; energy and transport. In the field of science and technology, despite the importance of making progress in pure science, emphasis in Africa at present has to be on applied research or towards the solution of practical problems, with the experience of Japan and to some extent the U.S.S.R. as useful examples, and in Africa itself the United Arab Republic. There are three issues: first, a mechanism for the transfer of industrial technology; secondly, the commissioning of applied research on behalf of Africa in the developed countries wherever the efforts involved are complicated and expensive, and thirdly, arrangements within Africa for the carrying out of applied research, including the adaptation of existing technology to suit African conditions.

In this area the developed countries can make a major contribution. First of all, in the transfer of technology they can simplify awkward problems of property rights in know-how and patents. Secondly, they can show themselves willing to carry out specific research on behalf of African countries. At present, much research on African problems is carried out in England and France, but is primarily directed to the solution of problems of interest to commercial bodies in these countries, e.g. corrosion of metals and the growing and processing of primary products such as edible oils, coffee and cocoa. In the third area, research in Africa itself, a start has hardly been made. Grouping of efforts by African countries is required and the developed countries can do much, partly by financial assistance, not necessarily at great cost, partly by lending key personnel and above all, by helping to train Africans on the job.

Education is a major subject which cannot possibly be examined in detail here. The shape of the educational system in Africa, particularly at the secondary and tertiary levels, is a determining factor in preparing the ground for future training of personnel at all levels for industry. There are two current tendencies which are on the whole not favourable from the point of view of industrial and indeed general economic development. One is perhaps rather too much emphasis, given shortage of resources, on universal primary education and the other is insufficient attention, particularly at the tertiary level, to scientific and technical subjects.[13] The contribution to be expected from outside Africa is very large indeed and will have to continue for three or four decades.

Another problem is that of manpower planning, which, as in the case of education, concerns economic development generally and not just industry. There have been few adequate manpower surveys and there is generally a lack of machinery for manpower planning. Not many African plans have much to say about manpower: effective liaison with educational planning and with the machinery for the establishment and carrying out of detailed training programmes. African countries are not, of course, wholly unaware of the need for such machinery. What is lacking is trained specialists in manpower planning. Here again much can be done by the developed countries, through both multi-national and bilateral technical assistance, in helping to draw up detailed manpower plans, in establishing permanent machinery for manpower planning and in training manpower experts primarily within Africa, but in certain cases through fellowships abroad.

Next comes the discovery of natural resources. It is commonplace knowledge that Africa is well endowed with most natural resources, which are inadequately explored and insufficiently exploited. Because of lack of knowledge, particularly of the resources of the smaller and poorer countries, it is sometimes argued that it is premature to envisage sub-regional arrangements for industrial development, since any agreements entered into might be unfair to some countries. This is surely wrong. The right approach is to give priority in further surveying to the weaker countries, particularly those in the hinterland of West and Central Africa. Since this kind of work is expensive in money and skilled manpower, such is rightly expected of the developed countries through multi-lateral and bilateral arrangements. The emphasis should perhaps be on the multi-lateral approach, e.g. the United Nations Development Programme and its Special Fund, since this avoids over-concentration on immediate commercial interests in the developed world. Furthermore, apart from specific surveys there is a case for setting up multi-national institutes in Africa and here again much can be done by countries outside Africa.

Energy and transport will have to be considered very briefly and almost in passing. Africa is rich in energy resources which are under-exploited and its transport system is at present, for historical reasons, based largely on the evacuation of natural resources for export overseas, with limited interconnections among African countries. A greater supply of energy at a reasonable price is an obvious necessity for industrial development. Transport is more complicated since there is something of a vicious circle. The justification of new transport links depends on more traffic and hence more industrial and agricultural production for African markets. The present African transport system is such as to inhibit the growth of African industry in particular. This circle can, of course, be broken.

Much of the effort of the international aid programmes, both multilateral through the International Bank and the United Nations Special Fund, and bilateral through FED, FAC, AID and the Commonwealth Development Corporation, has been directed towards improvement of physical infrastructure. Such a policy has not been wrong and there is much more to be done, especially in Africa, which has been less well favoured than Latin America and Asia. But the programmes could be better directed to specific problems of internal agricultural and industrial development, and sometimes conceived on a more economic scale.

There remain the instruments or agents of industrialization, perhaps the most important and difficult problem of all, and this means primarily institutions and people. First of all, there is development planning and programming. Almost all African countries have now drawn up development plans, largely with foreign assistance. This is not a particularly difficult exercise and there are two obvious criticisms. The first is that few of these plans envisage a coherent strategy for the transformation of the economy, notable exceptions being the United Arab Republic, Tunisia and, potentially Tanzania, Uganda and possibly Mali. The second is that in general, mechanisms for the execution of plans lag far behind the plans themselves. Here again, exceptions on the basis of practical experience so far are the United Arab Republic and Tunisia, and it is significant that in both these countries the public sector is important. Foreign aid remains necessary but will have to be different, not so much in quantity as in quality and perspective.

A further essential weakness related to industrial development lies in the realm of project preparation where reliance on the outside world is at present very great indeed. The successive elements in the process of project preparation have to be distinguished: the preliminary study; the feasibility study which in itself falls into two parts, the study of technical and of economic feasibility; and finally, the engineering study up to the point where detailed engineering designs, drawings and specifications are prepared and the financial plan drawn up. It should be possible for African countries within a relatively short space of time to be able to cope with the first two stages, resorting to specialized consultants for the final stage which is likely to be necessary for some time to come. Two things above all are required. First, training courses in project preparation and secondly, the setting up of national and sometimes multi-national agencies concerned partly to prepare feasibility studies and partly to be in a position to vet and control international vendors of projects and particularly machinery salesmen. What is required from the outside world is not so much feasibility and engineering studies, although in the short run these are clearly needed, as assistance to Africa so that it can step by step be in a position to carry out such studies itself and thus eventually become master of its own industrial fate.

Next comes industrial training at all levels—a much more comprehensive and long-term, though not necessarily more complicated business than is frequently assumed. More can be done by training within industry, particularly in large-scale foreign enterprises, by insistence on the part of African governments that whenever facilities are offered for the establishment of a new enterprise, a definite and comprehensive training plan should be a part thereof, so that within a limited period of years the whole enterprise can be not only owned but also managed and largely manned by Africans. Secondly, there is a need for training institutions, centres and short-term training courses within Africa, organized often on a sub-regional basis. Here again, this is a field where much is required and can be expected from the outside world both from multi-lateral agencies and from bilateral programmes. In this context, special emphasis should be given to management training and there would seem to be a case for the establishment of one or more management training institutes in Africa. Too much emphasis has been given to sending Africans abroad and it would seem appropriate that this should be confined to specialized training, at the highest level, of suitably selected candidates who are certain to return to work in appropriate and responsible positions in their own countries.

The next question is that of industrial promotion at all levels. There would seem to be a case for a national industrial promotion institute in every African country. The capital costs are not high but for the next few years external assistance in personnel is clearly necessary. This may be an area which is particularly appropriate to the United Nations Development Programme.

Assistance in terms of personnel, as distinct from finance, will be required for many years and this is perhaps the most important contribution which can be made to Africa by the outside world. In the short-run there is a sheer manning operation; in the longer run, which is two to three decades, this means the willingness of the advanced countries to supply personnel for fairly long periods, particularly as advisers and teachers, people who, by their very nature, are ready to respect the principle that African countries wish to run their own affairs but are ready to be assisted constructively in the process of Africanization, not only at the level of government and in the higher civil service, but also in the day-to-day management of economic life, and particularly in industry.

In conclusion, the main points of the argument may be summarized briefly. A proper industrial strategy requires emphasis on the production of intermediate and capital goods capable of transforming the structure of African economies, and according to the nature of the industries concerned, the grouping of African countries. There are then serious perspectives for rapid industrial growth. But without more emphasis on the pre-requisites and agents of industrial development, little is likely to be achieved. Finance is essential but much more must and can come from domestic saving than is generally recognized, much of it through the public sector. Realistically, most of the financing of basic industry will have to come from African sources, but much of what is needed to improve the human and physical infrastructure can continue to come from abroad. In each of the areas which can be regarded as falling within the pre-requisites—science and technology, education, manpower planning, the discovery of natural resources and energy and transport—the developed countries can be asked to make a major contribution in money and manpower for a long time to come.

Creating the agents for industrial development, appropriate institutions and people, is largely Africa's own business and the real test. But there is much that the outside world can do to help, partly through financial assistance and still more through disinterested advice and training.

REFERENCES

1 These problems are examined in detail in a study by the author on *Industry in Africa*, London, 1968, in the course of which full references are given. References in this paper are kept to a minimum.

2 Although the statistical evidence has been disputed, it is also argued that in recent years, at least, there has been superimposed on this basic trend a tendency for the terms of trade to move against under-developed countries. It by no means follows that this will continue.

3 See in particular G. Myrdal, *The Development of Under-developed Countries and Economic Theory*, London, 1957, and R. Prebisch *Towards a Dynamic Development Policy for Latin America*, United Nations, 1963.

4 See also F.Perroux, *L'Economie des jeunes nations* Paris, 1963.

5 A Maizels, *Industrial Growth and World Trade*, Cambridge, 1963. See also *Patterns of Industrial Growth* 1938, 1958, United Nations, New York, 1959.

6 See G. de Bernis 'Industries lourdes et industries legeres' in *Industrialisation au Maghreb*, Paris, 1963.

7 These were first pointed out by the ECA in *Industrial Growth in Africa*, United Nations, New York, 1963, and there have subsequently been a whole series of detailed sector studies, prepared manily within the framework of the four ECA sub-regions of Africa.

8 United Nations *World Economic Survey*, 1962, Part I-Developing Countries and World Trade, New York, 1963.

9 N. Kaldor, 'International Trade and Economic Development', *Journal of Modern African Studies*, Vol. II, No. 4, Cambridge, 1964.

10 In this context see the 'Report of the Advanced Seminar on Current Problems and Training Needs in Taxation Administration', held in Addis Ababa in December, 1965 (Document E-Cn. 14-FISC-I).

11 George D. Woods, 'The Development Decade in the Balance', *Foreign Affairs*, January 1966, Page 214.

12 See Dudley Seers, 'International Aid-The Next Steps', *Journal of Modern African Studies*, Vol. II, No. 4, Cambridge, 1964

13 For a discussion of these problems see recent contributions by Messrs. Harbison, Myers and Hunter.

NOTES ON THE COMMON MARKET AND AFRICA

by

DURI MOHAMMED

The acceleration of economic growth in most African countries depends upon the exploitation of their agricultural resources to enhance their industrial advancement. Agriculture at an early stage of development does not only supply the surplus food required for the industrial workers but has to produce export surplus through the marketing of food and industrial raw materials for the international market. The price these commodities fetch is a crucial factor in determining the economic pace in an open economy where imports have to be paid for by exports. Foreign currencies are needed (and used) not only for the importation of capital goods which are so essential for economic growth but also for the importation of consumer goods—simply because underdeveloped countries are equally deficient in consumer goods. Thus any fall or instability in their foreign currency earnings could have a far-reaching damaging effect on their economics and the rate of their economic growth. But foreign earnings and their effective utilization in the process of industrialization presents only one side of the problem. The industries once established have to market their products. There is no doubt that their products cannot compete in international market either in price or quality with those from the industrialized countries. Consequently the backward economies cannot share the international market with the highly developed capital intensive economies of advanced countries on a scale that guarantees their future growth. Neither can they compete in their own domestic market with the imported foreign goods because of the low cost of production of the latter. Therefore their infant industries have to cater primarily for the sheltered domestic market and there must be adequate provision to protect these industries if they are to be rescued from stagnation and saved from extinction. The task which this paper takes upon itself is to assess rather rapidly some of the economic implications of the European Common Market, or more appropriately, the European Economic Community, for the development problems of African countries.

The treaty of Rome, signed on the twenty-fifth of March 1959, for the creation of the European Common Market between France, Germany, Italy and the Benelux countries has opened one of the most important economic chapters in the post-war period. In this economic plan the seven European countries joined hands to plant the nucleus of the United States of Europe on the model of the United States of America, to enjoy the economics of mass production, free of tariffs and quantitative restriction and leading to eventual political unification. This grand design did not only prove to be important by itself, but confronted the outside world and in particular, the African countries with a difficult challenge.

Africa as it stands today is divided into three separate trade zones very much along the old colonial demarcation lines. Firstly, the ex-French territories having economic links and special preferential treatment with the Common Market countries. Secondly, the ex-British territories enjoying tariff preferences on their exports to the United Kingdom as members of the British Commonwealth of Nations. (Thus there are two separate preferential areas in Europe for many tropical products and especially for coffee, cocoa and tea). Thirdly, there are countries such as Ethiopia, Liberia, Morocco, Tunisia, Sudan, and the UAR which are left outside either major preferential area.

In the treaty of Rome, the member countries of the European Common Market agreed to free their trade not only among themselves but also with their associates, most of whom are in Africa. The member states are to apply to the associated countries the same rules and regulations for the removal of tariffs and quantitative restrictions that apply to themselves. Accordingly France, which already extends free trade to its own associates, will, in a series of stages, be applying the same policy to the associates of other Common Market countries. As far as the associated countries are concerned, the treaty provides for and justifies the practice of protection, but the paradox of it is that its implementation eventually leads to free trade. The overseas associated members may thus levy taxes which are in conformity with their development needs and fiscal policy. They can also employ tariffs within the community to protect their industries and to collect revenue. But these duties have to be non-discriminatory. Accordingly Madagascar has already introduced new tariffs which give free entry to all community products—but commercially nothing spectacular has happened.

The associate members are not only linked to the community through their trade relations but also through a development fund contributed by the European members of the community. This fund is established primarily to help finance the economic and social infrastructures of these countries in accordance with the Part IV of the Treaty.

What makes all these relations of Africa with the Common Market countries important is their preponderant reliance on foreign trade, and in particular, trade with Western Europe.

The African economy, which is mainly dependent upon primary products for its export trade, has to rely for the marketing of its products on an international market concentrated in one geographic area. And as the table indicates, exports provide a very large proportion of the total money income of most African countries.

Significance of Exports in Some African Countries

Algeria	10.2
Belgian Congo	48.3
East Africa	27.5
Ethiopia	11.8
Ghana	25.1
Madagascar	15.8
Morocco	20.7
Nigeria	16.2
Sierra Leone	34.7

Source: *United Nations, Economic Survey of Africa since 1950*. p. 15 and p. 175.

It is quite evident also that African trade is by and large conducted with the Common Market countries as the table below indicates.

Trade of Africa with EEC Countries

	*Exports to African Countries**			*Imports from Africa**		
	1958	*1959*	*1960*	*1958*	*1959*	*1960*
Belgium	237	186.4	163.3	278.4	329.2	382.7
France	1875.2	1772.3	2052.6	1525.1	1230.5	1430.0
Italy	214.3	210.4	243.4	245.5	284.2	322.1
Netherlands	182.4	182.3	206.2	176.8	203.0	179.6
West Germany	455.5	499.9	502.1	467.2	525.1	280.6
	2964.4	2851.3	3167.6	1693.0	1572.0	1595.0

*In millions of US dollars.

The question that arises from the above analysis is what kind of benefits the association can provide to the non-European members (associates). Broadly speaking, outside countries will be affected in two different ways by the advent of the Common Market. There will be 'trade diversion' as the result of the removal of customs barriers among the members of the community. This means that a member country, which formerly imported from a relatively low-cost country outside the community, now finds it less expensive to import from a member country. In such cases the union may be acting to the disadvantage of the third countries and may prove to be harmful to their economies. But the ultimate effect will depend on the height of the common external tariff which is eventually established. And each individual country has to examine its exports to the Common Market countries. The effect of tariffs on commodities like cotton and crude oil is certainly negligible, because the tariff for these commodities will be zero. On the other hand commodities like coffee and cocoa, imported from a third country, face nine per cent import duty while the associates enjoy free entry. This may cause trade diversion.

The Common Market may also be 'trade-creating', that is to say, the removal of restrictions on trade within the community might encourage production on a large scale and at high efficiency. This rise in productivity will certainly increase real income in the community as a whole, and possibly imports from the third countries. Consequently it may have a positive effect on the development of the third countries.

But the growth effects of the community cannot be separated from its terms of trade. The growth effects could strengthen the trends that make the union's term of trade *vis-à-vis* the third countries more and more favourable. This is because the selling opportunities of the community in the international market could expand tremendously as a result of economies of scale, specialization and better utilization of economic capacities. And with its tariff wall reducing importation from the third countries, real income may be shifted from the third countries to the members of the Common Market. In fact the integration may create a chain reaction in the terms of trade favouring the members of the community. One thing is clear. It will certainly improve the bargaining power of the community and more upward shifts may take place in its export prices, with a possible reduction in its imports from the third countries.

The benefits to the associate members are not obvious. Studies of the effect of economic unions on the economic welfare of the constituent units, their rates of growth and prospects of development have generally concluded that economic integration will most benefit those which are at much the same level of development. The integration of underdeveloped countries with highly developed ones will not assist the former, and may even hinder the more backward economies. It is appropriate here to quote Alexander Hamilton, writing in 1719 about the United States foreign trade policy *vis-à-vis* Europe. '*The United States cannot exchange with Europe on equal terms, and the want of reciprocity would render them the victim of a system which could induce them to confine themselves to agriculture, and refrain from manufactures. A constant and increasing necessity, on their part, for the commodities of Europe, and only a partial and occasional demand for their own, in return, would not but expose them to a state of impoverishment compared with the opulence to which their political and natural advantages authorize them to aspire . . . If Europe will not take from us the products of our soil, upon terms consistent with our interest, the natural remedy is to contract, as fast as possible, our wants of her*'.

The consequence of such integrations between economies at different levels of development are exhibited today in North and South Italy and in the North and South of the United States. Are we then going to perpetuate the North–South gap on a global scale?

In the treaty of Rome the signatory countries did not only agree to free trade among themselves but also with their associates—most of whom are in Africa. Of course the community has taken upon itself to promote the economic advancement of all parties to the agreement, and to assist the less fortunate members to bridge the gap which separates them from the more fortunate ones. But we have to remember that aid is only a peripheral source to be sought and indeed received carefully, but not as the major factor to enable us to jump over the hurdles of economic growth.

There are still many unresolved issues as far as the agricultural aspects of the union are concerned. Some of the community members do not only protect their agricultural sector but subsidize it heavily. Furthermore it would be a serious mistake to assume that the problems of low-income countries will be solved by free trade in tropical commodities or even by free trade in the whole range of primary products. It should be remembered that in Europe tropical products have long been a favourite source of government revenue, tapped not only by tariffs but also by internal taxes. On coffee alone, for example, Germany at the time of the Treaty had a 25% import duty and 47% excise tax. It has been calculated that in each of the three countries the combined impact of the two taxes was over 70% *ad valorem*. It is quite clear that both the tariff and the excise taxes were purely revenue measures, since none of these countries produce coffee. In a partial attack on the problem, President Kennedy in 1961 proposed that the U.S. and the Community jointly maintain a policy of free trade on those tropical products where no important domestic production is involved. Although this was primarily directed to customs duties it should apply also to excise taxes.

From the point of view of the African countries the elimination of tariffs is a very minor issue. Economic growth in these countries depends to a large extent on foreign currency earning capacity, and this is tied up for a long time to come with the expansion of agricultural export, the prospect of which is by no means bright.

This does not mean that agricultural products from the underdeveloped world cannot be marketed in the industrially advanced countries. Both kinds of raw materials, agricultural food stuffs and industrial raw materials, will continue to find a market in richer countries, but in each case at a falling rate. That is to say, as the incomes in the rich countries expand, the demand for food also expands but at a much lower rate. In the case of industrial raw materials the prospects are perhaps brighter but yet they are far from assuring. The assumption that the demand for raw materials within the industrialized countries will vary more or less proportionately with the changing level of industrial production is no more valid. The development of synthetic materials (notably artificial textiles such as rayon and nylon) have greatly reduced the dependence of industrial countries on a number of raw materials. Moreover in certain industries great economies have been achieved in the use of imported raw materials. Such developments in the United States have brought about a colossal reduction in the importation of industrial raw materials. Thus a vigorous expansion of exports of industrial raw materials is not very likely either. The abolition by all industrial countries of tariffs, consumption taxes and quantitative restrictions on tropical produce is only one side of the problem. More important is the world level of commodity prices. During the year 1958, the main tropical products, valued at $25 billion, proved subject to an average price fluctuation of 23%. In the same year the U.S., the U.K., and France, gave assistance amounting to $3 billion to the Asian and African countries, which are major areas of production of tropical raw materials. A drop of 12% in the average price was thus sufficient to wipe out the entire inflow of money into these countries from development aid. Therefore the most important thing is to set right the whole international economic framework into which African countries are going to fit, and the basic issue is not aid but trade.

It is becoming more and more evident that the relations between underdeveloped and advanced economies have been established on a double standard morality. What they gained in aid is completely overshadowed by what they lose in trade. It has been admitted time and again for the last fifty years, that the economic gap between the *haves* and *have-nots* has been widening. It has also been professed that this gap must be narrowed down in the interest of world peace and stability, if not for other reasons. So far none of the existing institutions have faced this challenge effectively. The Common Market is a trading arrangement primarily geared to improve relations between the developed economies which are considerably oriented towards exports of industrial goods. The association of African countries with such arrangements may prove damaging to their economy, and they may reap only transitory benefits—compromising their long-term development interests. If the union is to help the economic development of African countries, a totally different type of arrangement would seem to be required, sponsoring a fair price structure for commodity markets and constant protection for their industries.

REFERENCES

Sidney Weintrab, 'The Foreign Exchange Gap of the Developing Countries', *Essays in International Finance*, No. 48, Princeton September, 1965.

United Nations, *Economic Bulletin for Africa*, Vol. II, No. I, Addis Ababa.

Guy Benveniste & W.E. Moran, *Handbook of African Economic Development*, New York, 1962.

J.E. Meads, *U.K. Commonwealth and Common Market*, Institute of Economic Affairs, 1962.

S.K. Padover, *The Mind of Alexander Hamilton*, New York, 1958.

United Nations, *Towards a New Trade Policy for Development*, E-Conference 46-3. February, 1964.

Pieter Lieftinch, 'External Debt and Debt-bearing Capacity of Developing Countries', *Essays in International Finance*, Princeton March, 1966.

AFRICA'S PLACE IN THE ECONOMICS OF WORLD CATASTROPHE OR OPPORTUNITY

by

E. A. A. ROWSE

Introductory Note

The purpose of this paper is to revise, in the light of subsequent experience, an appreciation of the world situation, developed between August 1941 and December 1944. At that time it was anticipated that the population, which could be supported on the resources of the planet, might not exceed 5 milliard.

It has now been repeatedly stated that between 6 and 7 milliard consumers must be accepted as the probable total to be reached early in the twenty-first century. The 1965 Belgrade Conference of the United Nations on Demographic Trends and the Food Situation reaffirmed the Sakhatme projections of 1963; but included a paper by Dr. Boyarsky, which continued the line of demographic policy, followed by the Soviet representative at the Rome World Population Conference of 1955, that the rise in population would not be as dramatic as anticipated by the neo-Malthusians. Dr. Boyarsky claims, that well-known economic limiting factors will operate on the birthrates of the world and as a consequence the potential of rapidly advancing technologies will provide adequate living standards, given the maintenance of peaceful conditions over the planet. Can peace be preserved?

It is not by any means a certainty that the five-milliard population accepted by Dr. Boyarsky can be supported. In the case of a seven-milliard world by the year 2000, the tensions, which will be built up, will demand deep-seated adjustments, perhaps psychologically unacceptable. Failing a solution, the distribution of population on both land and sea must be subject to re-deployment. Peaceful or imposed by force.

It is now half a century since this problem of mass-movement of population came into focus once again after the lapse of seven and fifteen centuries. Twenty-five years ago its then current version, expressed in the word *lebensraum*, provoked an answer in Clauses 3 and 7 of the Atlantic Declaration of 1941. Promises given at a time of crisis have not been fulfilled. During the post-war period, Asian demographers, in particular

WORLD POPULATION TRENDS — GRAPH 1.

PROJECTIONS OF CONTRASTING ESTIMATES OF THE TOTAL CONSUMER DEMAND ON THE PLANET BEFORE AND AFTER THE TURN OF THE CENTURY.

THE INTENTION IS TO INDICATE CONJECTURAL, EVEN PROBABLE, DEMOGRAPHIC UPPER LIMITS OF THE EXPANDING MARKETS OPEN TO ALL PRIMARY PRODUCING AND MANUFACTURINC COUNTRIES.

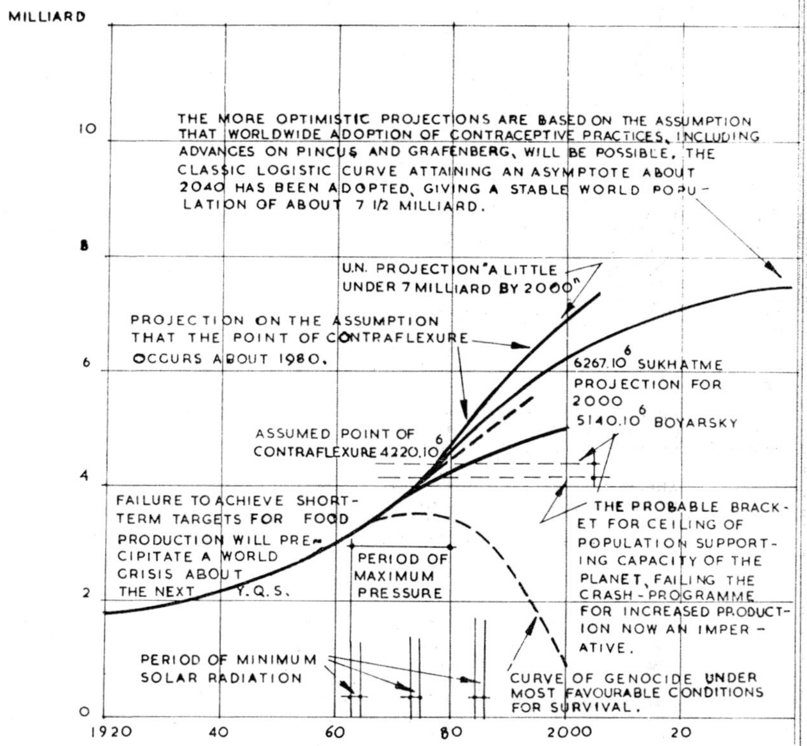

THE PERIOD, DURING WHICH THE EFFECT OF A DEVELOPMENT PLAN FOR THE CONSTRUCTION OF NECESSARY INFRA-STRUCTURE AND PRODUCTIVE CAPITAL EQUIPMENT, INSTALLED IN ALL DEVELOPMENT AREAS PRIOR TO 1970, WILL HAVE A CUMULATIVE INFLUENCE ON THE CAPACITY TO MEET A SEVEN-MILLIARD WORLD DEMAND, WOULD HAVE BEEN 1945 - 1965. THIS WOULD HAVE PARTICULARLY APPLIED TO HYDROLOGICAL CONTROL WORKS, FERTILIZER PLANTS AND TRANSPORTATION SYSTEMS OF COHERENT CONTINENTAL SCALE.
A CRASH PROGRAMME WILL NOW HAVE TO BE DIRECTED TO COVERING AS MUCH OF THE BACKLOG AS IS POSSIBLE.

E.A.A.R.

WORLD POPULATION BALANCE : C. 2000. MAP 1.

(FIGURES SUGGEST TOTAL POPULATION SUPPORTING CAPACITY)

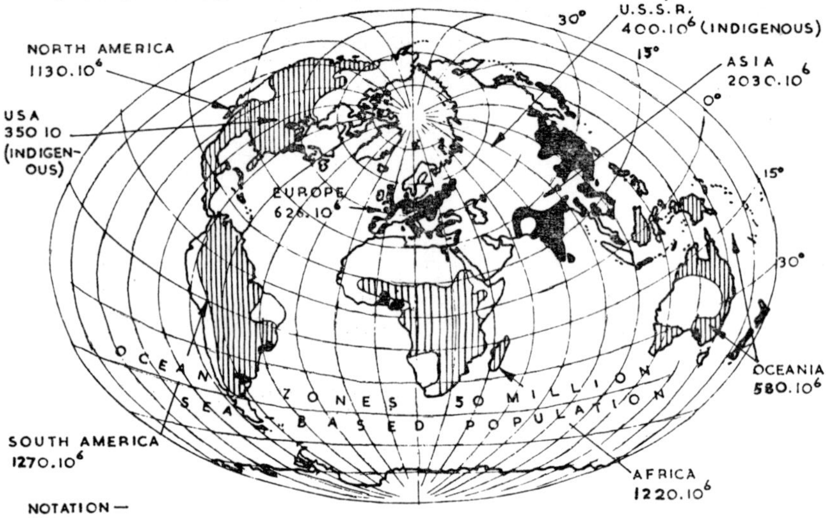

NOTATION —

'MALTHUSIA' — AREAS OF CONTEMPORARY CONCENTRATIONS OF POPULATION, BASED ON EXISTING OR INCIPIENT INDUSTRIALIZATION, IN WHICH DENSITIES WILL REQUIRE, DIRECT OR INDIRECT, EASEMENT.

'CORNUCOPIA' — AREAS OF UNDER-UTILIZED POPULATION SUPPORTING POTENTIAL, WHICH WOULD BE REGARDED AS RECEPTION AREAS FOR OVERSPILL OF SURPLUS FROM REGIONS OF ABSOLUTE OVER POPULATION, AS DEFINED BY A COMPETENT WORLD AUTHORITY; UNLESS AN EFFECTIVE SYSTEM OF TRADE EXCHANGES AND CREDIT LIQUIDITY CAN BE DEVISED.

CONTEXT —

THE HISTORICAL DEMOGRAPHIC CONTEXT OF MAP I STARTS WITH THE ANCIENT MASS-CULTURES OF SOUTH AND EAST ASIA, WITHIN WHICH THE GROWTH CHECKS OPERATED UNTIL A LITTLE MORE THAN TWO DECADES AGO. IN EUROPE THE GROWTH RATE BEGAN TO RISE FROM THE TWENTIES OF THE NINETEENTH CENTURY WITH THE IMPLEMENTATION OF HYGIENE REGULATIONS, MAKING MEGALOPOLITAN LIFE POSSIBLE. WITH THE RISE OF INDUSTRIAL WORKERS AND PERIODIC UNEMPLOYMENT, COUPLED WITH FAMINE, EMIGRATION FROM EUROPE AFFORDED RELIEF. UNLIKE THE VOLKEWANDERUNGEN OF THE ASIAN PEOPLES THE EUROPEANS MOVED FAR OVERSEAS. THE ECONOMIC AND STRATEGIC SITUATION OF THE SEVEN-MILLIARD WORLD MAY REPEAT FOR ASIA THE PROBLEMS AND THE SOLUTIONS, WHICH CHARACTERIZED THE FIRST MALTHUSIAN CRISIS, WHEN INDUSTRIALIZATION APPEARED TO OFFER A PANACEA.

MAP I. IS INTENDED TO EPITOMIZE THE IMBALANCE IN THE EXISTING WORLD DEMOGRAPHIC SITUATION, BROUGHT ABOUT BY THE INDUSTRIAL REVOLUTION AND THE ECONOMIC SYSTEM, WHICH CAN BE PERPETUATED, IF THE ASIAN MASS-ECONOMIES CAN ENTER INTO EQUITABLE TRADE RELATIONS WITH THE SURPLUS-PRODUCING AREAS : OR A MASSIVE RE-DEPLOYMENT OF WORLD POPULATION MUST BRING CONSUMERS TO NECESSITIES — BELLIES TO FOOD, HANDS TO WORK.

E.A.A.R.

FERTILITY BASIS : PEDOLOGY - PRECIPITATION.

MAP 2.

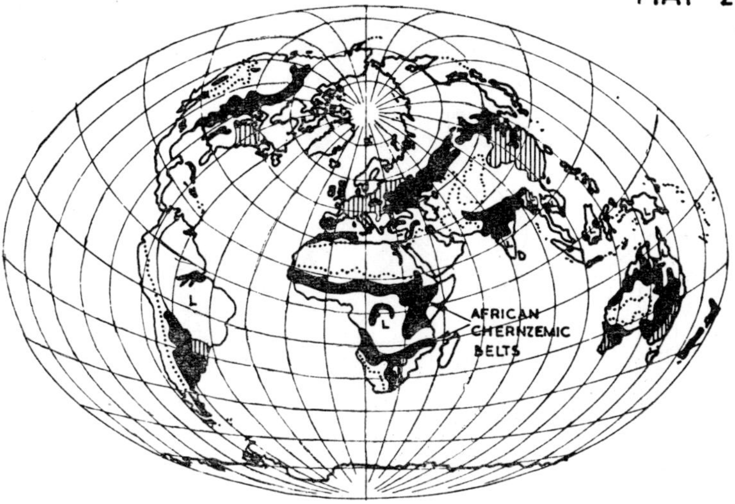

NOTATION —

(solid black)	CHERNOZEMIC AND CHESTNUT TO DARK-BROWN SOILS, INCLUDIND TRAP-BASED AND ALLUVIAL SOILS
(vertical hatching)	PODSOLS OF THE TEMPERATE AND SUB TROPICAL ZONES, REQUIRING HUMUS MAINTENANCE
L	MAIN AREAS OF INTRACTABLE LATERITES AND RAIN-FORESTS.
F	CONIFER FORESTS ON THE ARCTIC FRINGE
(dotted line)	250 M.M. ISOHYET AS THE SNATCH-CROP LIMIT.

THE NATURALLY FERTILE SOILS, FORMING THE BASE OF THE MAIN PRIMARY PRODUCING AREAS, WHICH WILL RESPOND READILY TO HIGH-INTENSITY APPLICATIONS OF FERTILIZERS, DO NOT TOTAL MORE THAN 2.10^9 HA. OUT OF THE PLANET'S TOTAL LAND SURFACE OF 125.10^6 S.KM. ALTHOUGH ESTIMATES OF 8.10^9 HA. CROPPABLE AREA HAVE BEEN MADE, THE FRAGILITY OF FOOD SUPPLY BASE FOR THE SEVEN MILLIARD WORLD IS OBVIOUS. IF FURTHER DETERIORATION OF THE SOIL-BASE IS ALLOWED TO OCCUR, THE RESULT COULD BE A DENSITY OF 3·5 PER FERTILE HECTARE. THE 960.10^6 KM^3 OF THE AQUASPHERE FORM THE RESOURCE-RESERVE, WHICH SHOULD BE POPULATED AND DEVELOPED.

MORE URGENT IS THE DEVELOPMENT OF THE CROPPABLE FRACTION OF AFRICA'S $11{\cdot}10^6$ S.KM. OF GRASSLAND SOILS TO YIELD THREE-TIMES, OR MORE THE PRESENT HARVESTS.

E.A.A.R.

TRADE PATTERN (1961).

MAP 3.

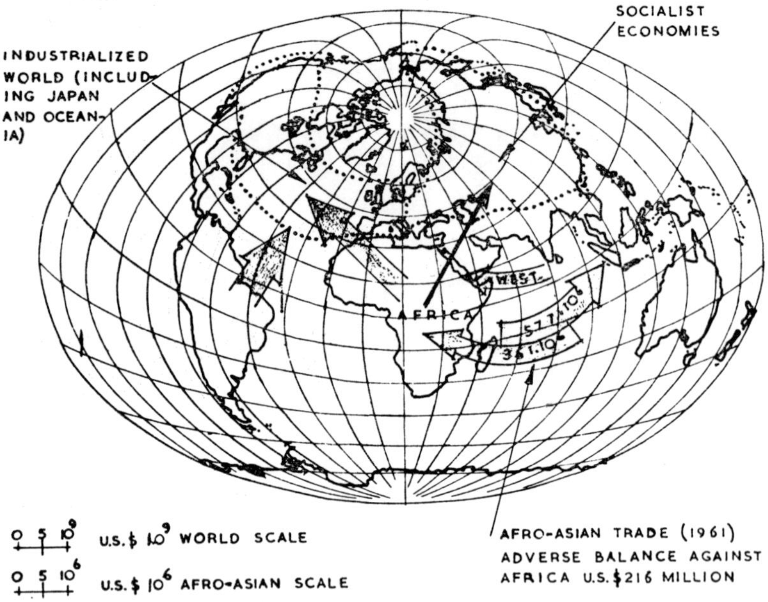

THE YEAR 1961 HAS BEEN CHOSEN AS A DATUM FOR COMPARISON OF TRADE TRENDS, BECAUSE AT THAT TIME THE FOOD CRISIS IN ASIA HAD BEGUN TO TAKE EFFECT IN INDIA ONLY, WHERE SHIPMENTS COULD HOLD STARVATION IN CHECK. FROM 1963 THE GENERAL SITUATION HAS CHANGED WITH FAILURE OF HARVESTS ON A WORLDWIDE SCALE. THERE HAS FOLLOWED THE ENTRY OF EURASIA INTO THE GRAIN MARKETS

THE DIAGRAMMATIC PRESENTATION IS INTENDED TO DEMONSTRATE—

(1) THE DISPARITY BETWEEN TRADE WITH THE INDUSTRIALIZED GROUP AND THAT WITH THE SOCIALIST COUNTRIES, INCLUDING MAINLAND CHINA, THE LARGEST POTENTIAL MARKET.

(2) THE TRADE EXCHANGE BETWEEN AFRICA AND ASIA CAN ONLY BE COMPARATIVELY REPRESENTED AT A SCALE OF 1:10 OF THAT FOR AFRICA AND THE INDUSTRIAL COUNTRIES.

A CURRENT PRICES SALES OF AGRICULTURAL PRODUCTS FROM AFRICA OF UP TO 2·7 MILLION TONS WOULD BRING THE TWO CONTINENTS INTO A FORM OF MULTI-LATERAL EQUILIBRIUM, YET TO BE DEFINED

E.A.A.R.

TRADE AXES OF 1980 - 2000 MAP 4.

ASSUMED RE-ORIENTATION ON NEW FOCUS

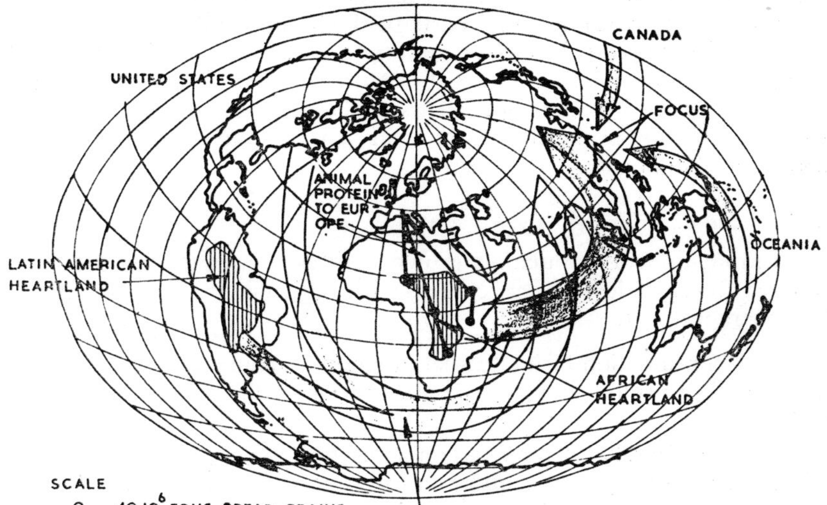

SCALE

0 40.10^6 TONS BREAD GRAINS.

NOTE: ROUTING IS DIAGRAMMATIC SOME SUPPLIES WOULD PASS THROUGH SUEZ.

IN SPITE OF THE OBVIOUS ECONOMIC AND POLITICAL DIFFICULTIES THE PROPOSAL OUTLINED SUGGESTS THE DOUBLING OF THE CURRENTLY FORESEEABLE SUPPLY POSSIBILITIES OF CANADA AND AUSTRALIA: ALLOCATING A SIMILAR FIGURE TO ARGENTINE AND UTILIZING THE FULL EXPORT POTENTIAL OF THE U.S. THIS INCLUDES YIELDS AS CALLED FOR IN ASIA AND, IF NECESSARY, THE CROPPING OF MARGINAL LAND IN ACCORDANCE WITH SOLAR RADIATION-PRECIPITATION CYCLE COUPLED WITH STORAGE OF CARRY-OVER RESERVES. ACCEPTING THE ALLOCATIONS GIVEN BELOW, THE AMERICAS COULD SUPPLY ALMOST ALL INDIA'S DEMAND, LEAVING AFRICA AND OCEANIA TO MEET NEARLY THAT OF MAINLAND CHINA. THE EXPANSION OF ALL POTENTIAL RICE PRODUCING AREAS MUST BE IMPLEMENTED IN AFRICA AND LATIN AMERICA, TO SUPPLEMENT THAT OF SOUTH-EAST ASIA (3 3/4 $.10^6$ TONS EXPORT, 1964) AND OCEANIA INCLUDING INDONESIA.

ASSUMED ALLOCATIONS IN MILLION TONS —

UNITED STATES	20	WITH A MARKED RISE (4:1) IN RICE EXPORT
CANADA	7	WHEAT
L. AMERICA	14	INCREASES OF RICE PRODUCTION IN AMAZON BASIN
TOTAL	41	
AFRICA	33	INCREASES OF RICE FROM CONGO AND MIDDLE-NILE
L AMERICA	10	AS ABOVE
OCEANIA	7	WHEAT AND RICE
TOTAL	50	GRAND TOTAL 91.10^6 TONS.

E.A.A.R.

Chandrasekhar, have looked squarely at the problems associated with global maldistribution of population and have warned the West what can be expected. If pressures continue to mount, given the existence of an effective nuclear potential wielded by an Asian Federation, an enforcement of freedom of movement to all parts of the globe would be possible and could not be opposed on moral or military grounds. In demographic cyclic terms the crisis can extend over a half-century (see Graph 4). It is, therefore, urged, that Africa's place in the events of the next four decades should be viewed realistically in the context of what may become a human tragedy of catastrophic proportions and finality.

World Population Trends (see Graph I)

The combination of population growth trends, illustrated by the graph, is offered for consideration, as covering the outcome of four combinations of demographic conditions:

1 A continuation of ineffectual attempts to control births, combined with a prolongation of the expectation of life at both ends of the span.
2 A deliberate attempt to attain an asymptotic condition by the third decade of the next century and to support the world population by trade exchanges or to carry out re-deployment on the basis of a rational demographic policy.
3 An even more drastic application of discipline to the limitation of births, freely accepted as part of an economic context consciously tolerated by the mass of the people (Boyarsky).
4 A cautionary indication of what can be expected, if a climatic escalation of war synchronizes with a food crisis of unprecedented dimensions during the next period of minimum solar radiation and the droughts which may accompany it.

In the case of alternatives (2) and (3), the danger of failure already exists. Those responsible for governmental control in the four reception continents may adopt the chauvinistic attitudes, which are even now denying human rights to indigenous populations or closing the door to the entry of Asians. As presented, Map 1 constitutes a challenge, calling for economic sanity or an open-door policy for population re-deployment in a seven-milliard world.

A search for a demographic equilibrium

The basic assumption behind the tentative balance sheet given below is that either directly by settlement or indirectly by trade, the habitable areas of the globe, existing or re-constituted, will, with some adjustment for sterile areas, support gross densities of the same order as those of Asia as a continental unit—57 per square kilometre. All currently under-utilized population supporting potential must be subjected to upgrading processes, scientific and technological, to place their full productivity at the disposal of the seven-milliard world.

On the above basis the following estimates, prepared in continental sub-regions, have been shown on Map 1, as representing an equitable global distribution of population-bearing capacity.

Breakdown of the Planet's Population-supporting Capacity—or Distribution (all figures in millions)

Continental Region	*Total Supportable*	*Indigenous, Internally Supported*	*Supported Externally or by Reception*
Under-utilized			
North America	1130	300	830
Latin America	1270	600	670
Africa	1220	500	720
Oceania	580	230	350
Marine based	50	—	50
	4250	1630	2620
Overstressed			
Asia	2010	4540	2530
Europe	626	—	90
Total	6886		2620

At below the seven milliard anticipated maximum, the breakdown offers only a prospect of equilibrium. Much refinement by a competent authority will be necessary, before a planet-plan can bear scrutiny on demographic and economic criteria of the standard required. Such a task might be carried out by the United Nations by 1970.

The total of 6,886 million takes the solution of the problem of absorptive capacity to the year 2000. As Graphs 2 and 3 illustrate, China and India could account for an extra 400 million after the turn of the century, before the asymptotic conditions, as hoped for, can obtain. The search for further margin must therefore continue to provide for a ceiling total of 7 to 7½ milliard about the year 2040.

If the enforcement of a rigidly static demographic policy is attempted, then the crop yields, shown on Graphs 5 and 6, must be attained. An achievement, which, even on agro-biological criteria, such as those advanced by Wilcox during the 1930s, looks highly unlikely.

East and West Europe, excluding the USSR, must and will become more self-supporting at a total of 626 million, if present trends in agricultural production are accepted as evidence. Trade on a two-way basis is assumed to be resumed on its former traditional exchanges. The existing

INDIAN POPULATION TRENDS GRAPH 2.

THE DISPARITY BETWEEN INDIAN AND AFRICAN POPULATIONS AND RELATIVE PRODUCTIVE POTENTIALS OFFERS OPPORTUNITIES FOR MUTUAL BENEFIT FROM EXPANDED TRADE HITHERTO NEGLECTED. THE BALANCE OF TRADE GAP BETWEEN INDIA AND EAST AFRICAN COUNTRIES HAS BEEN RUNNING AT AN ADVERSE ANNUAL FIGURE OF U.S. $10 MILLION PER ANNUM; YET IMPORTS OF COMMODITIES AS WELL AS MANUFACTURES FROM INDUSTRIAL COUNTRIES REMAIN HIGH, WHILE AFRICANS' SHARE IN TRADE FOODSTUFFS REMAINS DISPROPORTIONATELY SMALL.

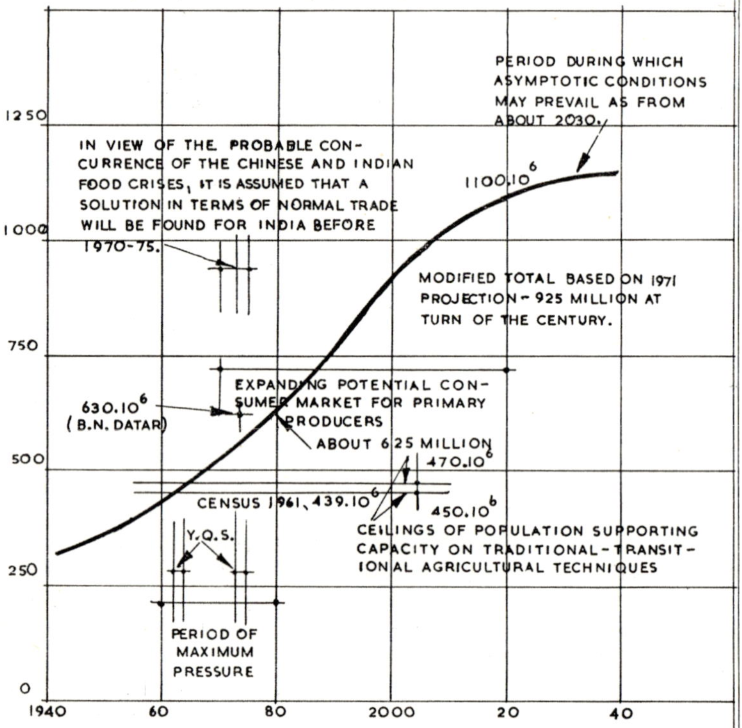

POINT OF CONTRAFLEXURE, WHEN POPULATION INCREASES SHOULD BEGIN TO FALL OFF, HAS BEEN POSTPONED TO 1985 DUE TO RESISTANCE TO CONTRACEPTIVE PRACTICES CONTINUING INTO THE 1970'S. IT CAN ONLY BE ASSUMED THAT THE ASYMPTOTE IN POPULATION TOTAL WILL BE ACHIEVED DURING THE THIRD DECADE OF THE NEXT CENTURY: OTHERWISE THE REPORTED GROWTH RATE OF BETWEEN 1·99% AND 2·15% WILL CONTINUE TO CANCEL GAINS IN FOOD PRODUCTION. THE EXPANSION OF TRADE, ON AN AFRO-ASIAN BASIS IS THE LONG-TERM SOLUTION, AFFORDING MAXIMUM MUTUAL BENEFIT.

E.A.A.R.

CHINESE POPULATION TRENDS GRAPH 3.

THE CHINESE NATURAL INCREASE FOR 1962 WAS GIVEN AS 2·3% PER ANN (U.N. LA SITUATION SOCIALE DANS LA MONDE, 1963)

IN 1961 IT WAS EXPECTED THAT THE POPULATION IN EAST ASIA WOULD INCREASE IN THE RATIO OF 2 1/2 : 1 BY YEAR 2000 (SUKHATME, 1961) ASSUMED TOTAL $650.10^6 \times 2 1/2 = 1625.10^6$

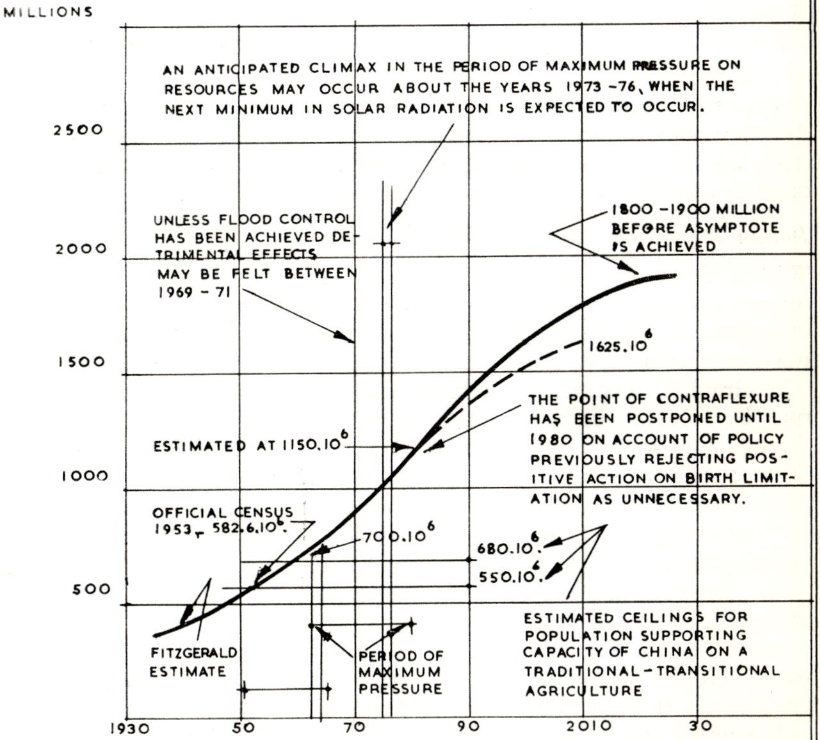

UNLESS TECHNOLOGICAL ADVANCE KEEPS PACE WITH POPULATION GROWTH, EVEN IF THE CRISIS OF 1970-80 IS SURMOUNTED AND A WORLDWIDE NUCLEAR CONFLICT ESCAPED, THE PROBLEM OF SUPPORTING MORE THAN 400 MILLION CHINESE, WHO MAY BE SURPLUS TO POTENTIAL POPULATION SUPPORTING CAPACITY OF THE PHYSICAL AND PSYCHOLOGICAL ENVIRONMENT OF CHINA, WILL HAVE TO BE SOLVED: TOGETHER WITH THAT OF INDIA AND A NUMBER OF OTHER OVER-POPULATED REGIONS.

E.A.A.R.

world pattern, as illustrated on Map 3, will be much modified by competition from the new focus of purchasing power for primary products, indicated as developing in south and east Asia (see Map 4).

In a seven-milliard world, emigration, if acceptable as a relief to the demographic pressures, would only be possible within limits mutually agreed, fulfilled between over-populated and reception areas. Such a movement by Europeans would be confined to the scientifically and technologically apt. It is assumed that historically the European out-surge has come to an end: at least in the aggressive form in which Toynbee has presented it.

If the crisis of the next two decades can be survived, it is permissible to dream of thermonuclear or geothermal power, desalination of seawater, desert rehabilitation on known and augmented water resources, together with bio-chemical engineering of foodstuffs. The world of the twenty-first century can be a good one—if anyone is left to enjoy it.

Indian Population Growth (Graph 2)

Within the world demographic frame, an indication of three trends is offered for consideration, as together they account for the greater part of consumer pressure on resources and therefore constitute the enormous mass-market open to Africa and all other primary producers (see Map 4).

Graph 2 illustrates the situation in India, under which the asymptote may be achieved early in the twenty-first century. At the Belgrade Conference Mr. B. N. Datar pointed out, with justification, that a total population for India of 630 million might be reached about 1975. This exceeds the most pessimistic estimates so far advanced.

The rising gradient of the logistic curve is based on the figures given in the Indian census and the higher brackets for the revised projections given as a demographic perspective in the Third Plan. In the Fourth Plan, modification of the totals will result from the limitation of births by means proposed by Dr. Chandrasekhar. The child-bearing group in India has been estimated at the 1965 figure of between 105 and 115 million. This can be covered by the new scale of contraceptive practices. A current birthrate, still running at a ratio of about 2 : 1 to the death incidence cannot encourage undue optimism.

Chinese Population Growth (Graph 3)

In their seaboard provinces and the foothills the Chinese command one of the most favoured areas of the world: since this basis has proved capable of supporting some of the heaviest rural population densities.

The basis of a demographic study of China was laid prior to the 1940s by Fitzgerald. A total of 450 million was suggested by U.S. sources about 1945. The recent announcement of a total of 700 million, emanating from Peking, is, as yet unsupported by adequate statistics. Experience has shown the wisdom of estimating upward, as likely to prove more realistic. The official figure has therefore been accepted. What Graph 3 suggests is, that a

JAPANESE POPULATION TRENDS GRAPH 4.

THE NATURAL INCREASE OF JAPAN WAS GIVEN FOR 1961 AT 881,000 OR 0·96% IT HAD FALLEN TO 0·9% BY 1965. THE TREND INDICATES A POSSIBILITY, THAT, IF ABORTION RATES CONTINUE TO FALL OFF; BUT CONTRACEPTIVE PRACTICES ARE EVEN MORE WIDELY APPLIED, THE ASYMPTOTE MAY BE APPROACHED AS FROM 1975. THAT IS ABOUT 50 TO 60 YEARS AFTER THE DEMOGRAPHIC CLIMACTIC COMMENCED. THIS TREND HAS BEEN ADOPTED AS A PROTOTYPE MODEL FOR APPROXIMATING THE ASYMPTOTE.

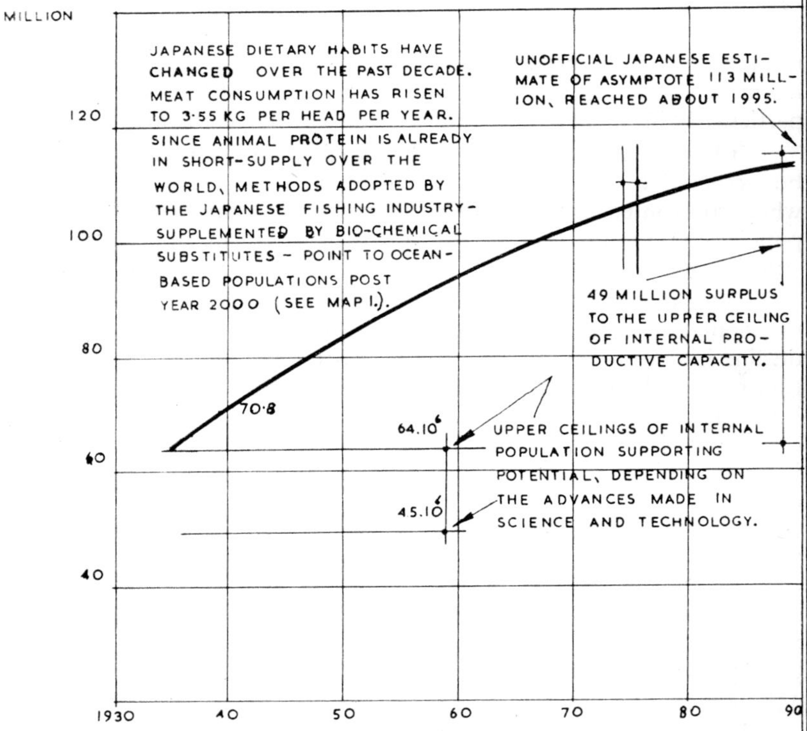

THE JAPANESE ECONOMY IS ALMOST SELF-SUFFICIENT IN BASIC FOODSTUFFS (RICE); BUT ONLY AS A RESULT OF GROWING IMPORTS OF ANIMAL PROTEIN (TERRESTIAL AND MARINE). AT THE TURN OF THE CENTURY THE NET DENSITY PER CULTIVATED HECTARE WILL BE $\frac{113.10^6}{54.10^6} = 21$. THE GROSS DENSITY WILL BE $\frac{113.10^6}{369,661} = 306$ PER SQ.KM. THE PRESENT DENSITY IS 250 PER SQ.KM. DEPRIVED OF ACCESS TO THE OCEAN FISH-FARMING REGIONS AND OF IMPORTS OF MEAT, THE JAPANESE, AND ALL SIMILARLY SITUATED PEOPLES, WOULD BE FORCED BACK TO THE POSITION OF 1941, WHEN THE ONLY RECOURSE SEEMED TO BE WAR.

E.A.A.R.

total Chinese population of about $1\frac{1}{2}$ milliard should be accepted for logistic estimating by the year 2000. What this means in terms of pressure on resources is considered below on Graph 6.

The alternative ceiling populations proposed is a justification for the implementation of an agricultural revolution of an unprecedented scale, is indicated on Graph 8. Africa: Surplus Producing Capacity.

Japanese Population Growth (Graph 4)

Since the introduction of the intra-uterine contraceptive in place of the Pincus pill, the possibility of reducing the natural increase of the high-birthrate zones has improved; but the extension of the expectation of life, particularly in the fall of infantile mortality, will cancel gains made.

It has been thought profitable to include an illustration of what might be expected from a highly disciplined, realistic and courageous people, when confronted with the full realization of what excessive pressure of population on limited resources really means in terms of human deprivation and demands on ingenuity in finding solutions for the problems involved.

Since the 1950s the Japanese have already demonstrated an approach to population limitation, which has shown absolute results in a marked decline in natural increase. Graph 4 incorporates variants in net reproduction rates and natural increases, extending the current trends, which have been introduced into the equations. The result has indicated asymptotic conditions about 50 to 60 years after the commencement of rapid population increase. This example may offer some confirmation of the assumption that other mass-populations will show similar tendencies during the third decade of the next century.

The dependence of the Japanese on marine-based protein supplies, points a line for development planning in terms of population based on, and employed in, ocean-scale fish farming, when 3 milliard of Asians turn to the biology of the aquasphere for an increasing proportion of their food supplies. A geophysical and bio-chemical study of the coral growths of Micronesia, paralleled by the development of the plankton belt of the Southern Ocean, would seem to be a line of advance, arising out of current oceanographic surveys.

MASS-MARKET

The demographic situation of the world has been briefly reviewed, in order to establish a context for, what may be termed, the economics of catastrophe—or opportunity.

On Graphs 2, 3 and 4 estimates of possible ceilings for population-supporting capacity on a transitional-traditional technology have been indicated. For India the margin supportable is very narrow (450—470 million): for China the possibility of expansion westward widens the bracket (550—680 million). In the case of Japan (64 million) the crisis was probably passed during the thirties. War ensued. These estimates were

INDIA: REQUIREMENTS FOR BREAD CEREALS (RICE & WHEAT) 1966-2000. GRAPH 5.

CULTIVABLE AREA 126 MILLION HECTARES
UNDER CEREALS 31 5 " " ON A FOUR-COURSE ROTATION
IT IS ASSUMED THAT THE AREA RETIRED FOR REHABILITATION WILL BE COMPENSATED BY SUCH RECLAMATION AND IRRIGATION WORKS AS ARE FOUND POSSIBLE ON A LONG-TERM BASIS.

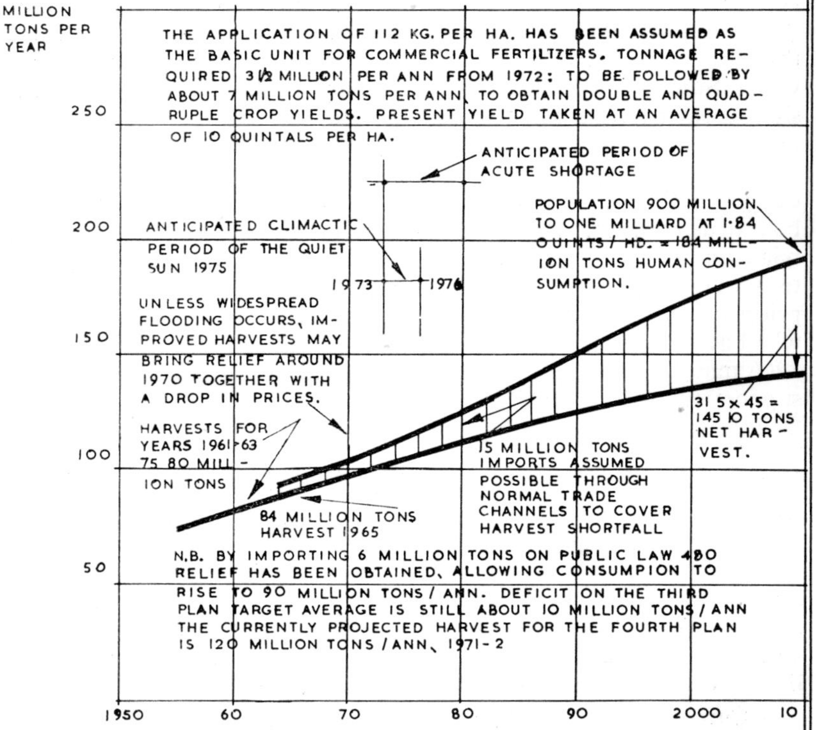

THE PER CAPUT CONSUMPTION HAS BEEN FIXED AT 1·84 QUINTS PER ANN. THIS MAY BE REDUCED TO 1·68 QUINTS, IF IT IS FOUND POSSIBLE TO ALLOW A CHANGE IN CULTURALLY DICTATED DIETS: OTHERWISE CONSUMPTION OF CARBOHYDRATES AND VEGETABLE PROTEIN MUST REMAIN HIGH. IN ANTICIPATION OF THE CONTINUATION OF SUCH A DEMAND, DEPENDENCE ON P.L.480, AS AT MOST A STOP-GAP MEASURE, SHOULD CEASE, AS IT HAS STULTIFIED AFRO-ASIAN TRADE EXCHANGES. BY STIMULATING PRODUCTION IN AFRICA THROUGH TRADE CHANNELS, INDIA WOULD BE PROMOTING FRIENDLY RELATIONS, AS EXPRESSED IN A TANGIBLE AFRO-ASIAN ECONOMIC PARTNERSHIP (SEE GRAPH 12 AND MAP 4)

E. A. A. R.

originally developed in Asia during 1943, when the lessons of the catastrophe of the Bengal famine were indelibly imprinted on the minds of all who suffered that experience. It is the intention of Graphs 5 and 6, to emphasize the need to continue preparatory programmes to face the dangers, as well as take advantage of the opportunities for world-wide prosperity, which are inherent in the Asian mass-markets.

It is reasonable to review the economic trends of mass-markets over two or more climatic cycles in order that the results of adverse conditions (flood or drought) can be corrected ahead of need. It has, therefore, been thought prudent to indicate on all graphs the next two or more years of the Quiet Sun, when widespread failure of rainfall may bring acute food shortages, at a time when there will be up to 700 million more mouths to feed. The period around the next solar radiation maximum may include one or two peaks about 1969–70, bringing heavy precipitation and the danger of floods. The years before and after this climax may be ones of bountiful harvests, which might result in a slackening of vigilance and a relaxation of the effort to increase production. Crop surpluses in the high-technology regions could rise to a point where glut conditions and falling prices due to maldistribution could again cause embarrassment to farmers, who have been counting on easy profits. The rundown of grain reserves of 1966 may be forgotten, particularly if economic stress causes cutbacks in support for prices. The provision of fertilizers, the erection of storage facilities, to maintain crash programmes, must be kept at top-gear tempo.

Indian Productive Capacity (Cereals—Graph 5)

The current near-famine situation in India has been aggravated by the inability of the responsible authorities to build up reserves of foodstuffs from internal harvest surpluses to meet emergency demand. The requirement would seem to be provision for one quarter of the population to cover a shortage of 25% of the average annual bread-grain ration over a period of 4 months during three successive years, when the monsoon may fail to the limited degree indicated by such allowances.

Current provision may be necessary as follows:

$$\frac{470.10^6}{4} = 117.5 \text{ million suffering from shortage}$$

at 25% of a daily ration of 0.5 kg = 0.125 kg
for a period taken at 125 days = 15.625 kg deficit
117.5 = 15.625 = 1,836,000 tons per year
over a period of 3 years, as a reasonable comparison with
what has happened in Asia since 1963, turn-over
reserves may be held at 5.5 million tons.

By the end of the century the above figure will be, on the most optimistic estimate, doubled if population projections as shown on Graphs 2

CHINA: REQUIREMENTS FOR BREAD CEREALS. (RICE & WHEAT) 1966-2000 GRAPH 6.

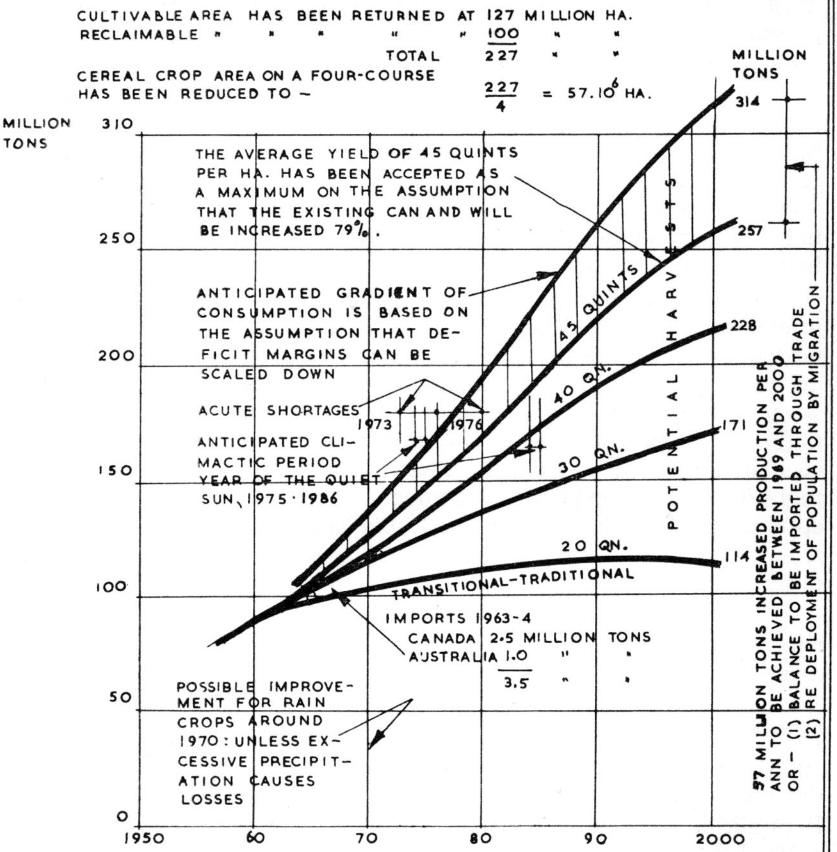

WARNING SERVED — IN THE PREVENTION OF CATASTROPHE THE KEY SOLUTION LIES IN AFRICA. IT IS NECESSARY TO EMPHASIZE THE MAGNITUDE OF THE TASK, WHICH CONFRONTS THE CHINESE AND INDIAN PEOPLES. THIS MAY BEST BE DONE BY CONTRASTING THE HIGHEST ACHIEVEMENTS IN AGRICULTURAL PRODUCTION WITH WHAT MUST BE ACCOMPLISHED AS AN AVERAGE: THE WORLD MAXIMUM FOR WHEAT 41 QNT./HA (DENMARK): FOR RICE 43 QNT/HA (AUSTRALIA). SUCH ADVANCES MUST BE IMPLEMENTED IN 30 YEARS. IF THIS PROVES IMPOSSIBLE THE SHORTFALL MUST BE MADE GOOD BY TRADE OR OUTRIGHT GIFT AND THE SYSTEMIZATION OF THE TRANFERS MADE PHYSICALLY POSSIBLE: OR THE ASIAN PEOPLES WILL MOVE INTO THE EMPTY SPACES UNDER A NUCLEAR UMBRELLA — OR DIE.

E.A.A.R.

and 3 are confirmed. The distribution of a part of such food insurance in African and Asian countries, producing surpluses of wheat and rice, forms a study, which has not yet been sufficiently developed. The eventual target must parallel storage equipment levels reached by advanced countries at present—of the order of one-seventh the export volume, distributed along the process pipeline to ports.

A sliding price scale, to cover periods of shortfall, may be designed to defray the extra cost of producing countries and relieve the importers of the full burden of year-to-year storage costs. In a seven-milliard world the severity of the results of failures of precipitation will be much greater than those previously experienced. Even before the 1980s, trade missions should not find negotiations on average long-term purchases as difficult as they have been in the past.

In the case of India, while the gap may vary, the attainment of a 120 million tons harvest, as hoped, may suffer a setback about the middle of the next decade. By the turn of the century, even if the tremendous rise in average yield (at least 4 : 1) per hectare has been maintained at the gradient suggested to reach 45 quintals per hectare, an uncovered gap of about 39 million tons per annum may form a permanent feature in the Indian economic system, to be compensated by imports and covered by the requisite value in export of manufactured goods. The necessary massive application of fertilizers at Japanese standards, offers a challenge to FAO and USAID in terms of 'give-away' programmes to raise productivity rather than attempt stop-gap food measures. (See Graph 9).

The case for a broadening and liberalizing of India's trade relations with all Africa, in order to stimulate the production of the food reserves, may be argued against an attempt at self-sufficiency (see Graph 10).

Chinese Productive Capacity (Cereals—Graph 6)

All the conditions discussed above, apply with even greater severity to the case of China. While the geographical area of the Chinese Peoples Republic is given at 9,761,012 square kilometres, the present realizable cultivable area, as given by the Institute of Agricultural Research, Peking, does not exceed 227 million hectares. Graph 6 is intended to epitomize the struggle the Chinese people will be called upon to undertake to support 7 to 8 people per fertile hectare about the year 2000.

The present distribution of population is markedly uneven, since 95% is supported by 58% of the land area. On the remainder above 1,000 metres altitude, deserts and severe winter conditions limit population settlement. The outcome in the seaboard regions is densities at 600 per square kilometre over areas nearly as large as a major European country.

The successive lifts in harvest totals, shown on Graph 6 are intended to demonstrate the gaps, which must be filled between Chinese accomplishment and rising consumption of food. A distribution of production quotas from surplus producing regions is illustrated on Map 4. The main burden is

AFRICA : POPULATION TRENDS GRAPH 7.

THE POPULATION OF AFRICA IS EXPECTED TO INCREASE IN THE RATIO OF 2 1/2 : 1 (SUKHATME) BY THE TURN OF THE CENTURY, THE CEILING MAY BE STABILIZED AT THE ASYMPTOTE BETWEEN 600 700 MILLION. THE PRODUCTIVE POTENTIAL OF THE CONTINENT, ON THE BASIS OF INTENSIVE APPLICATION OF SCIENCE AND TECHNOLOGY, HAS BEEN ESTIMATED AT A MEAN OF 1100 MILLION BASIC NECESSITY RATIONS. SURPLUS SUPPORTING CAPACITY ABOUT 500 MILLION.

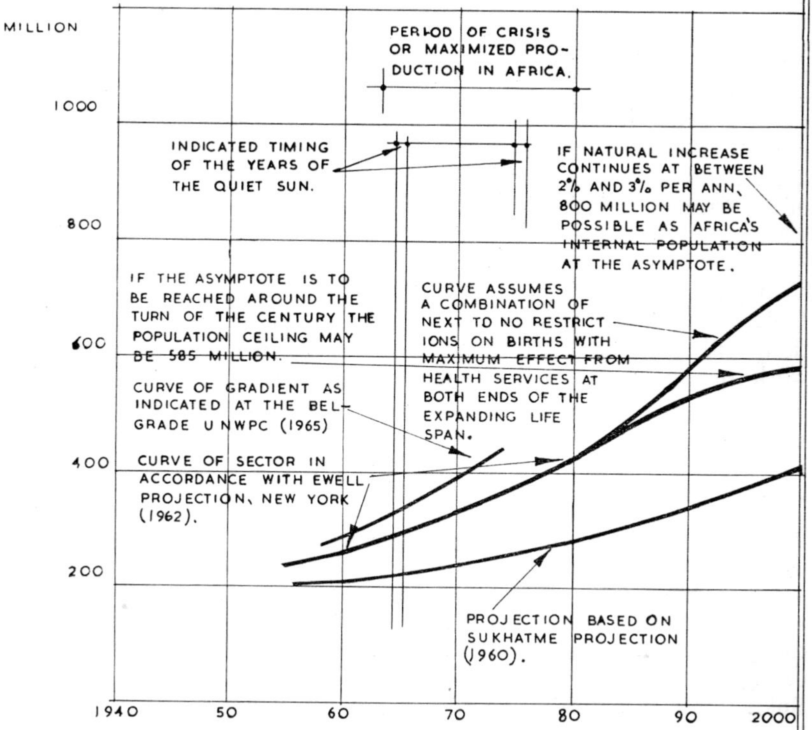

A THIRTY-YEAR PLAN FOR THE EXPANSION OF AFRICAN PRODUCTIVITY FOR THE WORLD MARKET IS NEEDED. IT MUST BE GEARED TO THE CONCURRENT INCREASES IN THE CAPACITY OF OTHER SURPLUS PRODUCING AREAS (THE AMERICAS AND OCEANIA) AND THE ACTUAL RESULTS OBTAINED FROM SUGGESTED RISES IN YIELDS TO BE ACHIEVED IN PRESENT DEFICIT AREAS. WORLD EQUILIBRIUM FOR BASIC DIET ESSENTIALS SHOULD BE REACHED DURING THE FIRST TWO DECADES OF THE TWENTY-FIRST CENTURY. THE SUKHATME ESTIMATES PROVIDED A BASIS FOR DEMAND; BUT CURRENT POLICY CHANGES IN THE UNITED STATES WILL — IF CONTINUED ON LONG-TERM — RECREATE GLUT MARKET CONDITIONS AND FRUSTRATE EXPANSION IN DEVELOPING AREAS.

E.A.A.R.

suggested as falling on Africa; but there is no intention of laying down the form of a rigid pattern of trade exchanges. The ultimate uncovered gap between demand and supply for food may be of the order of 57 million tons.

MASS-PRODUCTION

Of the three regions of potential surplus production, Africa forms the focus of this study.

The enormous purchasing power of the Asian foodstuffs market can only be maintained if bilateral or multi-lateral trade agreements make it possible for the Africans and Latin-Americans to digest the corresponding inflow of manufactured goods Asia can and will offer. Such a trend is recognized as likely to prove adverse to the interests of the developed economies of the West, unless these countries can move up in the grading of technology. They need to concentrate on the provision of sophisticated equipment of all forms for incorporation in infra-structure, plants and utilities for which they can accept in return animal protein and such minerals as African economies have in excess of their requirements. The supply of such scarce materials will put Africa in a strong bargaining position. Unless economic liberalization is granted and aided by the West, stultification will lead to frustration and the Afro-Asian association cannot work for the advancement of mankind, but towards aggression against the 'haves' of the world. This is the road to war and the annihilation of the species.

African Population Trends (Graph 7)

The demographic study of Africa is complicated by the lack of reliable data and statistical analyses, from which projections can be made. The situation has further been confused by the political instability of the past seven years. Graph 7 offers, therefore, what may be at best a warning, that the population of the continent at the turn of the century may reach ceilings of between 600 and 700 million, thus surpassing markedly the Sukhatme upper limit of about 400 million; although this seemed to have been taken at Belgrade as a datum, on which very considerable up-marking seems to have been accepted.

The economic pressures, cited by Dr. Boyarsky, as checks on natural increase, do not appear to operate in Africa, as they may be expected to express themselves in Asia under the sharpening deprivation, to be endured if economic planning does not bring relief to overcrowded populations. The trend of population growth to between 2% and 3% per annum, returned by several African countries for 1963, can, if continued, even treble the existing population next century. As settled conditions become more general, the upward gradient may be confirmed, as applying to the whole continent.

A series of more definite forecasts in perspective, adequately supported by statistical material and sociological research, is urgently required from

AFRICA : SURPLUS PRODUCING CAPACITY

GRAPH 8.

IT HAS HITHERTO BEEN ARGUED IN VARIOUS QUARTERS, THAT TO HOPE FOR SO MARKED A CHANGE IN AFRICAN PRODUCTIVITY, AS TO ENABLE THE CONTINENT TO COMPETE WITH THE ESTABLISHED SURPLUS PRODUCING AREAS, IS TO INDULGE IN FUTILE DREAMS. THE HISTORY OF THE UNITED STATES FROM 1850 TO 1950 – THE OPENING OF THE MIDDLE WEST TO 'POINT IV' – CAN BE REPEATED IN AFRICA; BUT SINCE THE TECHNOLOGY IS AVAILABLE, THE TIME-SCALE COULD BE HALVED.

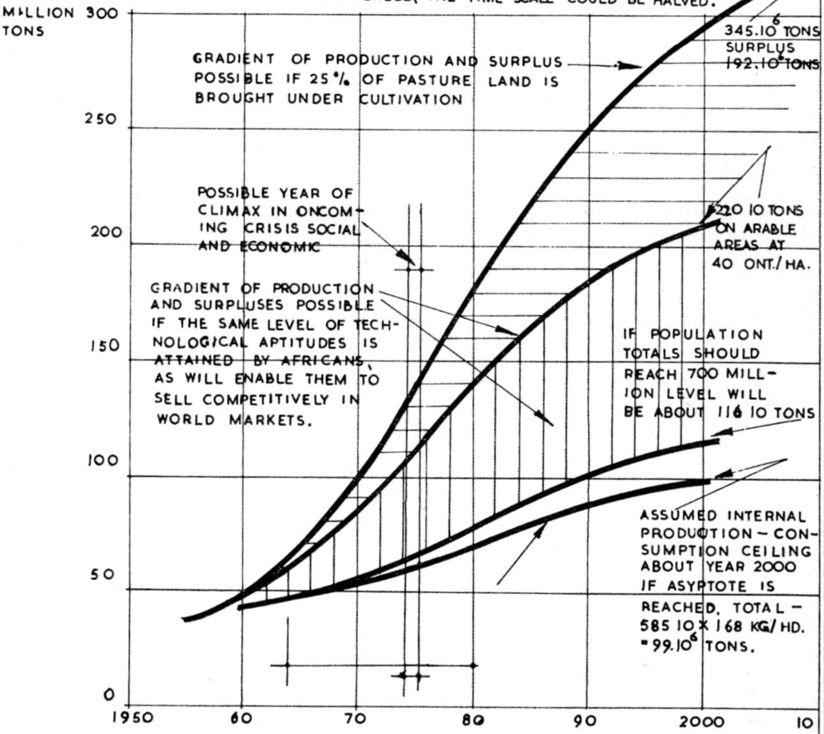

THE AREA OF CROPPED LAND RETURNED FOR AFRICA BY F.A.O. IS 219 MILLION HA. IF THIS CULTIVABLE POTENTIAL IS DEVELOPED ON A FOUR-COURSE ROTATION OF COMPLEMENTARY AFRICAN CROP COMPONENTS, UP TO 55 MILLION HA. CAN COME UNDER BREAD CEREALS AND FOOD GRAINS BY YEAR 2000. GIVEN A YIELD OF 4 TONS PER HA., PRODUCTION WOULD BE ABOUT 220 MILLION TONS. IF A PROPORTION OF 25% OF PASTURE LANDS IS RAIN-CROPPED OR IRRIGATED (AS IN THE CASE OF THE MIDDLE-NILE) THE AREA AVAILABLE AS A BUFFER WOULD BE 502 ÷ 4 = 125·5 MILLION HA. ASSUME AS YIELD A CONSERVATIVE 10 QUINTS PER HA. THE TOTAL MIXED CROP WOULD BE 125 MILLION TONS. A CONTINENTAL CROP OF THE ORDER OF 345 MILLION WOULD FEED 1·89 MILLIARD.

E.A.A.R.

competent African demographers, who can penetrate the psyche of their own peoples in their respective cultural contexts.

If the suggested Master Plan for African productivity (see Graph 8) is to be completed in time to meet the oncoming crisis of the '70s, as is evidenced in the schedule set out above, caution dictates the acceptance of the higher ceiling before asymptotic conditions obtain, as a basis for estimates of internal consumer demand.

African Productive Capacity (Graph 8)

A pedological survey on scientific lines does not exist for the greater part of the more fertile regions of Africa. Precipitation records for harvest projection are also conjectural over most of the continental heartland. A clearer realization of the magnitude of the under-utilization of productive potential is beginning to emerge.

The programme of expansion illustrated by Graph 8, suggests an ultimate production margin of 229 million tons of food. The upper gradient assumes the cultivation of 25% of pasture land found to be convertible. The same level of yields, as has been demanded of the Asians, has been applied. The intention is to open up the possibility, that, if survey justifies it, Africa could relieve Asia, by increasing its contribution by 33 million tons as an initial quota, if catastrophic crop failures should occur in that continent in the mid-term future. On the chernozemic belt, parameters may be close to those of North America, Australia and the Soviet Union, in all of which regions 'dust-bowl' conditions have been experienced. Under the pressures of the seven-milliard consumers demand of the year 2000, the temptation to over-crop may lead to disastrous losses of topsoil. While the continent may be regarded as the world's buffer against the imprudence of excessive procreation, this can be no excuse for the further deterioration of Africa's remaining fertility.

It is not yet apparent whether South America's productive potential can offer the same margin of safety as Africa's. The proportion of unresponsive tropical laterite soils is much higher than in the latter continent; but the shadow of encroachment by the huge forces for deterioration, which the Sahara exerts, must also be allowed for.

If the present policy of expansion of agriculture is to continue, as proposed in 1966 by the United States Secretary of Agriculture, Mr. Freeman, the result will be something like a standstill in much primary production in developing regions, which, if Washington returns farm support to previous lower levels, would profit from increased incomes and foreign exchange reserves accruing from overseas sales. The crisis of the next 'Year of the Quiet Sun' (1975) should see an expansion in African production of about 50 million tons of foodstuffs for export. If Europe and America sincerely wish for peace, the lessons which Map 4 attempts to convey, must be taken to heart. With the help of the West, there should emerge the basis of a fully articulated thirty-year production plan, such as is proposed on Graph 8 for Africa. Each of the surplus-producing continents should be the subject of a similar plan, the whole to be co-ordinated within a world frame. It should be noticed, that such a planet-plan is geared with concurrent increases (doubling) in the capacity quotas of the developed producing areas (the Americas and Oceania), which, therefore, will suffer no deprivation—if their agricultural communities show foresight and patience.

If the hope of fulfilment is not discernible to the destitute of the world, the war strategy, now being formulated in Peking, can be put into successful effect (see Graph 6).

Africa in the context of the mass-economy and market

The emphasis laid on the magnitude of the Asian mass-populations, their present distressful position and their potentiality as a market, is intended to urge with equal force the need for an African mass-economy, as well as others of a similar magnitude, capable of mass-production at continental scale. The difficulties of promoting intra-continental trade are already evident. At present African economies are too similar to allow of exchanges of significance. A broadening of external trade would have a loosening effect on informal relations. Africa as a coherent economic unit may still be a concept of the mid-term future. Such a status would make it possible to bargain on equal terms with the other five, existing and incipient, mass-economies. These by the year 2000 will each have an internal mass-production, consumer-market base of approximately the following strengths in millions—North America (350), West Europe (350), USSR (400), China (1800), India (900).

The three main criteria of a mass-economy are at present, an annual production of more than 100 million tons of steel, the utilization of 2 milliard tons of fuel equivalents. As an economic unit Africa would confront the world of seven-milliard in year 2000 with a population of up to 600—700 million. This is sufficiently massive to resist external pressures, such as the fifty-million population European countries have exerted on a weak sellers market for over a century. As a disparate collection of economically unstable states, a European legacy, lacking scientific, technological and management personnel, Africa can fall a prey to the Asian mass-market as easily as it has to the financial interests of the West. This seems to be the most powerful argument for African unity, that can be advanced on the available evidence. In a very dangerous world, it may be added, that the mass-economy of 200 million population is demonstrably the lowest magnitude, which can build up a nuclear potential effectively as a weapon of mass-destruction without ruining itself fiscally. To wield it will amount to self-immolation.

AFRICAN REGIONAL DEVELOPMENT

Africa is composed of eight regions of magnitudes not dissimilar. Four are major river basins (Nile, Niger, Congo and Zambesi), the others are the

WORLD REQUIREMENTS: FERTILIZERS. GRAPH 9.

THE JAPANESE RATE OF COMMERCIAL FERTILIZER APPLICATION, AS INDICATING THE REQUIRED STANDARD UNDER SEVERE PRESSURE OF POPULATION, HAS BEEN ACCEPTED AT 1000 KG. PER HA. AS AN ASIAN DATUM, ALTHOUGH NEW ZEALAND AND LOW-COUNTRY RATES ARE ALREADY RUNNING AT NEARLY DOUBLE THIS LEVEL. MASS PRODUCTION OF FERTILIZER IN ASIA IS UNDER DEVELOPMENT; BUT AN INTEGRATED CONTINENTAL SYSTEM OF PLANTS IS NEEDED FOR AFRICA.

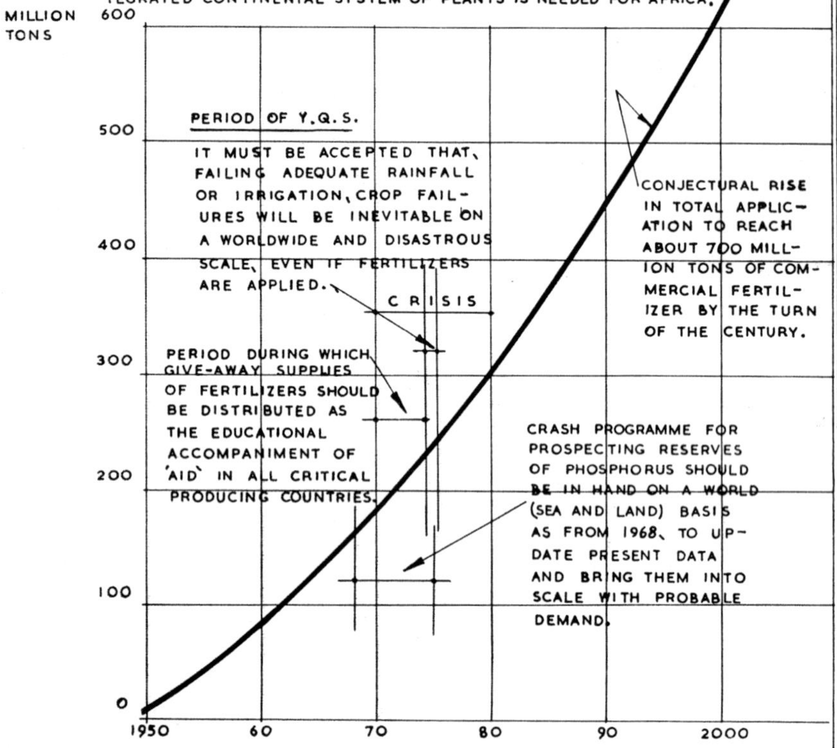

THE PRESENT UTILIZATION OF THE GREATER PART OF THE PRODUCTIVE SOILS OF THE PLANET IS STABILIZED AT EITHER THE IRREDUCIBLE MINIMUMUM YIELDS, CHARACTERISTIC OF SUBSISTENCE SHIFTING CULTIVATION, OR THE 20% IMPROVEMENT POSSIBLE AS A RESULT OF THE APPLICATION OF GOOD-FARMING PRACTICES, INCLUDING ORGANIC MANURES.

THE WARTIME CURVE OF YIELDS OBTAINED IN TAIWAN, WHEN SUPPLIES FAILED, HAS BEEN TAKEN AS A PROTOTYPE OF THE RESULTS TO BE EXPECTED, SHOULD RESERVES OF PHOSPHORUS FAIL.

E.A.A.R.

Lakes and Eastern Plateau, Peninsular Africa, the Northern littoral and—the great problem and perhaps opportunity—the Sahara. If the challenge of the seven-milliard world is to be met and the Asian market, in particular, supplied with the necessities of life, then time-phased production plans for each region, in terms of commodity quotas, should be worked out for implementation by the key year 2000. If this is done at the required detail over the coming two to three years, it is just possible, that Africa may be ready to answer Asia's call, which may otherwise, by the 70's turn to a ruthless demand, backed by force.

Land-base and its fertility (Graph 9)

Estimates made of the cultivable area of the planet range from one to two milliard hectares. FAO gives:

Category	milliard hectares
In land and tree crops	1.37
Permanent meadow and pasture	2.466
Forest	3.864
Unused, but potentially productive	0.6

Subsistence farming, which today occupies up to 85% of the labour force and their dependents in many regions, will, in certain cases, where the technological base has been created, give place to an almost direct reversal in terms of industrialized employment. As an indication of productivity possible, at the end of the last century one agricultural producer supported only 4 dependents, even on a relatively advanced technique, today the ratio is about 1:37. At the end of the century it may be higher.

Map 2 indicates the distribution of the chernozemic and podzolic soils, on which the concentration of science and technology would be most profitable. The laterites of the monsoon zones and rain forests need much more study before they are put under cultivation. The day may come, when existing technology may make the production of vegetable protein direct from forests a sounder practice than exposing ploughed soils to erosion by the thrash of tropical downpours.

The Parker estimate of world requirements for fertilizers gave about 120 million tons of commercial fertilizers as the transportation factor in the problem to be solved by 1980, Graph 9 shows what might have been a consistent curve for the doubling of yields on the world's cropped area, $1.37.10^9$ x 220 kg. per ha. average + 301.10^6 tons.

As the Parker curve of fertilizer application shows, to obtain a corresponding increase of 5:1 levels, shown on Graphs 5 and 6, would need about five times present applications of fertilizers in all developing countries; but optimum results are obtained between 0 and 75 kg. plant nutrient per hectare. The graph, therefore, postulates a turn to the category of pasture, where maximized returns can be more easily obtained by the same applications. This accounts for the suggested total of no more than 600 million tons per annum by year 2000. Since a serious backlog in fertilizer production has already developed, even the present crash programmes, now under way in all parts of the world, seem woefully inadequate.

On the fertile base in Africa's 3 milliard hectares an annual fertilizer application of 70 million tons commercial fertilizers has been estimated as necessary, including allowance for pasture enrichment and the feeding of rotation crops. The curve of increase in utilization would be proportionate with the world figure at a ratio of 10:1, world: Africa. Nearly half the fertilizer requirement will be for nitrogen. The ammonia based production process has ousted that of fixation by electrolysis; but in the case of the African heartland and similar regions, the cost of a haul of 1500 km. from the coast is likely to make the latter method more attractive. As a base load for Africa's hydro-power potential, taken at a global figure of 300 million H.P., fertilizer production may absorb three-fifths of that proportion generated in the headwater areas of the heartland.

Phosphorus presents a different problem in terms of proposed consumption. The land-based reserves are at present being estimated. The Moroccan deposits are returned at 20 milliard tons crude fertilizer. Coupled with the Uganda figures, Africa would seem to have three centuries of supply under its direct control. World production of phosphates, at 50 million tons (1963), has been growing at the rate of 5% per annum. It is reasonable to assume, that Africa will follow the same trend. Generally speaking, the situation seems under control at short-term; but, when it is remembered that the life expectation of a planet, even on the Bondi figures for a stellar regime, has been estimated at 10 milliard years, of which Earth has a future margin of five, the physicists and chemists have some enormous tasks ahead of them, on the exploitation of marine based phosphates, if the planet is not to become as sterile as its neighbour Mars.

Potassium production in Ethiopia and Congo Kinshasha is possible at about 1,200,000 tons crude potash per annum. The Canadian programme to produce at 6 million tons out of a world market of 11 million tons per annum may result in delay of development in Africa: unless emphasis is laid on the need to cover domestic consumption, on a 15–15–3 ratio for NPK application.

Africa, south of the Sahara, under exacting scrutiny, would be found to be capable of an immense rise in productivity, as the result of stimulation as suggested on Graph 9 (Fertilizers). If and when the existing gap in the time schedule for implementation has been closed, Africa will become a partner in an Afro-Asian combination, in time to avert the catastrophic disasters, which may otherwise occur during the seventies and eighties. What this means in terms of increased tempo of advance, is left for quiet consideration by those responsible, followed by action of the most vigorous form. It is Africa's potential economic strength, which must be developed, that a hope of salvation can be held out to the masses suffering from deprivation in Asia toward the end of this century.

AFRICAN TRADE BALANCES WITH THE WORLD AND ASIA. GRAPH 10.

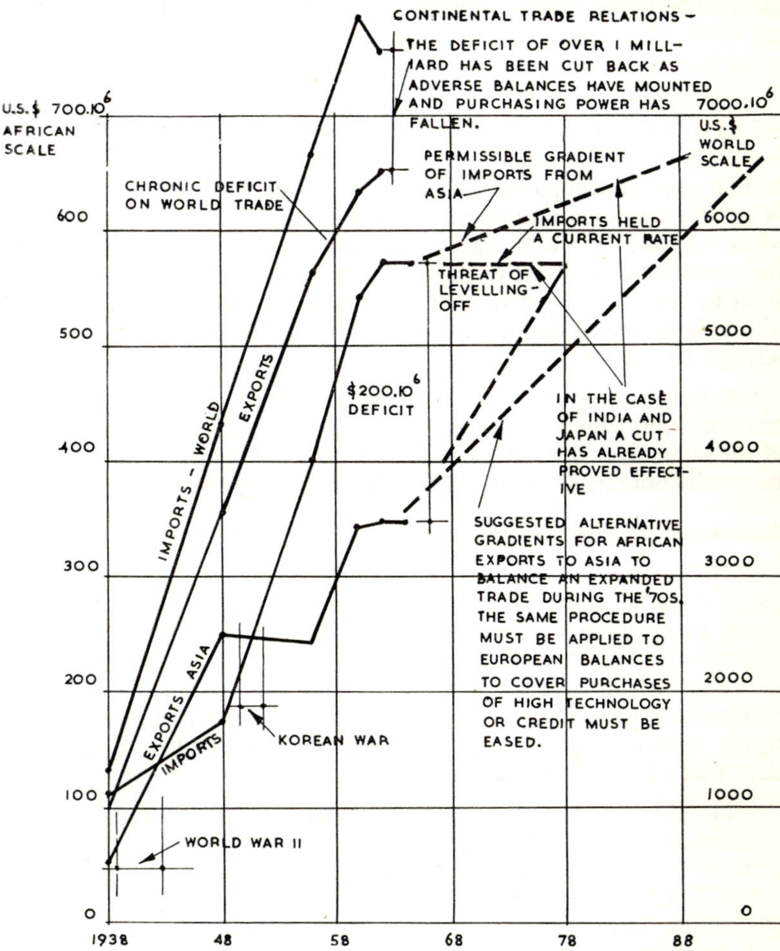

WHILE IMPORTS INDIA AND JAPAN HAVE RISEN IN SCALE WITH TRADE WITH THE WORLD EXPORTS TO ASIA HAVE FALLEN OFF SINCE THE 1950'S A TRADE IN BREAD CEREALS WITH ASIA (PARTICULARLY CHINA) AT 3 MILLION TONS PER ANN AT US $96/TON WOULD SET UP EXCHANGE TRIANGLES ON AN AFRO-ASIAN BASIS, WHICH COULD ULTIMATELY WIPE OUT THE IMBALANCE.

E. A. A. R.

The Ocean-base (Map 1)

The aquasphere is man's last recourse, if the gradient of world population growth continues upward beyond the limits suggested on Graph 1. Reference has been made to the conjectural figure of marine-based workers, engaged on the full range of industries extracting from the oceans, desalinated water, the mineral and biological resources potential. No indication has so far been given of a development programme of the required dimensions.

Consumption of fish at 16 kg. per head per annum is based on an estimated live-weight world catch of 50 million tons. Expansion may lead to a doubling of the total world take. Such an average daily intake of marine protein may be compared with the present Japanese consumption of about 44 kg. live weight per annum. But until refrigerated or dehydrated transportation has been fully developed, study of the problem of supply over the tropical belt has led to the confinement of the major disposal of seafoods to the littoral up to 1000 km. haul. Inland the lake, river—if not polluted—reservoir and the fish pond must be the main advance, until perhaps year 2000.

Supplies for continental interiors may be increased, in spite of their massive, unindented form, by the study of artificially promoted upsurges off the main river discharges. Such projects may produce, on a minor scale, the results obtained by natural causes from the Humboldt current off Peru.

Adjustment of imbalance by trade (Graph 10)

In spite of the obvious economic and political difficulties, the proposal outlined on Map 4 postulates the doubling of the currently foreseeable supply possibilities of Canada and Australia, allocating a similar figure to Argentine and utilizing the full export potential of the United States. In all cases this will include marginal land, cultivated on a solar radiation, precipitation cycle regime. Under such allocations the Americas could nearly supply India's demand around year 2000, leaving Oceania and Africa to meet that of mainland China.

The expansion of all potential rice producing areas must be envisaged in Africa and Latin America, to supplement those of South East Asia and Oceania. As examples of the imbalance in the rice trade, for the year 1963–4 Congo Kinshasha imported 38,900 tons, Somalia 36,678 tons and Sudan 5,670 tons. These are small figures, but in all cases, within the country itself or its regional fringe, a large surplus of rice should be possible.

The magnitude of the needs for food in Asia by year 2000 has been indicated in outline to scale on Map 4, to emphasize the completeness of the relocation of the focus of trade, which will result from the emergence of mass-populations in Asia as advanced economies. Even under the most optimistic assumptions on yields possible, the total requirement can be: India, 39 million tons per annum, China, 57, making a total of 96 million tons to be transferred from the producing regions to the consumers.

It may be argued that in view of the catastrophic food situation, which may be unavoidable from the late seventies onward, such restrictive practices as the four-course rotational regime should be modified. Soil fumigation and pesticides may profoundly alter ecological precautions hitherto necessary. But side-effects may occur. These may be of a hitherto unforeseen nature. For the purpose of this study and in view of the need to maintain other primary products, pending the emergence of synthetic substitutes, the limitation of 25% of land area down to cereals and grains each season has been accepted as a basis for Graphs 5 and 6, as well as the volume of trade for year 2000. Allocations have therefore been allowed to stand, even though they obviously strain production and transport capacities to the utmost and are at present largely politically impracticable.

A trade exchange of the size suggested can only be conducted on a basis of two-way traffic in reasonable equilibrium. The present suppliers of Asian food requirements are all included under the category of manufacturing nations. Some are in the high-technology bracket. Under the first heading, Canada, Australia and Argentine would be sensitive to the need to protect infant industries; although, with the United States, the possibility of trade in the sector of more sophisticated products could reward exploration and expansion over the coming decades. The fight for world exports markets is likely to be grim. If alternatives to the present situation are not found, it is obvious that the Soviet Union and China, in particular, cannot long continue the present pattern of trade; although it may continue to be imperative during a further crisis around 1975.

PEACEFUL MIGRATION—OR WAR

Repeated reference has been made to the need to facilitate mobility of population in the seven-milliard world, should it be found impossible to transfer supplies by trade to mass-populations of consumers suffering privation.

Twenty-five years ago it was thought necessary to suggest an extension of the functions performed by the International Labour Office of the League of Nations, in order to include the planning of migration on a world basis. This study, and the implementation of the solutions of the associated problems is today far more urgently necessary. Mass-movement, such as occurred at the rate of one million per year into the United States between 1900 and 1907, cannot be taken as a prototype. It was too small in scale, highly individualistic and therefore uncoordinated. North America was still comparatively virgin, as were huge areas in other continents. The same can be said of the Chinese move into Manchuria. In such cases it was possible to keep within the Issac limitation of immigration to about 1½% of the total population per annum, on the assumption that each entry created work for 1¼ other people. On such a basis all benefitted.

What may now have to be made possible, is the movement of distressed peoples, in unprecedented masses, seeking entry to areas, nearly all of which have already gone through a first phase of settlement. Friction of a most acute form will be inevitable, what may amount to world-wide chaos and catastrophe may be the outcome.

It is again pointed out with full knowledge of what this emphasis means, that Marshal Lin Piao has been charged with the formulation of the preparatory stage of what the writer termed twenty years ago—'militant civilian penetration'. To head-off the disaster of war, what seems to be required is:

> To determine if there is a break-point in time, beyond which trade in primary products and manufactured goods may prove ineffective to sustain a world population of around seven-milliard.
>
> To estimate the total optimum productive capacity of all potential surplus-producing regions.
>
> Beyond the point in time fixed under the first point, giving adequate warning, what may be the dimensions of the immigration problems to be solved by the respective reception areas.
>
> To set up within the United Nations an adequate organization to carry through this study in conjunction with all governments (including China) willing to co-operate.

Starvation and war are the catastrophes which threaten a seven-milliard world during the latter part of this century It is the author's conviction that these can only be avoided if, with courage and vision, a new economics of mobile demography can be brought to effective implementation.

THE TRANSMISSION OF INEQUALITY[1]

by

DUDLEY SEERS

In this paper, I describe a force which threatens to induce greater inequality of income distribution in poor countries, a slowing down of development and an aggravation of the political crisis of the Third World.

This at once calls to mind the belief of Marx that the mass of the population in capitalist countries would inevitably grow poorer, a belief attractive to revolutionaries, because it implied that 'internal contradictions' in capitalism would set the stage for the system to be brought to an end by a proletarian revolution. In the event, of course, these prophecies were not fulfilled. Capitalist economies have shown great social stability in this century, despite the strains of two world wars and the dismantling of colonial empires. Income has become more, not less, equally distributed.

Yet powerful tendencies to inequality *are* operating in the world and their effect is politically disruptive, though not quite in the way that Marx predicted.

It is now obvious that there is a basic tendency for the gap between average incomes in rich countries and in the rest of the world to grow, not merely absolutely but also relatively. There are many reasons for this, including political and administrative weaknesses in the governments of 'the rest of the world'. But a large part of the explanation lies in international economic relationships.

This is not the place to explore in depth how large this part is, or the way in which these relationships determine the rates of growth of various parts of the world economy. I have set out elsewhere the mechanism which I believe produces increasing inequality.[2] In summary, the explanation lies first in the tendency of the volume of consumption of manufacturers to grow more rapidly than the consumption of primary products, and second in the tendency for populations to grow faster in the countries which are poor than in those which are rich.

What I shall argue here is that this tendency to inequality between nations causes growing inequality inside the poor countries of the world, and that this in turn aggravates international inequalities.

First, some points of definition. In this paper 'poor' refers primarily to the countries of Africa and Asia (excluding Japan), but also to those of Latin

America in some degree, i.e. to a group which is conveniently known as the 'Third World'. (The word 'poor' is preferable to the euphemisms 'under-developed', 'developing', 'less developed', etc., which are vague and in some senses applicable to any country).

'Inequality' can, of course, have many meanings. What I have in mind here in principle is the ratio between the average professional salaries in a country and its average *per capita* income. This is somewhat imprecise, because what constitutes a professional salary is not always clear, and the average salary will be effected by the composition of the professions by age and by speciality. However, the international differences in distribution are so great that the ratio between any representative salary in a country and its *per capita* income would be usable as an indicator of inequality.

This definition has a number of implications. First, it measures the range of incomes, not the shape of the distribution; it leaves out of account the relative size of the group receiving salaries, which is also important for many purposes. But such a ratio tells us a good deal about a country's social and political structure. It is easy to grasp and visualise (in comparison to a coefficient which takes into account, as those of Pareto or Gini do, the shape of the distribution as well); because relevant statistics can be found. Moreover, *per capita* incomes are a yardstick used in other types of analysis, especially to measure differences between countries, to which the discussion of internal inequality should be linked.

Secondly it is rather restrictive. Company profits are very important in many countries—notably petroleum and metal producers. There are also other important sources of high personal income besides salaries—dividends and interest, profits of unincorporated businesses, rent from land and buildings. So this paper is not about the distribution of income as a whole. But, for reasons which will become clear, relative salary levels are both economically and politically significant.

THE STRUCTURE OF INCOME

One major explanation of the distribution of income in non-industrial countries is that there is an international market for those with certain professional qualifications, but only national markets for the rest of the labour force.

(i) *The International Market for the Professions*

Qualified people migrate from poor to rich countries, just as they do from the less rich to the very rich. But we tend to forget how novel is migration on this scale.

It is partly due to the proliferation of air travel since the war. It is cheap and easy to move to a job in another country; the spread of air services has helped in various other ways to extend the market for recruitment beyond national boundaries. Each profession is bound together by frequent conferences, which *inter alia* act as labour exchanges. And it is feasible now-a-days for somebody to travel thousands of miles just for an interview.

Another factor 'improving' the market has been the great extension of university scholarships. In 1964-5, there were 29 thousand students from the Far East (11 thousand from India) enrolled at 'institutions of higher learning' in the United States, 14 thousand from Latin America, 11 thousand from the Near and Middle East and 7 thousand Africans.[3] In Britain there were in February 1967 25 thousand students from poor countries altogether receiving University or 'further' education.[4] A student learns of the job opportunities open and meets a number of potential employers; he has an opportunity to establish himself permanently in the country, often in the very university where he studies, despite the fact that the purpose of sending him there is usually to enable him to be trained for work with his own government.

The type of education he receives may in fact make it hard for him to cope with his own country's problems; an economics student, for example, will find Keynesian economics—even 'development economics' as usually taught—a better preparation for an academic career in a rich country than for the practical tasks of economic development. A history Ph.D. may be quite unable to talk of the historical context of his country's problems. Even the courses available in his own country to a student of the Third World may be copies of those in a rich industrial country.

The international market is, of course, by no means perfectly competitive. Immigration laws limit the flow into rich countries; an immigrant, particularly one with a dark skin, may suffer from social handicaps such as discrimination in housing; families often find it hard to settle down, and education of children may be a problem; language difficulties restrict, perhaps drastically, the number of countries in which any individual can work. Many of the higher professional posts in the rich countries are, in practice if not in principle, reserved for their own natives, and so are virtually all posts in the civil service, the armed forces and establishments engaged in military research. Sometimes (as in the medical profession of the United States) foreign degrees are not fully recognised; the education available in the Third World is, in any case, often of too low a quality to prepare people for the competitive professions of the rich countries. Skills in the humanities are not readily marketable overseas. While fares to the North Atlantic area may be historically low, they are not negligible, especially for passengers from remote parts of the Southern Hemisphere and those who are still junior in their profession.

There are also attractions in working in one's own country. A job at home (especially in government service) usually provides more influence and perhaps more satisfaction than the posts open overseas, and it may offer greater security of tenure. Family ties may be powerful. Finally, of course, a young man may feel some obligation to take part in the development of his nation.

But on the other hand, the professionally qualified are in many ways encouraged to emigrate from the three poor continents. It is not unknown for a student to find after graduation that his own country has no suitable opening for someone with his particular qualifications, or political opinions, or his particular tribe or racial background. Professional people are attracted by the better libraries, better research facilities, better secretarial services and more extensive equipment available in Europe and North America, and especially by the larger and more eminent circles of colleagues. The citizen of a poor country may have developed a taste for life in or near the big cities of the North Atlantic area. Those from certain poor countries do not want to return home if their governments are uninterested in development or unable to guarantee public order.

Many acquire cars and consumer durables which it is difficult, or very expensive, for them to take back home because of import controls and high tariffs.[5] Some acquire foreign wives, and even those who do not may prefer their children to be educated abroad. Lastly, a young man, especially an African, may look on emigration as a way of escaping the responsibility of supporting his 'extended family'.

An African or Asian or Latin American now has in addition the opportunity of working for international organizations, which pay salaries close to those ruling in the United States. In fact, he may well, especially if he comes from one of the poorest countries, enjoy discrimination in his favour, because quotas, overt or tacit, limit the number of Europeans who can be employed, and governments actually exert pressure on agencies to hire more of their own nationals.

One consequence is that thousands of professionally qualified people from the Third World leave their own country each year. A high proportion of the students who go abroad to study never return home.

Data are only available on the United States, and only there for certain periods, but the volume is nevertheless astonishing. In the four fiscal years ending in June 1956, more than 18 thousand 'professional, technical and kindred workers', whose last permanent residence was neither Canada nor any European country, obtained immigrant visas for the United States. Within this total, the number of engineers and natural scientists was 3,462.[6] These figures include Japanese, Australians and New Zealanders, as well as some people who lived only temporarily in a poor country, after having been born and/or brought up elsewhere. They also include some who do not make use of their visas. On the other hand, they do not cover the large numbers who take jobs in the United States without obtaining immigrant visas.

The Bolivian, Cuban and Haitian doctors obtaining immigrant visas for the United States in 1965 were equivalent to half the output of their respective medical schools and the overall average for Latin America (excluding Cuba) was 10%. Half the qualified nurses of Chile emigrate, mostly to the United States, and the proportion is as high or higher for several Latin American countries. Over one-quarter of the interns and resident doctors in the United States hospitals are graduates of foreign medical schools, the majority from poor countries.[7]

The poorer the country, the greater the proportion that stay overseas. United States immigration data indicate 30% of Asian students apply for immigrant visas and in the case of some Asian countries the proportion who stay is from 60% to 90%.

Britain, France and other European countries also absorb additional thousands of professionally qualified people each year, mostly from very poor countries in Africa or Asia.

The 'brain drain' is a subject of increasing concern to European countries who lose a proportion of their own professionally qualified people. How much more serious it is for poor countries where chronic shortages of all types of professional people constitute an important, perhaps in some cases the main, constraint on economic development. As Professor Brinley Thomas has said, this is a 'perverse' movement in the sense that it moves resources to areas where they are less needed.

Among those with professional qualifications it is precisely those most useful for development who are in greatest international demand: for example, engineers, architects, chemists, physicists, agronomists, veterinary surgeons, experts in forestry and fisheries, geologists, hydrologists and statisticians.[8] Those who are less mobile, such as lawyers and service officers, may even be obstacles to development: many of those in the traditional professions have essentially static attitudes of mind, and see little advantage in development to compensate for them its strains and stresses. (A possible exception to this correlation between mobility and utility is the medical profession, which is subject to strong temptations to emigrate, but makes negative as well as positive contributions to development from a strictly economic point of view, so long as a low proportion of its activity is directed towards control of births compared to control of deaths. Another possible exception—unfortunately—are the economists!)

One consequence is that salaries in the poorer countries of the world are higher than they would be otherwise. The explanation is in part that shortages are aggravated, and partly that overseas salaries are imitated. It is not possible to pay the mobile professions such as doctors and engineers very much less than the salaries they would be able to earn overseas, salaries which often, as for doctors, incorporate elements of 'rent' due to restrictions on entry. Naturally, members of the professions which are less mobile, such as administrators with arts degrees, need not be paid nearly so much as their counterparts in rich countries. But the normal processes of setting civil service salaries maintain relationships between various professions, so that all—even primary school teachers and officers in the armed forces—benefit in some degree from the high salaries which have to be paid to those in international demand.

The professional markets of the richer industrial countries have been particularly closely linked with Africa and parts of Asia, where large numbers of expatriates have worked in colonial administrations. The salary scales in the various colonial services naturally reflected the possibilities open to the same people at home, with bonuses for expatriation or health risks. Many Europeans with university degrees in non-technical subjects (e.g. classical languages or literature) enjoyed higher standards of living if one allows for free or cheap housing and low taxes, than they would have, for example, in the less sheltered market of private commerce at home—especially if they had all been looking for jobs in this market.

When expatriate civil servants left in large numbers at Independence, Africans or Asians who replaced them naturally expected to enjoy the same standards. Anything less would have looked like racial discrimination. So a large section of the professional classes benefitted by the transfer of what are essentially foreign salary scales—in some cases higher.[9] The salaries on the non-mobile professions are particularly high now in Africa, in relation to the economic conditions of the countries where they work.

Another type of link—and this applies in all parts of the Third World—is that foreign business firms pay salaries to expatriates as high as, or higher than, they would for similar posts at head offices. Local employees of foreign companies who are promoted as part of 'localization' policies also receive these salaries.

This does not only apply to salaries; fees charged by doctors, lawyers, architects and others working on their own account reflect conventional scales in rich countries.

Additional links with the professional markets of the rich countries are now being forged, not only through the arrival of new firms but also through the technical assistance programmes, the size of which can in fact be partly attributed to the emigration of local people with professional qualifications. Those who work overseas under these programmes (or as part of agency staff or military aid missions) usually enjoy even higher standards of living than were customary in the colonial services. Local people with professional qualifications are therefore reminded of the opportunities available overseas not merely by the journeys they make with increasing frequency, but also by day-to-day contacts with those working alongside them.

(ii) *The Distribution of Personal Income*

Salaried staff are of course by no means at the top of the income ladder. Big landowners and merchants enjoy higher incomes, often much higher. Their significance depends on the local economic structure; it is marked in Latin America and parts of Asia, low in tropical Africa.

At the other end of the ladder are the agricultural labourers. In the typical unindustrialized country, a surplus labour force depresses incomes of those with little property or skill to a level near that of bare subsistence, as in the Marx-Lewis-Ranis model, especially if there is a shortage of food.

It is true that population pressure in the Third World has been relieved by migration of labour in the post-war years, e.g. from the Caribbean to the United Kingdom and the United States, from North Africa to France and from Central Africa to the gold mines of the Republic. Even at its peak, it was never very large in comparison to the total population of the Third World, important though it has been for particular countries.

One additional feature of the distribution of income in underdeveloped countries must be mentioned. This is that urban wage earners in factories or mines (and in some service industries) enjoy, even if they have little skill, much higher wages than those without this foothold in the modern sector. The institutional reasons for this lie outside the scope of this paper,[10] but there are also some that are analogous to the influences on professional salaries. Foreign companies, particularly in the petroleum and mining industry, pay unskilled labourers comparatively high wages, partly to buy industrial peace and partly to improve their local political position, affecting those paid in other sectors. More important trade unions in rich countries have often encouraged workers in poor continents to copy their methods and types of organization, creating privileged labour markets in one or two sectors of the economy. The International Labour Organization encourages the widespread adoption of standards essentially designed to prevent exploitation of workers in rich countries.

Within this rather privileged group of urban wage-earners, some are especially well off. Such international migration of non-professional workers as exists consists very largely of those with skills.[11] There are also in a few cases more direct links; thus wages received by skilled workers in the mining and construction industries of Central Africa reflect those which had to be paid to attract artisans from abroad. Premia for skills are big compared to those in rich countries; for some jobs, such as stenography, they are very high.

But this whole social group is, apart from the semi-industrialized countries of Latin America, typically small in relation to the large numbers in the towns, especially those recently arrived from the countryside, who have not been absorbed into the urban economy but live off it in some way, as relatives of those in employment, or as part-time employees in service jobs. The living conditions of many of these families, as of landless agricultural workers, especially in densely populated areas, are appalling.

The table on page 180 shows some data on employment incomes in the United Kingdom and two African countries. They are only very rough clues, because of the difficulty of finding comparable figures, and because they cover only three countries. But some points stand out very clearly. In Britain, the salary of the high-level civil servant or consultant is of the order of 10 times the nation's *per capita* income; in Uganda the corresponding figure would be 100. Ghana falls in between.

This reflects the fact that the international gap between salary levels is relatively very much less than between wage levels. Moreover, the gap is smaller for skilled workers than for unskilled—in the United Kingdom, wages of unskilled workers are some 6 to 7 times as great as those paid in the two African countries. Yet, in East Africa at least, even messengers in government service and unskilled labourers are relatively well off in comparison to the mass of the population in the rural areas.

The situation seems to be not essentially different elsewhere. The range in French-speaking Africa may well be even greater than in the former British territories.[12] An important unpublished study[13] by Harold Lydall reaches the conclusion that there is a much wider dispersion among employment incomes in Brazil, Chile, Mexico, India and Ceylon, and among household incomes (or expenditures) in Ivory Coast, Korea and Phillipines, than for rich countries. The only partial exception is Argentina which shares an income dispersion more like those of the North Atlantic area. Mr Lydall uses as a measure of inequality the ratio between various percentile incomes from the top and the median income. This is fundamentally rather different from the concept of inequality used in this paper (because it will be affected by the shape of the distribution) but clearly the two are related.

Data on the distribution of total *personal* income (i.e. including property, incomes, etc.) indicate that in countries of Asia, as for other parts of the Third World, there is a much more unequal distribution than in developing countries.[14] This would be at least compatible with the above thesis, since income from employment is nearly always the most important source of personal income.

INCOME DISTRIBUTION AND ECONOMIC DEVELOPMENT

Let us now look at the dynamics of income distribution, first briefly considering how the distribution of income affects development, and then examining the forces changing the distribution.

(i) *The consequences of inequality*

One possible mechanism of growth is, of course, for savings to be accumulated by the rich and invested in private capital formation; moreover, big income differences can act as incentives. Was this not, it is argued, the way in which countries such as Britain developed?

(In parenthesis, the historical record is far from clear. Two countries which apparently—there are no statistics—failed to achieve a more equal distribution in the past century, Spain and Portugal, have fallen far behind the rest of Western Europe. There are, of course, also non-economic reasons for their classic stagnation, but these examples suggest that a highly unequal distribution acts as a barrier to progress, at least over certain stages of development.)

To take the point about incentives first, a certain degree of inequality is needed to stimulate effort, including the effort to get higher qualifications. Some inequality will naturally result if a period of fast development starts with a shortage of qualified people because of reliance on expatriates or weak scientific faculties in universities. It is also necessary to provide those holding responsible jobs with enough comfort and time to do them properly, and to buttress their resistance to corruption.

These arguments can be exaggerated. The degree of inequality needed to induce people to study and work hard is probably not very great—certainly not as great as it is in many underdeveloped countries today. There is a limit to how much one should bribe people to make them incorruptible. But nevertheless, although the inequality needed for these purposes is a matter for judgement, and indeed must depend on the local social context, it is not zero. Neither the Soviet Union nor the countries of Eastern Europe, although they do not rely on personal saving to finance development, have insisted on anything like equality between professional salaries and wages. Indeed in 1964, the Czech Government deliberately set about increasing inequality.

On savings, the argument is much more dubious. One point should be firmly emphasized at the outset. The classical mechanism of development relied not so much on the savings of salaried professional people as on a large class of self-employed business men (and at a later stage on a big corporate sector), with the opportunity and the incentive, indeed necessity, to reinvest profits in their own businesses. It is therefore, hardly applicable to most underdeveloped countries.

But this process of growth is unlikely to produce fast enough growth for poor countries today, anyway, when the population and its aspirations are both rising rapidly. Here I have to broaden the scope of the discussion temporarily to talk about the distribution of income as a whole, though the points which will now be made apply in some degree to relative salary levels too, which naturally play an important role in shaping the total distribution.

The circumstances are less favourable today for this type of development. During the early stages of the industrialization of Western Europe, the industrial countries of Western Europe were not confronted with still richer countries overseas. The upper classes of the Third World today aspire to foreign standards of consumption which leave them little margin for saving. For the decade 1950–1959, despite highly unequal distributions of income, none of the poor countries for which figures were available, except South Africa, averaged personal savings at more than 7% of personal disposable income.[15]

In as far as they do save, the local rich—whether salary-earners, landowners or merchants—invest much of their savings in gold or even foreign securities. (There is, after all, an international market in capital as well as professional services.) Moreover, because of the embryonic state of local capital markets, savings that remain in the country tend to be devoted to building (e.g.) luxury residences which are of little consequence for development.

A particular drawback about the income distribution to be found in the poor countries of today (which would not have been nearly so true of Western Europe in the nineteenth or early twentieth centuries) is that because those with the big incomes are influenced by overseas standards, they have a high propensity, not merely to consume, but to consume imports—e.g. motor cars, refrigerators, air conditioning units, wine and whisky. The presence of large numbers of expatriates has contributed greatly (and continues to contribute greatly) to the formation of these tastes; so has education overseas. It seems only natural to many civil servants that officials of their rank should use cars and drink whisky. Some governments actually stimulate car purchases by making loans at low interest rates (usually the legacy of the practice of colonial governments).

In addition, because of real or imagined differences in quality, those with high incomes often buy imported goods which are competitive with local products—such as clothing, beer, confectionery, bakery and dairy products, and tinned fruits and vegetables. And they spend heavily on foreign travel. Even wage-earners in the modern sector usually have quite a high demand for imports, e.g. for wheat bread. Household budget data are not sufficient to enable the propensities to be quantified but it can safely be assumed that the lower the income the smaller the propensity to import.

This goes beyond personal consumption. Those whose tastes have been formed abroad are often able to induce governments or firms to undertake large outlays on imports, which are, if not superfluous in themselves, luxurious in design for the purposes they will serve. Technically advanced equipment such as computers and automatic lifts are popular. But the greatest waste of expenditure is on modern military weapons such as jet fighters, aircraft carriers, tanks, etc. Here the demonstration effect (e.g. through joint military exercises) is powerful.

These patterns of expenditure are hardly compatible with rapid economic development, which requires foreign exchange to be reserved for commercial vehicles, industrial machinery, tractors, fertilizers and other intermediate products that cannot be produced at home. It is true that priorities can be imposed by import and exchange controls; but when these are applied in a poor country, the result may be the corruption and demoralization of the controllers, which can spread through the administration, rather than a change in the composition of imports.

Rapid development also requires markets sufficiently homogeneous to permit mass production of domestic industry. The rich could hardly supply sufficiently big markets to stimulate rapid industrialization even if they were eager to buy local products. There needs to be some concentration of purchasing power at the lower levels. The consumption of clothing by the lower paid wage-earner creates considerable markets, and even purchase of light durables, such as bicycles and transistor radios, offer possibilities of import substitution. By contrast, local manufacture of the heavier and more expensive consumer durables, such as cars, is usually highly uneconomic. The pattern of industrialization found in the more developed countries of Latin America, and attributable largely to the income distributions there, is wasteful of both financial and human resources.

Inequality brings other well-known handicaps which can only be touched on here. The distribution of income distorts the techniques and structure of production. The artificially high salaries and wages paid in the urban industries of the Third World inhibit their development directly by making them uncompetitive with overseas manufacture; those that do develop tend to be highly mechanized, so unemployment is aggravated and wages depressed outside the modern sector. At the same time, many country dwellers are attracted to the towns—these are often the least uneducated, precisely those most needed to modernize agriculture; this also happened in Britain in the nineteenth century, but growing exports of manufactures could pay then for increasing imports of the food needed by the urban population.

The traditional path of development seems unlikely, therefore, to produce a fast enough rate of growth in the Third World today. But I do not rest my argument on a sweeping generalization, which is supported by little actual evidence and which some might find unacceptable. The point is that most governments of poor countries, especially in Africa, under the spur of the problems created by the pace or population growth and the increasing impatience of the masses, have already adopted a different route, one with a leading role for themselves in investment and organization: indeed the need for rapid structural changes in the economy and the absence or weakness of a local entrepreneurial class capable of developing industry give them little option.

But high salaries are hardly compatible with this pattern of development. In the first place, the necessary government savings on current account are very difficult to achieve as services are developed, if the salary bills for civil servants, teachers and military officers are heavy. This path also requires widespread political support, including the willingness to accept certain sacrifices, for example some restraint on the part of the urban workers in demanding wage increases. Such support is more difficult to win and hold if the government permits a very high degree of inequality in the income structure of its own public service. It is true that sacrifices can be imposed on the population by military regimes, which have in fact become the typical form of government in the Third World. But many of them, especially in newly independent countries, do not have sufficient force at their disposal to rule for long in the face of widespread opposition from their urban proletariat.

If ministers and civil servants are separated too far economically from the majority of the population, they will be unable to understand the problems of the common people, especially those in the rural areas. They may hardly be able to communicate with them, let alone formulate workable policies for modernizing rural society. They will tend to be sceptical about the possibility of development, to underestimate the potential power of nationalism, to despise rural life (and rural dwellers) and to disparage manual effort.

The administration can hardly mobilize the public if it is, or even merely appears to be, a remote and unsympathetic bureaucracy.

(ii) *Determinants of changes in distribution*

Yet the forces at work are tending to produce greater inequality in poor countries, not less. There are three main reasons for this: salaries in rich countries are now rising rapidly, the international market in professional skills is becoming more perfect, and the pace of population increase in the poor countries has become very fast.

(The total pattern of income distribution in poor countries may well be growing more unequal for additional reasons—because of the growth of property income and of the profits of the self-employed, which are big in some countries, notably the semi-industrialized countries of Latin America, and could well be climbing rapidly, especially where there is also a labour surplus. But these reasons lie outside the scope of this paper.)

Before looking at the consequences, let us examine the mechanism through which inequality grows. Suppose first that the ratio of salaries to *per capita* income in a rich country remains constant, and secondly that the average *per capita* income has a chronic tendency to rise more quickly there than in a poor country. Then salaries in the former will tend to rise relative to all income in the latter.

The assumption that the structure of employment incomes in industrial countries remains unchanged would, of course, be invalid if professional salaries were rising more slowly than average incomes. They certainly were rising more slowly in the first half of this century. A study by Tibor Scitovsky summarises the data available on the main industrial countries.[16]

Guy Routh's study of changes in employment incomes in the United Kingdom goes into some detail, and the same conclusion stands out clearly.[17]

It looks, however, as if it is no longer true. The sustained pace of development over the two decades since the end of the war has caused a serious shortage of many types of professional worker. This has been aggravated by the rapid expansion of universities, the soaring outlays of foundations, and the fast growth of military and 'space' research. New advances, particularly in medicine, have led to the adoption of techniques which require large numbers of highly skilled people, in some cases teams of specialized experts.[18] Finally, formal qualifications (such as doctorates) are increasingly often required for professional posts, reinforcing the monopolistic element in professional salaries. These are rising rapidly now in the North Atlantic area, especially the United States.

Inside this group of countries, moreover, the professionally qualified are highly mobile. No other well-to-do country can allow its professional salaries to lag far behind those of the United States.[19] Recent increases in university and medical salaries in Britain, for example, were partly justified by the need to stop the 'brain drain', and these influence the whole structure of salaries.

Scitovsky's paper contains only fragmentary data, but suggests that the general downward trend in relative professional salaries, a trend which was marked for virtually all professions and all countries in the decades before 1950, did not continue after 1950. The unpublished study by Lydall, cited above, suggests that although in the United Kingdom, the United States and Canada the distribution of employment income became much more equal between the 1930's and the end of the war, it became more unequal again in the 1950's, as it did also in France, though not in the Netherlands. A study by H. P. Miller came to the same conclusion about the United States.[20] Routh's study shows that in Great Britain salaries of both 'higher' and 'lower' professional employees increased faster than average employment incomes between 1955/6 and 1960, partly reversing the previous decline in their relative position. Official indexes for the United Kingdom imply that average wage earnings and average salary earnings increased at about the same rate from 1955 to 1965, but details of the salaries index reveal that clerical employees' earnings grew much more slowly than those of the salaried employees as a whole, implying that salaries of technical and administrative employees (including employees with professional qualifications) rose more rapidly than wage earnings over this decade.[21]

Tax structures are also no longer becoming noticeably more progressive. There is not a great deal of scope for further increases in direct taxation in rich countries when rates of about 50% apply at the margin to the higher professional salaries. Moreover, the general tendency seems to be for tax-free 'fringe benefits' to increase.

Finally the market for professional services has improved. Travel costs are falling relative to salaries. The average passenger revenue per passenger mile has in fact declined absolutely (in the case of BOAC by 29% between 1956–7 and 1965–6). This is largely due to the spread of concession fares, but economy class return fares have shown only moderate increases, or have fallen, as shown by the following specimen figures:

	1955	*1965*
London-New Delhi	£236	£260
London-Nairobi	209	241
London-Kingston	253	217*a*)
Paris-Abidjan	179	186
New York-Buenos Aires	309	225*b*)

a) low season *b*) Jets—£202 for propeller flights

Immigration laws in rich countries have been changed in ways that make it easier for those with professional or technical skills to leave the Third World for good, or harder for those without such skills to do so. In October 1962, a supplementary law in the United States allowed easier entry for professional personnel, and under the new Immigration Act of 1965, 17 thousand immigration visas each year, or 10% of the total, are reserved for professional people, irrespective of their race or nationality, other than those from the Western Hemisphere, where special conditions apply. Students already in the country on F visas can apply for these 'third preference' immigration visas themselves, instead of having to be nominated by an official body on grounds of national interest. Indeed in some cases students have been advised by immigration officers that an immigrant visa is easier to obtain than an extension of their present visa.[22] All employable immigrants, apart from relatives of US citizens or permanent residents, require certificates by the Labor Department showing that they are needed to fill labour shortages. Developments in Canada have been similar.[23]

In Britain the development has been rather one of restricting entrance of unskilled than facilitating immigration of the skilled. The Immigration Act of 1962 created a system of vouchers which reduced the immigration of those without either jobs already promised (Category A) or professional qualifications (Category B). In fact from September 1964, vouchers were only issued to those two categories, and in 1965 the number of vouchers was reduced (from about 21 thousand a year to 8,500) with Category B getting priority.[24]

At the same time population growth has accelerated in poor countries—from 2.1% overall to 2.5% in the decade from 1950–55 to 1960–65. This has helped to slow down the rise in *per capita* incomes, and has acted as a brake on the wages outside the modern sectors of economies.

THE POLICY PROBLEM FOR GOVERNMENTS OF POOR COUNTRIES

(i) *The Central Dilemma*

These developments pose serious dilemmas for governments in the poorer continents. If they do not raise local professional salaries, they lose badly needed personnel, in whom they have invested a great deal of resources. In most poor countries, particularly in East and Central Africa, manpower plans are showing increasing shortages, for many years ahead even on the assumption that no qualified personnel are lost by emigration.[25]

On the other hand, if governments do raise professional salaries, inequalities are accentuated. The rise spreads to officials with less economic justification for an increase, including those who owe their jobs to nepotism or to degrees in subjects which are of little practical use, except for occupations such as diplomatic representation. It continues down through executive and clerical grades and strengthens the pressures of organized urban workers for higher wages.

The consequences follow from the analysis above. In brief, import substitution and export promotion become expensive; the growth of employment is inhibited; much of the increase in purchasing power spills over into demand for imports; the problem of financing the expansion of government services, partly in imitation of those in the rich countries, grows worse. There are also potential dangers of inflation. Rises in money incomes from any source leads to attempts by others to obtain increases sufficient to protect their real incomes and makes chronic inflation a real possibility (in countries with monetary autonomy); this type of mechanism, though operating usually under the stimulus of rises in incomes other than salaries, has been an important factor in the inflationary process of Argentina, Brazil, Chile, Colombia and Uruguay.[26]

There is very little published evidence on how governments actually handled this dilemma or on changes in income distribution,[27] but the picture seems to be broadly as follows. Up to the time of independence colonial governments made a series of salary increases, and retained their expatriate staff. The arrangements for independence included however, in the case of British colonies, substantial lump sum payments ('golden handshakes') which actually encouraged officials, including those with technical qualifications, to leave. After becoming independent, some countries (notably Zambia) continued to raise salaries, including those at higher levels. The degree of inequality therefore greatly increased in the post-war period. Although this trend is now ceasing, and price inflation (especially in Ghana) has eroded their real value somewhat, salaries offered to young African graduates returning to their own country are usually not unattractive, especially since they can advance to senior posts quite rapidly.

In countries which have been independent for some time, however, including India, but notably Latin America, salaries in the public sector have not kept pace with other incomes. This has been specially true of countries experiencing price inflation, and qualified personnel naturally prefer working for private business or foreign countries. In some cases, governments have retained their staff by turning a blind eye to their taking on a growing volume of outside work.

There is some evidence on the growing migration of manpower to rich countries—and most governments have in fact, if not consciously, chosen to pay this price. The number of immigrant visas into the United States to natural scientists and engineers whose previous permanent residence was neither Canada nor a European country rose from 682 in 1952–3 to 1,274 in 1960–1; including some of social scientists, the total was 1,438 in 1961–2 and 2,294 in 1962–3, the rise in the latter year being due to a big increase in Asian immigrants, following the new regulations in 1962 mentioned above.[28] Following the 1965 law, the number of foreign students (of all faculties and from all sources) who proposed to stay in the United States after graduation rose from 6 thousand in 1964–5 to 11 thousand in 1965–6.[29] In Canada the number of professional and managerial immigrants (from all sources) rose from 6,592 in 1961 to 10,799 in 1963.[30]

There are fewer data on British immigration. The total number of engineers and scientists migrating into the United Kingdom rose sharply in the 1950's but then levelled off. The flow, however, is considerable. Out of 8,500 vouchers issuable under the new Commonwealth Immigration procedure, 5,425 were issued in Category B (for the professions) in 1966, the first full year.[31] This included 1,974 doctors, a number believed to be considerably higher than in former years—these included of course all Commonwealth countries, and about one quarter of vouchers issued are normally not taken up.

This dilemma looks like becoming still more acute in the future. The rate of growth of income per head in rich countries is about 3% a year and even if professional salaries there only rise at that rate, they will rise by a third in a decade. In fact the shortage of professional personnel in rich countries is likely to grow, with a consequently continued strong market for their services.[32] During this time, partly because of the rate of population growth, and partly because of shortages of professional manpower, *per capita* incomes in the Third World may well not rise by half as much. Meanwhile travel costs are also likely to continue to fall relative to salaries, as bigger airliners come into operation.

I have been writing as if governments could choose whether inequality or loss of manpower was the greater evil. In the years ahead, they can hardly avoid either.

It might seem as if a policy of salary restraint (or increased direct taxes) would correct the distorted income structures of newly independent countries. But in fact the effect of such policies would only be small in the foreseeable future.

The Uganda Second Five-Year Plan, pointing out that 'it is quite usual for people to earn as much as over thirty times their domestic servants' wages, and domestic servants are not the lowest paid groups,' does propose an egalitarian incomes policy. The rises in pay envisaged from 1966 to 1971 are as follows: 3½% a year for those with under £90, 2½% for those with £90 to £210, 1% for the £210–£600 group and no increases for those with more than £600. *Per capita* national income would rise at a slightly slower rate than 3½% a year.[33]

However, it will be difficult to implement such a severe restraint. Governments are highly dependent on their senior civil servants, who also exercise considerable political power, and are usually well organised. Some African governments which have tried to reduce salaries have fallen (though President Nyerere succeeded in Tanzania). The result could also be—there are plenty of Latin American illustrations—a decline in the quality of the administration.

In any case, if it were possible to hold the top salaries steady while waiting for the lower incomes to catch up, the income structure would only change very slowly. If the Ugandan national income target quoted is achieved, and higher salaries successfully contained, a Permanent Secretary's salary would still at the end of five years be over 90 times the *per capita* national income. Even assuming the *per capita* income continued to grow at $3\frac{1}{2}\%$, and this severe salary restraint could be maintained so long, it would take more than 60 years before the ratio became 10 to 1. Inflation, which will be a serious danger in Africa and Asia in the 1970's, would be almost a boon in such circumstances if it had no other ill effects.

In countries which have been independent for some time, it will be hard for governments to avoid raising their salaries more rapidly than wages, partly because of the growing international mobility, but also because of the continued rise of salaries in the private sector, which is less protected from the market forces which are pulling apart the income structures of poor countries. Yet a policy of raising relative salaries would not stop the 'brain drain'; from the foregoing analysis it is clear that some of the attractions of work overseas are non-monetary.

The political dangers in this set of developments, apart from their economic implications, are obvious. It is true that economists are professionally prone to economic determinism, but anyone familiar with almost any part of the Third World will be aware of the real menace they pose.[34]

There are many possible cumulative processes. If growing international inequalities aggravate internal inequalities and check the rate of development, political unrest may make it still more difficult to keep high-level manpower in a country so that the income distribution becomes still more unequal, import propensities still higher and development even slower, leading in turn to further economic and political problems and causing greater international inequalities.

(ii) *Are there any solutions?*

Anyone who poses a fundamental policy problem is expected to face the challenge; what can be done about it? Before indicating some ways in which governments of poor countries could ease the central dilemma, let me make three points. The first is that it is not really for outsiders to work out policies for dealing with major social and political problems; the people of the countries concerned are in a far better position to do this—and after all they have to live with the consequences. Secondly, there is no reason why there should be a general solution, in the sense of a set of policies which would be generally applicable and also consistent with economic development and political stability. Thirdly, if there is such a solution, it cannot necessarily be foreseen at this date; not much thought has been given to the problem yet.

I can only indicate very briefly here some possible lines of solution with notes on the contribution which each could make.[35]

Educational Development

The most obvious policy is to increase the supply of technically and professionally educated people in the poorer countries. The educational development now in progress will ease shortages and help to change the balance of the local market for their services, and this could be accelerated. The provision of more university places will reduce the danger of losing talented people.

There are a number of reasons, however, why one cannot expect an increase in the number of educational establishments, desirable though it is, to solve this problem in the foreseeable future. The first is that to build up an adequate stock of professional manpower will take decades, especially in East and Central Africa, since the needs will be growing all the time.

Secondly, the increased supply will be of little help if a large proportion emigrates, and we have seen that this is very likely. Thus even countries such as Argentina, Chile and India, with large university systems, suffer from chronic manpower problems; much of their graduate output helps to ease the manpower shortages in far richer countries.

The third difficulty is particularly intractable. The very shortage of high-level manpower is one of the factors responsible for the rising salaries that teachers receive, which in turn inhibits sufficient expansion of education to produce the high-level manpower which is needed.[36] So there is a cumulative element here—the more pressing the shortages, the more difficult it is to solve them.

Fourthly—and this is particularly relevant in Africa—the appearance of large numbers of graduates will create increasingly severe promotion 'bottlenecks' in the civil service and the educational system. The top jobs are often held today by very young people, who no doubt expect to keep them for another three or even four decades, during which time many people with at least comparable paper qualifications will be building up comparable experience too. This could create dangerous political frictions in the heart of an administration.

Finally, the educational system is, to a greater or lesser degree, inappropriate to the needs of any poor country. In many of them (India and Nigeria are conspicuous cases), the secondary schools and universities are still pouring out people who have little prospect of jobs at salary levels they consider appropriate, although shortages of technical and professional people remain severe. So a mere expansion of educational output would be of limited help in easing shortages; it may even not greatly reduce inequalities, if salary levels prove rigid.

One major need is to change drastically the balance between different subjects, emphasizing much more heavily the physical (and social) sciences. At the beginning of this decade only 26% of those graduating in 47 poor countries (India not being one of these), took degrees in engineering, agriculture or the natural sciences, as against 31% in industrial countries.[37]

Perhaps even more important is to adapt the length and content of courses to development needs. It may be better to produce 1,000 medical assistants a year capable of dealing with common illnesses and of dealing with preventives against endemic diseases, rather than 100 doctors educated to 'Western' standards, who might well emigrate.

The key to many of these problems lies however in the content of secondary education. A few secondary boarding schools could be selected to emphasize strongly both nationalism and technical subjects, and provide a rather spartan, even quasi-military, system of discipline. This would help accelerate development, especially rural development. Those produced by the educational system would then be less able to market their services overseas, and less interested in doing so; they would also be less influenced by foreign expenditure patterns and attitudes to development.

Such reforms can in principle be made quickly, though education ministries, schools and universities alike will naturally resist ferociously any major structural change—as they do all over the world![38] And we run into the time lag problem again; it would take many years before the manpower stock could be materially affected.

This suggests the need for large-scale adult education. Apart from its 'vocational' contribution, it involves the public in the development process. But its contribution to the manpower problem must be to reduce technical rather than professional shortages. This is of course important in itself, but it does not contribute greatly to easing the central dilemma.

Manpower Controls

This leads one to consider ways of restricting the mobility of professional labour. Such restrictions were not common practice during the early stages of European industrialization, except in the case of those with trade secrets, but there were after all few major possibilities then of improving one's lot by emigration.

The commonest method actually used now is 'bonding' those who receive Government scholarships, so as to ensure that they work in their own countries for a period after completing their education. Some countries, such as Iran, reinforce bonding by requiring a financial guarantee for bonded scholars, which is forfeited if they take up jobs abroad—though it is hard to estimate the cost of the loss of a trained man; in some cases, the discounted flow of additions to national income which he could make possible if he stayed in his own country might amount to millions of pounds. In other countries (e.g. the UAR) bonding is supplemented by control on overseas employment using as an ultimate sanction the withdrawal of passports. Another possibility is to induct people going overseas for high-level education into military service before they depart.

It is true that such measures restrict traditional human liberties, but on the other hand a check to development through the loss of qualified manpower exacts a terrible price in terms of needless poverty. A more cogent argument is that the scope for policy may not be as great as it appears to be, in countries with many contacts with the richer nations. It is dangerous to keep too many at home against their will. Although the Cuban Government has lost much badly needed professional manpower by allowing emigration to the United States (except for a period following the missiles crisis in 1962), while pursuing a vigorous policy of equalizing incomes, it may have gained on balance by getting rid of what might have been the core of political opposition.

Restrictions on choice of job within a country, such as were adopted in industrial countries during World War II, may be more effective. They would reduce the temptation to private business to bid up salaries and help to prevent waste of trained manpower, and high rates of turnover.

A Selective Salary Policy

A Government can arrange that taxation falls more heavily on wealth and unearned income than on salaries. More important, salary increases can be restricted to the professions which are mobile and necessary. One way of achieving this is to create professional cadres with special salaries outside the civil service proper—in development corporations, for example (as many Latin American governments have done). Such policies can also be applied in other salary structures over which the government has control or influence, especially the universities, which can achieve the same objective (with less envy from other professions) by increasing the facilities available for key faculties.

Discriminating policies of this kind would reinforce other lines of solution. They would encourage school children and students to study the priority subjects, and they would make it easier to operate manpower controls.

THE CONTRIBUTION OF RICH COUNTRIES

The proposals I have outlined would not amount, however, even taken together, to a general solution in most countries. Even if they were adequate, it would be very hard for newly independent governments, which have to face a number of problems at the same time, to carry them out. These governments need to build national unity, avoid food shortages, and provide enough employment, as well as solve the central dilemma which has been described.

The question that obviously arises is: what can the rich countries do to ease the dilemma? At present they are getting into the rather ludicrous position, unsatisfactory to all parties, with one hand taking (for example) doctors from overseas into their own countries, while financing with the other the heavy costs of providing doctors under technical assistance programmes. This alone poses the need for rethinking policy.

Capital aid can be considered a form of repayment for the value of those who migrate; one possibility would in fact be for governments or rich countries to pay an indemnity for each graduate or skilled person they absorb.[39] If spent on strengthening educational institutions, overseas aid can contribute directly to solving the problem outlined here. Training schemes can help repair the damage.

However the contribution of aid is bound to be limited in the next few years. Rich countries are not contemplating big increases in capital aid. Many recipient governments lack the capacity to produce sufficient projects. In principle this capacity can be increased by technical assistance, but in practice governments are often unable to make even the right job specification for technical experts, or to check the suitability of those who are offered. Moreover if foreign experts become too numerous, local personnel spend a large part of their time briefing newcomers, and later coping with their reports and recommendations. A government needs in any case to put some limit on the technical assistance it receives if it is to keep its national identity and preserve the nationalist mainspring of the development process.

The usefulness of aid depends very much on its type and source. If donors supply the wrong type of technical assistance or send the wrong people overseas, or if they abuse capital aid by favouring (perhaps for their own strategic convenience) governments which resist necessary social reforms, or if they provide aid on onerous terms, or if they fail to guard against corruption, the results may well be greater inequality and slower development. The same will happen if overseas students are provided with courses which have not been designed to help them serve their own country, but 'alienate' them, or if immigration authorities permit them to stay after the courses are over.

While recipients of aid could do much to put their own house in order, especially by co-ordinationg their approaches to various agencies, governments of rich countries should help more constructively with the manpower problem. In the first place, they should find out how much damage their immigration policies are doing. How many skilled people from poor countries are they absorbing themselves, as a result of retaining students, or in others ways? There is a great need for better statistics; the United States is in fact taking steps to provide these.

Secondly, carefully tailored programmes of training and scholarship should supplement the facilities available to students in their own countries, and indeed make it unnecessary for many foreign governments to set up expensive faculties such as medicine and engineering. But this is not merely a question of supplying places at their own technical colleges and universities; syllabuses need to be worked out for the use of overseas students.

Thirdly, students should be returned home at the end of their courses, as is done by the Australian Government, unless an extension (e.g. into post-graduate work) has been specifically approved by their own government. Those who come on short-period courses of training do normally return home—the problem is more those who come on scholarships, or privately financed, for university degrees. Deportation may at times work cruelly, if it means returning someone to a country where he is a member of a minority which is discriminated against, or where he has inadequate scope for his professional skill (though the cure for this is to make sure he gets the right training). In fact some exceptions might have to be made, though making them puts the rich government in an invidious position. Moreover the onus is precisely on the most highly educated citizens to help modernize the political system of their own countries. So exceptions ought to be strictly limited, to cases where those returning home faced the possibility of death sentences or long terms of imprisonment, or had talents which could only be developed in a large industrial country (e.g. someone with capacity for research in the natural sciences).

A more conscious strategy of this kind implies finding out from governments of overseas countries their manpower needs, which in many cases would involve helping them to estimate these, and then taking measures to help governments keep their graduates at home. This would greatly reduce the political and administrative problems of applying the manpower controls and salary policies outlined above.

It would perhaps be politically unrealistic to expect governments of rich countries to go farther and take account of the deteriorating world situation in forming their own domestic economic policies. It would of course help if the monopolistic elements in the professions were removed, so as to slow down the salary increase, but this would be a big task, requiring detailed study of recruitment procedures and professional practice in each field, followed by legislation that would be vigorously opposed by the professional trade unions. The central dilemma would also be eased if governments of rich countries tried to control the rise in salaries, but this would be difficult, especially in the United States, precisely where it would be particularly helpful, so long as the private sector is so powerful and shortages of certain skills remain so severe.

Governments of rich countries could however be expected to accelerate more rapidly the rise in their own production of graduates in professions such as engineering and the sciences, so that they become less dependent on taking graduates from countries where the need is much greater; here again the key to the world problem is the policy of the United States.

These measures, which could of course be advocated on other grounds, would reduce the danger of economic and political chaos in the Third World on a scale that would be harmful to all nations, rich and poor.

IMPLICATIONS

I will close by drawing attention to some of the wider implications of this analysis for economic theory and for the future outlook.

(i) *Theory*

Migration and income distribution will attract much more attention in economic development, precisely because increasingly serious difficulties will arise in these fields. The development of the economics of manpower leads inevitably into them.

The international distribution of income is important. One line of argument is that all will be well if *per capita* incomes in poor countries rise, and that it does not matter whether this rise is as fast as the rate of growth of rich countries. This argument is politically questionable anyway, but it does not stand up on economic terms either, when one allows for the transmission of inequality. Different rates of growth in the world are creating severe and growing tensions inside countries, impeding their development, and thus further widening the gap between the growth rates of rich and poor countries.

The histories of today's rich countries cannot be copied. The problems facing poorer countries today are profoundly different, because of the existence of countries already rich, from those faced earlier by those who led the world as they industrialized. Emulation of foreign salaries, consumption patterns and attitudes are major new influences (and there are others).

This subject yields one more illustration of the inadequacy of existing economic theory, developed in industrial countries.[40] Although textbooks on (say) the theory of distribution or the theory of wages (or the theory of inflation) have titles which may lead a student to think they are universally relevant, they usually ignore factors important in the Third World, notably external influences. Virtually all growth models treat labour as homogeneous, and many even omit to mention income distribution (except perhaps to assume that saving is positively associated with inequality) and thus altogether miss the significance of its relation to import propensities.

Yet a great deal of what has been said above does not only apply to the Third World. The central dilemma confronts all the richer countries except the United States, and applies particularly to Britain. The upward pressure on salaries in certain mobile professions, transmitted from the faster-growing United States, tends to spread to salaries in other professions and in 'administration', and eventually to wages. Similar dilemmas arise—a choice between losing doctors or disrupting the incomes policy. With this pressure on salaries, it is difficult to see how a moderate degree of price inflation could be avoided, even if there were no other upward pressures.

(ii) *Policy and prospects*

Just as it is dangerous to take theories over from industrial countries, so it is dangerous to take over policies. The traditional 'laissez-faire' solution of letting salaries rise and curbing inequality by direct taxation cannot solve the problem. If net salaries keep pace with those paid abroad, the foreign exchange and fiscal problems of development will be virtually insoluble.

A country's incomes policy, its education plan, its manpower controls and its programme for making use of foreign scholarships need to be worked out as a whole. An economic plan is seriously defective unless these are covered in some detail, and economic strategy will be largely ineffective unless the government is determined to carry them out. This is also true for industrial countries, especially Britain.

The emergence of an international market for professional skills increases the need for internally co-ordinated policies. It is surprising that this central problem of development has been so neglected by UNESCO and UNCTAD (although in the latter case one explanation is the heavy influence of Latin America, where problems of the supply of foreign exchange appear, at least, to be more a severe limitation on development).

The case for free (or non-discriminatory) trade is seriously impaired by the single fact of different degrees of mobility of different types of labour.

The future depends largely on whether the younger generation of professionally qualified people see the central dilemma and draw the correct conclusions—namely in their country's interests (and indeed in the long-run interests of the new elite itself), not to exploit their full bargaining power or to seek employment abroad. Their reaction depends in the last resort on the strength of patriotism, and therefore very largely on the quality of political leadership.

Table

Illustrative salaries, wages and per capita incomes in the United Kingdom, Ghana and Uganda (1966)

(*£ per annum*)

	U.K.	*Ghana*	*Uganda*
Professional salaries			
High-level Civil Servant	5350	2000	2800
Doctor: (Consultant)	4500	3000	2240
(General Practitioner)	2750	1850	1460
Engineer	2000	920	1320
Wages Skilled Industrial Worker	1100	475	350
Unskilled Industrial Worker	800	137	110
Agricultural Worker	700	100	n.a.
Messenger	600	100	110
National income per capita	525	85	25

Sources to Table

This is an illustrative table, based on published salary scales and on information supplied by the High Commissions of Ghana and Uganda in London. In some cases, proxy figures are used (e.g. midpoints of pay scales or averages for different periods). It should be borne in mind that salaries of established civil servants are pensionable. Further details are as follows:

Civil Servant	*U.K.:*	Fixed salary for Under-Secretaries (excluding London allowance).

	Ghana:	Midpoint of Permanent Secretary scale (£1500—£2500).
	Uganda:	Fixed salary for Permanent Secretaries. It is assumed that the responsibilities of Permanent Secretaries in African countries of this size correspond roughly to those of Under-Secretaries in the United Kingdom. In practice the former are usually younger and less experienced.
Doctor (Consultant)	*U.K.:*	Ministry of Health unofficial estimate for 1965 of the average earnings of consultants in full-time government service. The range was £3200—£4885, with 'merit payments' (i.e. additions for extra qualifications) of up to £925. In 1966, substantial increases were awarded, which are not included in the figure shown in the table—they did not come into effect until 1967.
	Uganda:	Midpoint of Consultant Scale (£2175—£2300).
(General Practitioner)	*U.K.*	Ministry of Health unofficial estimate of National Health Service G.P.'s average earnings in 1965. In 1966, large increases were awarded, partially backdated, which are not included in the figure shown.
	Ghana:	Midpoint of Medical Officer scale (£1080—£1620, plus £500 tax-free bonus at all levels).
	Uganda:	Midpoint of Medical Officer scale (£1128—£1791).
Engineer	*U.K.:*	Wimpey's average rate for civil engineers.
	Uganda:	Midpoint of Engineer's scale (£837—£1791).
Skilled Industrial Worker	*U.K.:*	1965 average earnings of skilled engineering workers. (Source: Ministry of Labour).
	Uganda:	Midpoint of the scale for industrial foreman (£102—£597).
Messenger	*Ghana:*	Based on the government rate of 7s. 6d. per day.
	Uganda:	Midpoint of the government scale for general labour (£96——£136).
Unskilled Industrial Workers	*U.K.:*	1965 average earnings of unskilled engineering workers. (Source: Ministry of Labour).
	Ghana:	Based on the standard industrial rate of 10s. 6d. per day.
	Uganda:	Midpoint of the government scale for general labour (£96—£136).
Agricultural Worker	*U.K.:*	April—Sept. 1965 average earnings of agricultural workers (Source: Ministry of Labour). This figure does not take account of payment in kind.
	Ghana:	Based on the standard agricultural rate of 7s. 6d. per day.

REFERENCES

1 When this paper was read at the Haile Selassie I Prize Trust Conference in Addis Ababa, October 1966, I was working for the British Government.

I wrote this paper in my personal capacity and it should not necessarily be taken to reflect the views of the Ministry of Overseas Development. I would like to acknowledge very useful comments of Mr. Streeten, Mr. Foggon and Mr. Wilmhurst and the research assistance of Mr. Greenfield, Mr. Minford and Mr. Bryden.

I opened discussions on this subject at meetings of the Economics Faculty, Cambridge, and the Political Economy Club at Oxford. I gained a great deal from the discussions. Some of the themes have subsequently been developed further, with later references in 'Graduate Migration as an obstacle to Equality' to be published in *Essays in Honour of Thomas Balogh* (ed. Paul Steeter).

2 See *Economic Journal*, March, 1962. 'A model of comparative rates of growth in the world economy'.

3 'Open doors, 1966: Report on International Exchange' (Institute of International Education). These figures exclude those who had already made plans to stay in the United States after their courses ended.

4 Minister of Education and Science, House of Commons, 28-2-67.

5 This may seem trivial but it was given as the main reason in a report on a sample among Chileans resident in the United States 'La emigracion de recursos humanos chilenos de alto nivel a los estados unidos' by Gutirrez and Riquelme, *Ciencia Interamericana*, 1965, Vol. 6. No. 2.

6 *Scientific Manpower Bulletin*, February 1958 (National Science Foundation).

7 'Foreign Students: Exchange or Immigration' by G. Henderson. *International Development Review*, December 1964; *Wall Street Journal* 21-11-66; 'Foreign Aid and the Brain Drain' by J. A. Perkin, *Foreign Affairs*, July 1966, Dr. Halsey Hunt, Dr. Charles Kidd, Dr. Kelly West and Professor Shear in 'International Migration of Talent and Skills' (Council on International and Cultural Affairs of the US Govnt, October 1966).

8 In the *American Economic Review*, (May 1966), Grubel and Scott argue that emigration of highly skilled people (the 'brain drain') involves a lower cost to their native country than is usually thought. They assume, however, that the skill of the emigrant can be replaced quite rapidly and that 'externalities' can be ignored. Despite the apparent generality of the text and title ('The international flow of human capital') the argument applies, if anywhere, only to the rather special case of migration between industrial countries; it certainly does not apply to emigration from poor countries to rich.

9 The process and problems of 'Africanisation' and 'Asianisation' are analysed in depth in 'The British and their Successors' by Richard Symonds, London, 1966.

10 See *Wage Trends, Wage Policies and Collective Bargaining: the problems of underdeveloped countries*, H. A. Turner, Cambridge University Press, 1965, and *Wage levels, employment, productivity, and consumption*', an unpublished paper by Reginald Green prepared at Makerere College, Kampala.

11 Over half of the Jamaicans migrating to the United Kingdom in 1953-5 were classed as skilled workers, the stock of masons, mechanics, electricians and carpenters in the island falling as a consequence. *Study of External Migration to the United Kingdom: 1953—5*, by G. W. Roberts and D. O. Mills (UCWI, 1958). A 1961 survey showed a rather lower proportion, 32%—see R. B. Davison in *West Indian Economist*, July-August, 1961.

12 In *Guinee et L'Emancipation Africaine*', Paris, 1959, Sekou Touré pointed to civil service salary scales in which top salaries were fifty times as high as those at the bottom.

13 This has subsequently been published with the title '*The Structure of Earnings*' Oxford, 1968.

14 See, for example, *Quantitative aspects of the Economic Growth of Nations. VIII Distribution of Income by Size* by Simon Kuznets, *Economic Development & Cultural Change*, January 1963. An article by E. Ahiram in *Social and Economic Studies* for June, 1966, shows a very marked inequality for Jamaica (in 1958) but less so for Trinidad.

15 *World Economic Survey*, United Nations, 1960.

16 See 'An International Comparison of the Trend of Professional Earnings,' *American Economic Review*, March, 1965, Tables 5 to 9, drawing on work at the Institute of Business and Economic Research at Berkeley.

17 *Occupation and Pay in Great Britain, 1906 to 1960*, Cambridge, for the National Institute of Economic and Social Research, 1965.

18 Research and development expenditures in the United States grew from $5 billions in 1953 to $17 billions in 1963 from *Review of Data on Science Resources*, May 1965.

19 The pull of the United States on the professional manpower of other rich countries is brought out clearly in 'The Immigration of Scientists and Engineers to the United States, 1949-61' by H. G. Grubel and A. D. Scott, *Journal of Political Economy*, August, 1966.

20 *American Economic Review*, December 1960.

21 From October, 1955 to October, 1965, average salaries of all kinds (clerical and professional) rose by 79%; female clerical salaries rose by 77% but male clerical salaries by only 58%. These averages are affected changes in the industrial structure (and in the occupational structure within industries) but the differences between the increments in male clerical salaries and total salaries is sufficiently marked to imply that a weighted index for professional salaries would show a faster rise than 79%—yet the average earnings of wage-earners only rose by 78% over the same period.

22 Professor Bridgers in 'The International Migration of Talent and Skills' (*op. cit.*).

23 See 'Canadian Immigration Policy: An Analysis' by M. F. Timlin in *International Migration*, nos. 1-2. 1965. The key change there was Order in Council, no. 86 of 1962.

24 'Immigration from the Commonwealth'. Cmnd 2739.

25 See, for example, *Manpower Report* (Government of Zambia, 1966).

26 See 'Une hypothèse de travail; l'inflation, conséquence monétaire du comportement des groupes sociaux' by Henri Aujac in *Economie Apliquee* (April-June, 1950) and *International Economic Papers*, No. 4. One could elaborate a theory of the 'transmission of inflation' from abroad: apart from international influences on salaries, commodity price fluctuations or price rises in imported manufactures or forced import substitution (due to exchange difficulties) can provide disturbances which set off a self-perpetuating inflationary cycle.

27 Mr. Lydall, who has surveyed the field of data on changes in income distribution, shows in his study only one relevant piece of information; a slight increase in the dispersion of employment incomes in Argentina from 1953 to 1961, which could, however, be attributed to statistical errors or to political changes that followed the fall of President Peron. See also 'Income Distribution in Argentina', *Economic Bulletin for Latin America*, ECLA April 66.

28 Sources: National Science Foundation *op. cit.* also 'Scientific Manpower from Abroad' (1962) and *Review of Data on Scientific Resources*, July, 1965.

29 'Open Doors' (*op. cit.*).

30 Timlin (*op. cit.*).

31 Source: Ministry of Labour.

32 'Resources of Scientific and Technical Personnel in the OECD Area' (OECD 1963), also the 'Report on the 1965 Triennial Manpower Survey of Engineers Technologists and Technical supporting staff' (Cmnd 3103).

33 'Work for Progress' (Government of Uganda, 1966).

34 The dangers are heightened by a further influence. Given the slow growth of agricultural output, the combined effect of population growth (especially urbanisation) and of the rise in urban salaries and wages has exerted an upward influence on food prices. This not only acts, as it has in India and Latin America (especially Brazil, Chile and Colombia) as a cause or aggravation of inflation, it also has further distributional effects because it benefits landowners, cash farmers and traders (not usually among the poorest social groups) at the expense of the unskilled labourer.

35 I shall not discuss here the big contributions which agricultural development or population control can make to reducing inequalities or to economic development generally. This is not because these are unimportant (on the contrary), but because they lie somewhat outside the main field of this paper.

36 Another factor is upgrading. See 'Employment, Wage Levels and Incentives' by Richard Jolly (an unpublished paper presented to a symposium organised by the International Institute for Education Planning in Paris in May, 1966). I have gained a lot from many discussions with Dr. Jolly on this whole group of subjects.

37 'Science and technology in Economic Development' by H. M. Phillips in *International Social Science Journal*, UNESCO (vol. XVIII No. 3).

38 Dr. Balogh, who has taken the lead in changing received doctrine on this issue, describe the conformity of the 'post liberation establishment' in *The Economics of Poverty* Weidenfeld and Nicholson, 1966 Chapter VII.

39 See 'From the other side: A European View', a paper on this subject by Brinley Thomas, in *Annals of the American Academy of Political and Social Science*, September, 1966. In 'The International Migration of Talent and Skills,' Dr. Kelly West estimates the annual value of foreign physicians entering the United States, in terms of the cost of producing substitutes in America, as of the order 'of 100 million dollars a year', or more than United States aid in the medical field. About three-quarters are from poor countries.

40 See 'Limitations of the Special Case' by the author (*Bulletin of the Oxford Institute of Economics and Statistics*, May, 1963) and 'Economistas latinoamericanos en Estados Unidos' by Anibal Pinto and Osvaldo Sunkel, course material used in the Latin American Institute for Social and Economic Planning.

REPORT ON THE ECONOMIC SITUATION OF AFRICA

COMMISSION B

The main emphasis in the papers presented on economics and in the trend of discussions is a recognition of the serious nature of Africa's present economic situation. In particular African agriculture is not responding to demand, leading to rising food prices and expenditure of foreign exchange on imported food. Industry remains at a low level of development and is still mainly in the hands of foreign enterprise both with respect to conception and execution. One of the main obstacles to industrial development is the small size of African markets. Another is shortage of skills at all levels.

A strategy of economic development has to recognize that, owing to the respective income elasticities of demand for manufactured products and primary products, the prospects of Africa earning sufficient to meet its foreign exchange and investment needs from the sale of traditional primary products are diminishing. It is this rather than the terms of trade which is the primary factor. Consequently there is a need to transform the structure of African economies. However, since—for Africa at least—the possibilities of selling manufactured goods in world markets are not promising for a long time to come, there is a need for and also scope for the export of manufactures from one African country to another. This means that African industrialization has to be pressed forward, but within the framework of groupings of countries. Structural change also means the modernization of the agricultural sector and in particular the production of staple foodstuffs for the African market.

There is no fundamental conflict between agricultural and industrial development and both have to be promoted. One of the keys to agricultural development is the growth of demand for agricultural products which can only come from development in the non-agricultural sector. A major factor in industrial development is the production of inputs for agriculture, particularly fertilizers, pesticides and agricultural machinery.

A proper industrial strategy requires emphasis on intermediate and capital goods capable of transforming the structure of African economies and from the nature of the industries concerned, the grouping of African countries. Only in this way can markets of sufficient size arise and thus make possible the setting up of industries where economies of scale are important. Furthermore, grouping of countries is urgent since as time passes uneconomic industries are set up and integration becomes more difficult. There are then considerable perspectives for rapid industrial growth. But without more emphasis on the prerequisites and agents of industrial development, little is likely to be achieved.

Finance is essential, but much more finance, especially for basic industries, must and can come from domestic savings than is generally recognized. In each of the activities which can be regarded as prerequisites—scientific and technological research, manpower planning, study of natural resources and energy and transport—it is realistic to expect that a major contribution in money and manpower can come from outside Africa. Creating the agents for industrial development, appropriate institutions and personnel, is largely Africa's own business and the major test. But there is much more that the outside world can do to help, partly through financial assistance and more through disinterested advice and training.

The essence of the agricultural problem in Africa is that, while the sectors catering for exports overseas are well developed, even though—as has already been pointed out—the future market prospects are less promising for traditional primary products, much more has to be done to tackle the problem of producing staple foods for African domestic markets. Research and development in this field has been limited. The reciprocal relationship between agricultural and industrial development has already been indicated. The main problem which lies ahead is to correct the failure so far to bring the African peasantry into the development process, and to create at least a minimum dynamic and effective political link between the peasantry and government. A major stimulus to raising the agricultural growth-rate in Africa must come from incentives from the non-agricultural sectors, in other words, the growing markets which will arise from industrial development.

Improved transport, particularly from the producing areas to the towns, is also a major requirement. Agricultural productivity can be raised by an application of modern in-puts, such as fertilizers, pesticides and machinery. It should not be forgotten, however, that the availability of skilled labour and the deployment thereof still remain a constraint in African agricultural development.

Compared to the tremendous needs for staff, the research problems which constitute an important bottleneck and, above all, the problems of organization, population increase is not a major problem facing African agriculture. In fact, with the exception of a few areas (e.g. Eastern Nigeria and parts of highland East Africa, the UAR and Mauritius) population in most areas may be regarded hopefully as a stimulus to production and to innovation. Most of the innovations which are emerging clearly indicate the need for more careful farming which in turn presupposes an increase in labour requirements. The training of agricultural specialists at all levels, including extension workers, will remain a serious problem for many years to come. Part of the shortfall can be made good by continuing imported skills. Probably this means a concentration of skilled resources already available on key areas.

In the longer run it may be possible for Africa to become an exporter of certain food products to other parts of the world which are suffering seriously from pressure of population on land, e.g. Asia. A view on how far this is possible must await more intensive research.

Turning now in more detail to African foreign trade problems, exports in recent years have been rising more rapidly than from other developing areas. However, this is mainly due to petroleum and masks the relative decline in exports of traditional primary products. It follows that a large number of African countries are beginning to suffer from foreign exchange constraint. In other areas where foreign exchange constraint has not been apparent the shortage of domestic savings and skilled labour are the effective constraints to growth. In this regard detailed country studies are needed.

Given the limitations on exporting primary products overseas, to which attention has already been drawn, and the difficulty of Africa becoming competitive in world markets for manufactures for many years to come, this means that arrangements will have to be made for African countries to export their products to each other and, therefore, promote regional and sub-regional groupings. As in the case of other under-developed countries, Africa can benefit from the solution of two problems which can be discussed in the framework of UNCTAD. One is commodity arrangements for primary products, but it should be borne in mind that Africa has sometimes a comparative advantage and, therefore, should be in a position to insist on a favourable position in such arrangements. Further, more could be done by African producers accounting for a large share of world out-put of primary products to obtain higher prices for their primary products by co-operation among themselves. African producers should now be in a position to insist on further processing of certain raw materials for exports; in this respect the reduction of tariffs in developing countries is probably required.

The increasing internationalization of the world economy has given rise to stimuli which have accelerated the process of growing inequalities of income within the developing economies and not least in Africa. This applies with special force to professional incomes. This distorts the whole pattern of consumption and inflates imports. Steps have therefore to be taken to counter the growing inequality of incomes. There are two main measures which can be taken. The first is an increase in the level and rates of taxation. It is true that those with professional skills are frequently in a position to take steps to maintain their net incomes, even though the level of taxation is increased. Nevertheless, there are a wide range of measures which deserve further investigation, the cumulative effect of which would be to increase tax receipts. These include personal income tax, company taxation, incentives to attract private savings to go into industry and agriculture rather than land and property. In effect a selective incomes policy is required, and measures have to be taken to stimulate private savings.

Secondly a large part of the problem of growing inequality of incomes arises from the sheer scarcity of high-level skills for economic development. It follows that appropriate educational reform is not only vital, but also in the long run a means of diminishing the inequality of incomes.

From the point of view of economic development, the essence of educational reform consists of the following:

Less relative emphasis on conventional primary education leading to further education, and much more on education appropriate to peasant producers whose education will not go beyond the primary stage.

Much greater emphasis on maintaining the targets for secondary education, which are not being met, and also far-reaching changes in the secondary syllabus.

Greater emphasis, especially at the level of university education, on scientific and technological subjects.

Planning of educational policies as a function of a manpower planning policy which not only estimates future requirements in detail, but also takes into account the aims of African countries to change the structure of their economies.

Proper integration between manpower planning, educational training through African institutions, the treatment of educational training abroad as a derived function, and centralized control of overseas education within such a centralized policy, including suitable arrangements for the bonding of students sent overseas.

A dynamic employment policy which ensures that those educated, particularly at the advanced level, are immediately absorbed in the economy.

The primary general conclusion is that the time has come for a general stocktaking of the nature of the African economic problem; that attention should be focussed on the future and that much more will have to be and can be done by the African countries themselves. There are, however, a number of spheres in which continuing assistance from overseas countries is of great importance.

In summary, one might put first finance. Although external finance is required for industrial development the main emphasis should be on finance for the further development of infrastructure, and especially human infrastructure. Much more of the financing of both agricultural and industrial development will have to come from African domestic sources.

Secondly, skills present a greater constraint than capital. Greater emphasis should therefore be placed on technical assistance than has been the case in the past. The main areas to be tackled are science and technology, partly through research of interest to African countries carried out from overseas and partly by support for African scientific research institutions; support for the reform and execution of African educational programmes; training in manpower planning; assistance in resources surveying; support for African institutions for the promotion of agricultural and industrial development; assistance in the establishment and development of training institutions of all kinds; help in creating African enterpreneurship and ability to organize production in both the private and public sectors.

Thirdly, it is suggested that African governments should carry out a detailed and objective appraisal of the effects, positive and negative, of foreign aid programmes.

COMMISSION C

SOCIAL AND EDUCATIONAL SITUATION

CONSIDERATIONS OF SOME OF THE IMPORTANT SOCIAL FUNCTIONS OF AFRICAN EDUCATION

by

GERMA AMARE

It is realized in almost all underdeveloped countries of the world today that education is the keystone of national development. Educational development is often identified with national development. Kojo Bosio of Ghana, once Minister of Agriculture and Chairman of the Commission of University Education, stated in 1961: '*Of all national instruments, education is one of the most crucial and the pace of our educational progress is the pace of our national development.*' The rapid educational development in all parts of Africa today is due to this great faith placed in education as the sole means of social progress.

In this paper I shall deal with what seems to me to be the best way of utilizing modern education as an effective instrument for development in Africa today. I shall do this by pointing out certain commonly held misconceptions regarding modern education, its functions, its scope, and its content. I shall be drawing my material mostly from Ethiopian experiences.

EDUCATION REGARDED AS CONCERNED ONLY WITH CHILDREN

First, there is the general tendency to regard modern education as a function that is entirely concerned with the improvement of the intelligence of only the young in society. This tendency has largely been responsible for confining educational activities within the four walls of schools. It hardly needs to be emphasized that for a number of reasons the education of adults is as important as, if not more important than, that of children. For one, the leaders in a society exert greater influence upon the young than do the schools. This is particularly true in Africa, where the family ties are so strong and the ideas of the elders are so highly respected. Consequently, the new ideas gained from schools might be largely dispelled under parental influence. Joyce Cary in his work *The Case for African Freedom* makes a very important and relevant point when he says:

> *An African child, like an English child, with new ideas on any subject, is very likely to be laughed at, or to be told that he is talking nonsense. His elders know better.*

Thus elementary education of children loses seventy or eighty per cent of its effect without adult education for their parents. In fact, it is largely wasted. For children in Africa, as in England, are fond of their parents and respect them. The prejudice of a mother, especially with her own daughters, will outweigh years of careful and expensive instruction. A suggestion from the father that new ways of farming may offend local spirits of which white men know nothing will instantly destroy all the influence of an agricultural instructor. Prejudice, superstition, fear and ignorance must be attacked in their strongholds, the adult minds.

What is more, it is much easier for educated parents to influence their ignorant children than it is for educated children to influence their ignorant parents. In most cases, the education of a father is much more useful than that of his children. The influence he exerts upon the whole family would automatically revolutionize the attitude of all members of the family. By virtue of the tremendous influence he exerts, his enlightenment determines the whole course of events that take place in the family. Likewise, the education of a chief of a tribe or the head of a clan amounts to the education of the whole tribe or clan. It is in considering this very key position held by the elders in African communities that Joyce Cary goes on to say:

It is not too much to say that if available funds allowed only for children's education or adult education, the latter would be the best choice. For children eagerly learn from parents, but parents seldom consent to learn from children. The very fact that children are the first to offer a new idea is, often enough, all over the world, to bring it into derision.

For the reasons outlined above it can be stated with some degree of certainty that an educational program that excludes adults is doomed from the start. It is highly improbable that underdeveloped countries will ever be able to reach a take-off stage in national development so long as the adult population that constitutes at least 50% of a country's population is neglected.

EDUCATION EQUATED WITH LITERACY

The second and most significant misconception of education is the tendency to equate it with literacy. This is the unfortunate consequence of the tendency to regard literacy as a measuring rod for social progress. Without ever belittling the importance of literacy, it can by no stretch of the imagination be accepted as the equivalent of education. The Amerindians, who were responsible for the creation of the great Andean civilization with its complex administrative systems, did not know how to read and write. In this tendency to equate literacy with education is a potential danger, the danger that 'African education may begin and end in a great outlay of paper and paste . . .' However, 'no amount of paper or talk will ever make a primitive African understand why it is better to save soil, to drive his furrows across the hillside than up and down, to teach him the need for preserving cover belts . . .'

What is called for here is a broader definition of education—an education that is directed at raising the level of intelligence of the masses. This approach to education is highly commendable because it makes it a social function. Only by according to education a social function is it possible to solve many of a society's problems. This is a fundamental fact that has generally been recognized by individuals who are well acquainted with conditions in underdeveloped countries.

Robert Theobold is one such man. He suggests that for any headway to be made in such countries a change in the attitude of the masses is a prerequisite. Cary likewise maintains that 'modern . . . civilization required a modern mind, modern ambitions and needs . . .'. Only education that is directed at raising the level of social intelligence can create this modern mind. In the *Second Five Year Development Plan* that came out in 1958 in Ethiopia, it is stated that 'education in Ethiopia cannot be considered as an end set apart from the general requirement of socio-economic conditions. It has primarily to serve the needs of the country's development and there make its fullest contribution to the achievement of national goals. From this it is easily perceived that education in Ethiopia has to be taken in its broadest sense. It does not only imply the activities of the educational institutions proper but of necessity, also, stretches over the whole set of activities ranging from training manpower for the various jobs and skill-levels to the various forms of broadening the educational and cultural level of the people'.

It is generally agreed today that a change in the attitude of the masses is a prerequisite for progress. But the methods of approach have varied enormously. Some have suggested a vigorous and nation-wide campaign against illiteracy. Others have found the solution in fast industrialization. In practically all instances, however, the tendency has been to require people to change in a manner laid down by the authorities at the top without due consideration being given to the needs of the people and their problems. Communities are required to accept innovations that have no immediate relevance to the solution of their urgent problems. When such measures fail to bring about any significant change, the blame is often[7] directed at the people who are considered stupid and unresponsive.

There are innumerable instances where this has been the case. The nomadic Somalis roaming in the bleak deserts of Northern Kenya have suffered and still do suffer from lack of water. Hundreds of cattle and human beings die every year because of this shortage. This is their immediate need. Yet the Kenyan government has shown greater concern about the spread of literacy among these people than providing for their more urgent needs. The shortsightedness of this approach was well expressed by an educated Somali from this area, when he stated:

. . . these people (the Africans in Northern Kenya), and particularly their leaders, consider that education is all important. While not belittling the value of education, water and grazing are to us of infinitely greater importance. They are matters of life and death to us, our cattle and our camels in our thirsty country. Our people can, if they must, live without schools. They cannot live without water and grass.

This imposition upon the people of certain changes which they can see no real need for has been the basic kind of approach of modernization in most underdeveloped countries. Not surprizingly, the reactions of peoples have, in most instances, been negative to such methods.

It has aroused the resentment and suspicions of communities towards their government authorities. Consider, for example, the consequences of building a modern brick school in the middle of an impoverished community. For the maintenance of the school it becomes necessary to derive more taxes from an already impoverished peasant. Thus, the peasant becomes poorer and poorer in spite of the provision of more educational facilities for his children.

More agonizing still, it becomes necessary for the peasant to do without the services of his youngsters who in the past helped on the farm. He is even placed in a situation where he might never again see his children, who, after getting used to life in modern schools and in the cities, refuse to take up the occupation of their parents.

Consequently, for reasons which are quite understandable, the peasant becomes antagonistic to any innovation. Thus, the peasant is compelled to regard the interest of the state as distinct and apart from his own. He develops a feeling of enmity and suspicion towards his government. He, as a result, becomes ultra-conservative, holding fast to everything from the past and rebelling against everything new.

IMPORTED EDUCATION CONSIDERED TO BE THE BEST

A further misconception widespread in Africa is to regard the education that has been imported intact and unchanged from abroad as the best education. This attitude is largely a legacy of colonial times. The education introduced in hitherto colonial countries of Africa was a replica of some European system of education. Thus a British colony has a British education system and a French colony a French system, and so on. Ethiopia presents a peculiar situation in that it contains examples of educational systems found in most of the western countries: Great Britain, France, America, Sweden, Italy, Germany and Canada.

This has been a most unfortunate situation. It is unfortunate because as long as this newly-introduced education remains detached from the real conditions of Africa it will remain a cause of many frustrating and threatening problems, rather than a means of solving them. George Counts, quoting Montesquieu, who stated that the 'laws of education ought to be in relation to the system of government,' rightly comments that such a statement is only a partial truth. He suggests that education should not only be in relation to the government but also 'to the whole system of society, with its social heritage, its institutions, its body of values, and its power structure'. He goes on to state that '. . . this means that a program of education entirely suited to one society might destroy the other'. A great American scholar, J. B. Conant, in his work, *Education and Liberty*, considers the danger of importing educational concepts which he believes are not 'exportable commodities'. Hence, the urgency of adapting education in Africa to the needs and conditions of the continent.

After having briefly outlined some of the prevailing misconceptions concerning modern education in Africa, let us briefly consider how education could best be employed in the service of African development.

COMMUNITY DEVELOPMENT

The futility of trying to improve people's living conditions by way of impositions has largely been instrumental in the formulation of a different approach to the problem. Edward Lindman, Richard Poston, Carl Tayler, Paul Miller and others emphasize the great importance of starting from the needs and problems of a community in any undertaking designed to raise the level of intelligence of underdeveloped peoples.

The most promising aspect of community development lies in the fact that it attempts to put an end to the usual procedures of fragmenting social progress into separate units that have to be coped with by isolated measures. Here, development is regarded as a comprehensive undertaking intended to raise the level of the community as a whole and in every respect, educationally, economically, culturally, etc. No attempt is made to isolate the educational undertaking from the economic undertaking or to improve agriculture while neglecting problems of sanitation, but rather to cope with all community problems as a whole.

People now recognize the futility of teaching people how to read and write, while various kinds of diseases take a heavy toll; or of trying to cope with the health problems of a community and thus contributing to the rapid increase in the rate of population growth, while neglecting the improvement of the means of production to sustain this increased population. This recognition makes the approach of community development most commendable.

It is often argued that no underdeveloped society can, at this stage, afford to attend to all community needs at once. Priority must be given to certain pressing problems. This is a legitimate contention. People must first have enough to eat before they are introduced to the more sophisticated aspects of civilized life. But there is often a gross mistake inherent in this argument. The argument is often based on the assumption that a government's task is to give and that of the people is to receive. This attitude has often had a most unfortunate effect on human development. So long as a nation's people remain passive recipients and the role of the government is that of an active donor, hardly any definitive progress will be made. A reciprocal arrangement of giving and receiving must be developed.

This can come about when the needs of the people are considered the focal point of any development, and the people themselves become vitally involved in their own affairs. John Dewey often emphasizes the important fact that people in a society should not be blind receivers of the good that is provided by the state, but should be participants in the creation of that good.

Development that revolves around the basic needs of the public creates in the people a genuine interest in their own betterment. People who have previously been passive recipients of government plans and endowments (that in most instances had no direct bearing on their essential needs) will now eagerly participate because they envisage a goal which they, through their own efforts, can achieve. Community development, therefore, becomes a sort of self-help with some outside assistance. In the last analysis, the mounting burden imposed upon the government would not be as it was expected to be.

The realization that one's condition can be improved through self-help and the application of one's own intelligence would be a notable step forward. It creates a certain dissatisfaction within people and an impatient desire for change. It creates an awareness of one's own ignorance.

One of the far-reaching effects of an approach based upon self-help is the fact that it makes people aware that their living conditions can be improved. The age-old enemy to progress, in these underdeveloped nations, has been the acceptance of a condition of life as predetermined and God-given. To attempt to change this condition of life is not only considered impossible but also blasphemous. The realization that one's conditions can be improved through the application of one's own intelligence creates a certain confidence in one's own abilities.

Finally, a development that focuses attention upon the needs of the community and attempts to satisfy these newly discovered needs by way of self-help, will assure the gradual emergence of an independent and self-determining society aware of its needs and with the initiative to meet these needs without always having to depend on outside assistance.

COMMUNITY SCHOOLS

In a community development undertaking the community school plays a central role. As is well-discussed by Olson and others in their book on school and community, the community school plays two roles:

> *. . . Educating the children in the community and . . . serving as a community center. As a community center it serves members of the community as a meeting place, where they can discuss problems of common concern or where they can come to watch movies or demonstrations on certain innovations and the like. They may even come to watch how childen are formally educated in classrooms.*

The curriculum, in such community schools, except for the fundamentals, is adapted to the specific needs of the community where the school is located. Thus, a community school situated in a cattle-breeding area would necessarily be different from one located in a grain-growing community. The emphasis would be placed on the main occupation of the people concerned. Even among the community schools located in agricultural areas there could be differences. In one area the problem may be that of irrigation, while in another stress would be placed on the rotation of crops, or erosion and so forth.

Community schools may also differ in the languages employed in teaching the subjects. For maximum efficiency it would be necessary to employ the mother tongue for the children of the particular community, at least in the very early stages of their education. They will certainly have no need for a foreign language at this early stage. A foreign language may be introduced as a subject and not as a medium of instruction.

In Ethiopia an encouraging step has been taken along this direction. English was used up until a few years ago as the medium of instruction in the elementary grades. Now under the proposed 6–2–4 system of education, Amharic is to be used as the medium of instruction in the elementary grades.

The most important single factor in the success of a community school is the teacher. The ideal teacher is one who is a native of the community, who speaks the language of the people and understands their way of life. He should be one in whom the people have absolute trust and one whose leadership they will accept.

The duties of a community school teacher do not end at the close of the day nor are his functions limited only to the imparting of certain set knowledge to the young of the society. On the contrary, it extends far beyond that of the school walls. He is a true liaison officer between children and their parents, between the school and the community-at-large. By organizing various school activities which are open to the public, he tries to interest the parents in the education of their children. By way of periodic visits, he tries to create a certain understanding between the two generations. In short, the teacher of a community school is a bridge between the modern and the traditional.

Working with the teacher may be other personnel such as health officers, agricultural advisers, and others. All of them work in a cooperative spirit to lift the community in every way possible.

Finally, the community school building should be modelled on the style of architecture prevalent in the community. This is, of course, in contrast to previous practice, when very impressive and expensive European-style school buildings were erected in very desolate communities. Here, the tendency was to place the school on a pedestal as something apart from the rest of the community. This tendency proved not only an expensive practice, but was also detrimental to pupil adjustment.

While this does not necessarily mean that such community schools should be deprived of the conveniences of a modern school, they should reflect the general condition of the community. Mud-walled and thatched-roof schools, if properly built, could serve the needs of the students just as well as brick-walled and tin-roofed schools. In this way, the school becomes an institution that is an integral part of the community.

At the completion of their community-school education, the able students are allowed to proceed with further education. How many will be allowed to continue with their education and in what areas will be determined in accordance with an already laid-out national plan.

The majority of children, who upon completion of their community-school programme are not allowed to proceed to further studies, will be required to remain in their own communities and will be encouraged to utilize their knowledge in helping their parents, for example, by establishing model farms of their own. It is most unlikely that they would like to leave their communities for the cities, since they have no need to do so. They will find employment in their community, which they may not find in the cities.

The government, in its turn, could utilize innumerable incentives to induce youngsters to stay and help their community and themselves. This is done in some African countries like Zambia, by creating large farm settlements on unused tracts of land for younger people to work with the use of more improved implements. Callaway reports that in some places 'experiments have begun in which villages provide land for their own school leavers, and the government gives initial support with subsistence payments to the settlers and by providing subsidized seedlings and advances for buying tools'. At other places 'cooperative buying of requisites and selling of products is introduced'. In places like Dahomey and the Ivory Coast, the government extends credit to young farmers and gives a certain amount of technical advice on production and marketing. A further incentive that could yet be tried is the establishment of a Young Farmer's Club, where these young farmers could hold recreational, as well as instructional meetings.

Innumerable are the desired outcomes of this kind of approach toward national development. For one thing, the problem that arises out of the exclusive upbringing of children by their parents would be greatly minimized, if it ever occurred at all. The community school, by being part-and-parcel of the community, reflects all the conditions of life of the area or district. Consequently, children would face no problem of adjustment.

Furthermore, such a cooperative effort on the part of the school to include parents would better expose them to change. They will become as impatient for change and progress as their youngsters. They will be able to modify their values and attitudes together with their children. Consequently, the agonizing problems that arise out of conflicts of values between parents and children will be greatly minimized.

As was pointed out earlier, only a select few proceed from the community schools to the higher schools. The number to do so, not only at this stage but also through the successive stages up the educational ladder to the university level, is determined by the needs of the country and the resources available. For example, the *Second Five Year Plan* in Ethiopia envisages the need for 1,833 university graduates and 11,700 technicians and employees with completed secondary education, 900 highly skilled and

2,700 skilled and 29,500 semi-skilled workers for the various jobs that will be created in the coming five years. With this national goal in mind the educational institutions of the country must make the necessary adjustments and try to operate within the framework of the general national objective. In this way the problem that arises in connection with the emergence of an unemployed semi-educated class is minimized.

THE NEED FOR CONTENT REVISION

While some progress is being made to fit education in Africa into the framework of economic needs and resources, there is unfortunately a marked lag in the revision of the content of the curriculum to include studies dealing with various aspects of Africa—its history, geography, art, music, literature, etc. One of the great challenges of education in Africa today is to re-establish the lost personal integrity and wholeness of the African, for as Prof. Dike has pointed out, '*Our newly acquired independence must be without meaning if . . . it implies nationhood without two of its fundamental components, a distinctive history and culture; if it implies mere imitation of Western ways*'.

Colonial education had its positive aspects. The statistics show how far advanced the ex-colonial countries are in education when compared to these countries that have not been colonized. Those responsible for the liberation of their countries were by and large the products of that education. It cannot be denied, however, that the negative aspects of colonial education far outweigh its positive aspects.

Education during the colonial period was so much tied up with political and economic motives that it was used as a powerful instrument for the perpetuation of the *status quo* and the furtherance of the economic and other interests of Europeans. '. . . *The conception of the aim of education,*' writes a British educator, was '*that it should make useful citizens, and when we say useful citizens we mean literally citizens who would be of use to us. The conception was one of exploitation and development for the benefit of the people of Great Britain—it was to this purpose that such education as was given was directed.*'

By limiting the educational opportunities of the African only to the first few grades so that when he went out he retained a perpetually dependent economic position, and mainly by glorifying the achievements of the west and belittling those of the African himself, it was possible to rob the African of his dignity, and his pride in his history and his culture. '*The African had everything to learn*', writes Herskovits in his *Human Factor in Changing Africa*, '*and nothing to teach, either to their own children or to the rest of the world. The prevalent point of view exemplifies, in almost classical form, the conception of the African as envisaged in the nineteenth century theory of social evolution: a straggler in the march of mankind toward civilization, whose progress was to be shaped by those who brought him the benefit of the higher order.*'

Everywhere in Africa, dependent or independent (for the schools in the independent countries were run by Europeans who entertained the same view as those in parts of Africa, and who also knew little about Africa), the schools taught their pupils about European culture, history and geography, art, music and literature and nothing about Africa. In Ethiopian schools up to very recently, the only subject related to Ethiopia which was taught in the schools was Amharic, which was never considered as important as the other subjects.

Consequently, Ethiopian children grew up more conversant, to quote Donald Levine '*with the history of Rome and the life of Abraham Lincoln than with the geography of their immediate community or the history of their own country*'. Prof. Dike, speaking about the same subject, pointed out that: '*In the past the school-child in French-speaking Africa was always taught about "our ancestors, the Gauls" and the English-speaking African has been more concerned with the history of Henry VIII than Uthaman dan Fadia*'.

The detrimental psychological effect that this system of education has had on the African child is quite clear. Aimé Césaire, though not an African himself, but an individual who was subjected to the same process of indoctrination as an African, relates in his book, *Cahier d'un Retour au Pays Natal,* how all his life he hated himself for being black and despised his origin. But finally, he accepts himself, takes pride in what he is and '*gains personal integrity and wholeness*'.

The great challenge to African education today is the reinstating of this lost personal integrity and wholeness of the African. This is recognized as the most important function of education by almost all political and educational leaders today. Senghor of Senegal pointed out at the West African Language Conference held in Dakar that '*If the African of this second half of the century is to take root in order to develop, it is evident that she must first know herself before she can realize herself: she must take stock of her riches before trying to cultivate them by the assimilation of foreign techniques*'. At the Third All-African Peoples' Conference the following resolution was passed: '*The Conference demands the reorganization of education in such a way as to remove from curricula all ideas tending to give the African a sense of inferiority, and re-establish authentic history*'. In his historic address to the Summit Conference of African Heads of States in 1963 Emperor Haile Sellassie said, '*We seek, at this meeting, to determine whither we are going, and to chart the course of our destiny. It is no less important that we know whence we came. An awareness of our past is essential to the establishment of our personality and our identity as Africans*'.

The logical starting point of the much-talked-about African unity is the cultivation of a deeper knowledge in the African about himself and about his African neighbour. What do Ethiopian children in the schools know about Kenya, or Nigerian children about Ethiopia, or the Congolese about the Sudan? We were all taught something about Egypt and the civilization that flourished there. But this was taught to us not as African history but only as a prelude to European history. Egypt was never presented to us as representing Africa. All these factors led the African to regard as the best education that which had been imported from abroad.

For a combination of reasons the study of Africa is now gradually assuming an important place. The individual and group efforts of serious scholars have drawn the attention of the world to the rich and yet largely untapped knowledge about Africa. It has now become evident that man's store of knowledge could be greatly increased by a scientific study of African culture, its history, sociology, geography, etc.

The recent theory of Leakey and others that the human race might well have had its origin in Africa has made the continent a focus of interest for the scientific world. Furthermore, the emergence of many countries in Africa as independent nations has made necessary a better familiarity with Africa on the part of the rest of the world. For these and similar reasons the hitherto widely entertained idea of Africa as the 'dark continent' is gradually being dispelled. African studies are gradually occupying an important place in the syllabuses of universities elsewhere in the world as well as in African universities.

The problems of language, of textbooks and of teachers are still main obstacles to the progress of education in Africa, it need hardly be said.

There is hardly anyone who is not convinced of the need to employ African languages in African countries in place of the foreign languages that were superimposed during colonial times. The effort of reviving and re-studying African culture is very much tied up with the revival of African languages. The acceptable thing would be to employ African languages in the schools, both as media of instruction and as subjects, as well as official languages.

But there are practical difficulties that have to be contended with. Most countries in Africa are multi-lingual. To try to adopt one of these languages, even though it may be spoken by the majority, may be to invite civil strife. The political repercussions that imposition entails are so great that many African politicians have preferred to go on employing the already existing foreign language until the foundation of national unity is well consolidated. Some countries in the world have peacefully accepted one indigenous language as a national language. The experiences of other countries like India and Ceylon, however, have not been so pleasant. The transition from a foreign language to one dominant indigenous language in Africa will certainly be smooth when it is implemented at a time when tribalism has given way to nationalism. (Ethiopia is quite fortunate in this regard. Amharic has been accepted as the official language since 1270.)

A further obstacle is that few African languages have scripts of their own. Many African languages use the Roman alphabet and it may will be that other languages in Africa will have to do the same. Again, Ethiopia is fortunate in that Amharic has a script of its own, and because of culture contact, the language has been enriched as has no other language spoken in Ethiopia.

The limitation in vocabulary and expression, particularly for scientific subjects, limits the use of African languages in schools. This however need not be a major obstacle. Just as modern European languages borrow words and expressions from each other and derive part of their vocabulary and expression so can African languages by borrowing from each other as well as from European languages. Amharic is certainly a rich language because of the many words it has taken from Arabic, Portuguese, Italian, French and English.

No less difficult is the problem of new textbooks and reading material specially written for use in elementary and secondary schools in Africa. There are many scholarly books written on Africa, but these are so specialized and technical that they are hardly suitable for school libraries.

It is the right time to suggest that African governments subsidize the establishment of a small committee of African textbook writers to undertake the task of writing textbooks and reading material on various aspects of Africa—history, geography, art, music—for use in *African* schools.

Lastly, it is no use repeating the well known fact of the great shortage of teachers in Africa today. The problem is not only the shortage of teachers of good standing, but mainly of teachers with some background knowledge about Africa. Almost all teachers now teaching in African schools today follow the old curriculum which included practically nothing on African studies when they took their training. Many are graduates of foreign colleges and universities. The rest are expatriates. It is hardly possible to include new courses in the curriculum of secondary and elementary schools unless teachers are prepared to teach these subjects and are able to use the new textbooks that will have to be produced. This calls for reorganization of the courses given to teachers in teacher training institutions.

These are major obstacles but, unless they are overcome, what Sir Eric Ashby said of West African universities will remain true of African schools for many years to come:

There are no West African universities yet. There are British and French universities in West Africa but they are importations; they are no more indigenous than the motor-cars. They have junior modifications, of course, just as motor-cars have sun-hoods and chocolates (I am told) a higher melting point. But the West African university is still to be born.

A worthwhile effort, and one to which African educators should direct their attention, must be to try gradually to give Western education in Africa an African character. This requires a great amount of research, and greater cooperation among African scholars to try to develop material for use in all African schools and find means by which education could best be of use in meeting Africa's needs. The educational problems of African countries are so similar that a collective endeavour at tackling these problems would be much more effective than individual efforts. There would not be so much duplication of effort nor such great expenditure of money by individual countries. All the effort and individual financial contributions could be put to far more productive use.

THE FOREIGN EDUCATOR IN AFRICA

by

PAULOS ASRAT

Foreign educators have played and will continue to play significant roles in the education systems of Africa. For centuries non-African missionaries have influenced the destinies of individuals and of nations in the continent. Teachers brought to Africa by European powers have worked hard to design systems of education for African nations, based mainly on the systems of education in their own countries, and on the aims and policies of colonial times.

Today, after most of Africa has become politically independent, there are still thousands of non-African teachers helping in the education of African youth. European and American missionaries continue to have a great impact on African education. Expatriate teachers paid by African governments, and representing every continent, occupy key positions in the education systems of Africa. Young volunteers flock into the continent from Europe and America with the expressed aims of helping African nations with their educational problems, of maintaining peace in the world, and of winning more and more African friends for their countries. There are also a great many United Nations' personnel serving as advisors and experts in the various fields of education in Africa.

The writer of this short memorandum will attempt to raise some fundamental questions related to the role played by non-African educators in Africa. Lack of pertinent facts about the subject and the inadequate experience of the writer have severely limited the discussion. The main aim of the paper, therefore, is to stimulate further discussion and studies on the important topic under consideration. With this in mind, the following headings will be discussed briefly in the succeeding paragraphs:

understanding the educational aims and needs of Africa

the need for more emphasis on the education of African youth for continental and world citizenship

responsibilities of the host country towards foreign educators

the future of foreign educators in Africa

EDUCATIONAL AIMS

A clear understanding of the broad aims of education and of the specific objectives of the school system in which he works is a major responsibility of any professional educator. The general aims of education in Africa are more or less the same as in the rest of the world. Education should aim at producing people who can think objectively and who are emotionally mature. It should help individuals to appreciate fully their duties as citizens, and their traditional and cultural values. In short, it should provide for the full development of all the abilities of the individual to enable him to live an upright and meaningful life, and to help him to contribute successfully to the material, social, political, cultural and spiritual progress of his country and the world at large. Education should produce people of sound principles and good will, people whose actions are based upon understanding, deliberation and intelligence, and people skilled in working with each other.

In addition to the universal aims of education, certain specific objectives deserve special emphasis in Africa. These objectives will no doubt vary from time to time and from country to country. But the most common ones in present-day Africa appear to be the following:

Education for freedom. The struggle for freedom from ignorance, from poverty and disease, and from enslavement to others will have to continue until the battle is won completely. Education should play a major role in promoting the struggle for freedom, as well as in preparing Africans to use and to safeguard such freedom as they have gained.

Education for national and continental unity. A continent which is so much divided into tribes, religious groups, social and economic classes, and many other cultural and political units has no alternative but to formulate well-thought-out programmes of education to bring all these groups together. This is perhaps the only successful way of creating harmony among African countries and at the same time wiping out the alien subversive elements which are now common. More positively, Africans needs to understand to live together freely, peacefully and happily. They need to convince themselves through education that there is plenty for all of them and for the future generations in Africa. The only things required are cooperation, intelligence and hard work. Through special programmes of education for post-colonial Africa they should work out priority needs for their own countries and work out at the same time a way of living together with non-African countries.

Education for the understanding and respect of the African personality. Today the African is no longer the same as he was during colonial times. He has changed tremendously. Today he is a scientist a lawyer, an educator, a statesman. Even the dish-washer or the houseboy has the right to change his trade if he wants to. He is his own master. This means he has become a new person. Now, what is this new personality? How does it compare with the personality of colonial or pre-colonial times? What is the meaning of being an African, a black man, today? Education should try to find answers to these and similar other questions and communicate the answers to the African as well as to the non-African for mutual understanding, respect and assistance. By and large the present African has won his human rights. He must learn how to use his rights with responsibility and tolerance to others.

The educator, whether he is an African or a foreigner, is the key to the whole educational process. If he has a thorough knowledge of the aims and objectives of education, if he is constantly alert to the educational needs of Africa, and if he has the necessary personal and professional qualities, he is more likely to succeed as an educator in Africa. Specifically, the foreign educator should pay special attention to the following points which might help him in his professional duties: He should view his personal and professional affairs in the light of a thorough understanding of the social, economic, cultural and political factors prevailing in Africa. He should have an understanding and appreciation of people who are different from himself in racial, religious, cultural and national background. He should be proficient in the activities for which he is employed, and in the techniques of imparting knowledge to children and adults. He should be a person whose actions are governed by professional ethics. He should try constantly to understand the purposes, programmes, limitations and administrative organization of the school system in which he works, and he should participate professionally in planning improved educational activities for African children and adults.

Education for Continental and World Citizenship. Today African countries should guard themselves against the danger of being too much preoccupied with their own internal problems and of not paying enough attention to their leadership roles in the rest of the world. Until now African nations were fighting against colonialism, against invasions, against injustices and against economic slavery. They were fighting to be free, and they have won much of the battle. But they are now confronted with a new kind of war—perhaps more subtle and more dangerous than any previous war. It is seen creeping into Africa to divide Africans, to create confusion, and eventually to weaken the continent so that Africa will become a new battlefield of foreign ideologies and even of physical wars. This is the worst type of colonialism that can be faced by any country or continent. To avoid it Africans need to frame educational programmes specifically designed to avoid pitfalls that would be a threat to their peaceful development.

There are at least two ways of carrying out the process of education for national, continental and world citizenship. One is curative in nature, and the other preventive and progressive. The foreign educator can play an important role in the application of these methods. He can help Africans forget as quickly as possible their sufferings in the dark ages in Africa.

He can assist Africans in having their wounds healed—wounds brought about by slavery, moral and social injustices, and by the physical and mental tortures of colonial times. In short he can help in undoing some of the bad things colonizers have done to Africa. He can assist Africans to recover from the psychological shock of inferiority complex they were forced to suffer for centuries. Just by being a professional person and by serving in Africa as a living example of good, honest and understanding human beings the foreign educator can influence Africans to substitute their fear and suspicion by trust for people, and their hate by love for all mankind, regardless of the differences in race, colour, religion, nationality or any other background.

Hence, the foreign educator is an ambassador of good will representing his country in Africa. If he is an educated person he has a lot of truths to tell to Africans, so that they can understand and appreciate their own countries and the world better. If he is a person of good principles he can teach Africans about the dignity of man, about the wealth of the world's culture and about the continuing progress of science so as to help them acquire the feeling of being one with the whole of mankind. The qualified foreign educator is also an indispensable person who can teach the people of his own country about Africans and their problems, about African dreams and expectations, and about the African personality and culture. In carrying out this difficult responsibility the foreign educator will be required professionally to paint only the true picture of Africa and its citizens, and to avoid completely the undue sensational tendency of certain film producers and storytellers. The question of understanding the world and of identifying oneself with it is not funny; it is a very serious question. A productive and peaceful life in this world requires broadmindedness, tolerance, respect for the dignity of man and an appreciation of the different cultural values. This is why the foreign educator is fully challenged to do all within his power to help Africans understand the world, and the world to understand Africans.

RESPONSIBILITIES OF THE HOST COUNTRY

The success of African education is measured to a very high degree by the efforts Africans themselves put into it. Foreigners cannot and must not carry the educational burdens which Africans alone should carry. Foreign educators should assist only in the areas of education where their assistance is clearly required and in the areas considered to be of value by Africans. Foreign educators are guests of African countries, and as such they cannot be masters of African education. There should be a marriage between the know-how of the foreign educator and the eagerness of Africans to develop their countries. They need to be told by the host countries exactly what they can do and what they cannot do in the field of education. They could get constant advice and guidance so that they will understand clearly the short and long term educational plans and objectives of the country they assist. They must be helped to have a thorough grasp of the country's educational, social, cultural and political problems if they are to do a good job in producing well-disciplined, understanding and productive citizens. They should know about African history and geography, and African cultural values.

Another area of responsibility for the host country is to formulate and administer carefully thought-out personnel policies governing the recruitment, retention and dismissal foreign teachers. One serious problem affecting the services of foreign teachers in Africa is the big turnover rate. No sooner have they learnt about the educational aims and problems of an African country than a great many of foreign teachers leave the country only to be replaced by a new batch. Satisfactory solutions should be found by each host country in Africa in the interest of the school child and the education system. In particular, attention should be drawn to the recent recommendations of ILO/UNESCO regarding the status of teachers.

The supervision of the activities of foreign missionaries is a source of great responsibility for the host country. Missionaries can be of great assistance in carrying out the educational plans for any African country if they are properly supervised and guided. In the past one of the main aims of missionaries was to convert pagan Africans to some religion. How much is this aim maintained today? When is this process of converting Africans going to be over? Should missionaries be allowed to do the work of converting people from one religion to another? Or should they help in the education of only those who follow their religion? How closely should missionaries follow the official curricula of the country in which they work? These and similar other questions need to be answered and clear policies established if missionaries are to help rather than hinder the progress of education in African countries.

THE FUTURE OF FOREIGN EDUCATORS IN AFRICA

It is easy to conclude from the foregoing analysis the importance and desirability of the continued presence of foreign educators in Africa. Mutual understanding and respect are better achieved by living and working together as colleagues and friends. From this point of view African educators should also be encouraged to travel in other continents and work in the field of education.

Foreign educators can also contribute a great deal to the expansion of education in the African continent. Satisfying the strong desire of its citizens for an expansion of education of quality is going to remain one of Africa's most serious problems for many years to come. Thousands of qualified teachers are required each year to work in the elementary and secondary schools, and in universities. In fact, compared to the shortage of trained teachers the number of available foreign educators in Africa is very small.

Another problem is related to the quality of the foreign personnel in Africa. Not all foreign teachers in the continent are trained educators. The question is whether Africa should continue to have its systems of education serve as laboratories to inexperienced foreign teachers or whether it should attract only qualified educators even if their number is very much limited. It is a question of quantity versus quality. In the opinion of many educators quality comes first. And this applies not only to government-employed and volunteer teachers but also to missionaries.

The educational problems of Africa cannot be solved overnight. A lot of patience, hard work and thoughtful planning are required. The needs of each African country will have to be classified in priority order. It seems that for many years the most serious problems will be in the areas of teacher education, and technical and vocational training. The successful implementation of the social and economic plans of Africa depends upon an adequate supply of skilled and professional workers. When such professional people are available in large numbers, African nations will become more and more self-sufficient, and like the advanced countries in the world will depend less and less on foreign personnel to carry out their educational programmes. Until then, it may be desirable for even the least qualified foreign teacher to work in Africa under proper supervision and guidance.

To arrive as quickly as possible at a satisfactory rate of educational progress Africans should continue to seek more assistance from better qualified and experienced foreign educators; especially in the fields of university training, teacher training, and technical and vocational training. If this scheme is successful the number of qualified African educators will gradually increase while the number of unqualified foreign teachers in Africa decreases, thus enabling the continent to satisfy its educational needs slowly but surely.

MACRO AND MICRO COOPERATION AMONG NATIONS

by

DAN AVNI-SEGRE

Few are the words that have entered the political dictionary of the sixties of this twentieth century with so wide a range, so deep a hope and, by now so many cynical undertones, as the word 'cooperation'.

The fact is that international cooperation is as old as the Bible, as old as the technical cooperation established between King David and King Hiram of Lebanon, and between his son, King Solomon and the beautiful Queen of Sheba. Yet we need no deep knowledge or sophistication to agree that, in a profound sense, international cooperation is a new phenomenon; in fact it was virtually unknown in its present form up to the middle of this century. In its present form it is linked with two very important historical events: the American post-war aid to developed countries and the emergence of the independent under-developed countries in the second half of this century.[1]

Often, but in my opinion quite mistakenly, the novelty is ascribed to size. Ministries and international organizations for cooperation have been created. Thousands of people staff them. One hundred thousand experts[2] are scattered throughout the world to organize and foster a colossal enterprize of international assistance which, for donors as well as for recipients has sometimes come to mean the practice of more or less veiled control by the strong nations of the world over the poorer. There are those who protest that there is too much international help, and those who believe that there is not enough. Theories of international cooperation, analyses of the problems produced by the new science of giving, are propounded, and no less enthusiastically criticized.

The critics are generally not opposed to aid but to the theories about aid.[3] After all, as the representatives of the affluent third of humanity, they know perfectly well that, if it wants to survive, it must learn to get along with the other two-thirds that, with a few exceptions, is getting poorer and more impatient every day.

The recipient two-thirds, on their part, realize perfectly well that the basic motive of the donor is self-interest. Even when they agree that this typical aid is in their own interest, they are invariably resentful, because of procrastination.[4]

Any type of cooperation, even the most sincere, requires time to yield results. Time means frustration and the cooling off of enthusiasms, unless there is direct personal involvement where the physical presence of the donor himself makes up for many of the weaknesses of the theoretical planning. It is, however, far from easy to build a bridge or operate a factory merely on the basis of such personal involvement as the 'Peace Corps' personnel, or similar bodies. The inescapable truth is that international cooperation as an aim in itself does not exist.

Donor governments and institutions are out to achieve something useful for themselves. They measure their work in terms of the tangible, politico-economic results.

The development experts reason almost exclusively in terms of the equipment of a society and this 'equipment conception' is closely related to the idea of efficiency.[5] The idea of 'efficiency', used as a yardstick of development, is a very complex and dangerous one. On one side, it is linked to the concept of technical advancement, that vital ingredient of success required by all developing states. On the other, it is closely connected in the minds of the inhabitants of most underdeveloped countries with the notion of the superiority of the recently ousted white foreign ruler. In one respect and in one only, the colonizer never had any doubt about himself or his mission, which is to say, his notion of complete technical superiority over the colonized. This behaviour of absolute self-assurance gave the local population the impression that the white man was undoubtedly better in everything bearing on efficiency. Foreign efficiency is still taken for granted today, even when local products, like canned fruit, cigarettes or textiles, often outclass the imported commodities, but are still rejected by the local market in favour of imports from 'advanced countries'.[6]

This complex outlook is certainly not restricted to Africa only. I am positive however, that as long as the idea of international cooperation is tied up with the feeling that the donor countries have a complete technical superiority, there can be little genuine cooperation. Curiously enough, when viewed from the donor's point of view, cooperation often appears to him as a symptom of his own inadequacy: he usually doubts the usefulness of his own donations.[7] There are frequent instances in which the donor party criticizes himself both for his incapacity to understand the recipient party, and for his subsequent inefficiency in helping them. Academically, this criticism is highly gratifying, but it raises the question: why should the cooperation be offered by efficient partners go wrong in so many instances.[8]

I would like to introduce explicitly here a conceptual distinction which is adumbrated in literature, the clarification of which might help: *macro-cooperation* and *micro-cooperation*. I hardly need explain the terms.[9]

Macro-cooperation is, by its very nature, a massive operation organized by big operators who can organize it because they are big. This applies to governments as well as to private or public agencies. There are, of course, small operators as well, who try macro-cooperation. If, for instance, the government of a small country sends a ship or an ambulance to another government as a gift or a loan, it is 'macro-cooperating' on a modest scale. For a 'macro' operation is, first of all, one that can be measured in quantity, in statistical, economic and technical amounts. It all goes back to the underlying concept of 'tools' or 'tooling', which is the principal object of interest for development experts, in macro-cooperation. 'This equipment, this tooling, embraces not only the methods of production of a given society but the "thinking" connected with it'.[10] Since every society has its own 'society equipment' and therefore its own thinking, its own 'group complex', the transfer of the technique, has to face the stiff resistance from the different 'group complex'.

Melville Herskowitz dealt with this resistence in a very pertinent paper in which he stressed 'the fallacious concept of cultural inferiority or superiority', and the danger of replacing racism by culturism.[11] Technical changes, whether imposed or accepted, always imply a deeper cultural adjustment and therefore a battle of the group-subconscious. The unwillingness of Malagasy farmers to part with their (economically speaking) quite useless herds of long-horned bulls cannot be adequately studied in rational economic terms. Only powerful, socio-psychological subconscious group resistence can explain it.

The simplest and most straining and constant obstruction in the way of macro-cooperation is that, by its very reliance on modern techniques, it usually includes regular evaluations of time and space; these differ from the one which the recipient populations conceive and apply.

I have quoted the example of the Malagasy long-horned bull. It is in that island that I saw two most interesting experiments in cooperation of an entirely different kind. The first was conducted by a well-known Malagasy diplomat-scientist with a group of local traditional healers; the second by a distinguished lady physician from the University of Milan with the help of a group of Malagasy doctors. In the first, the objective was to sort out and test the plants possessing pharmacological values used by traditional healers; in the second, the aim was to look for the defining types of neurosis which could throw some light on the clashes between western and traditional cultures and societies.[12] I noted two striking features in both these experiments: a laudable lack of 'resistence complex' between the western and the traditional techniques and a regrettable, almost complete lack of publicity for the remarkable results achieved. These are what I call examples of micro-cooperation, and these are some of its difficulties.

The main reason for the lack of publicity which I mentioned and which characterizes most cases of 'micro-cooperation' is probably that the people engaged therein and the recipient countries sharing it, not only do not possess adequate means of propaganda, but are also so widely scattered that it is difficult to ensure organized coverage. Comparatively little is known about the cooperation of Taiwan with African countries, in spite of its very consistent success in the field of rice-growing.[13] Much less is known on the highly original system of banking and credit cooperative interstate bodies established between the Upper Volta, Togo, Dahomey and the Niger, with the very constructive cooperation of Tunisian banking institutions. A thin veil of unsought-for silence cloaks the interesting experiments in regional cooperation between Malagasy and Mauritius in the fields of tourism and dairy industries. Of all things, not much is heard about the extensive project of cooperation between Yugoslavia and African countries, particularly East Africa.[14]

Why is micro-cooperation both remarkable and yet unnoticed? Micro-cooperation seems to be, first of all, a kind of 'cooperation in movement'.[15] It can be defined as cooperation between two or more independent societies which, themselves, are caught up in a process of swift structural development and national evolution, and for that very reason it is suitable for 'a continent in a hurry' such as Africa.[16]

When developing countries are engaged in mutual help, both donor and recipient occasionally find it difficult to establish models of cooperation of a repetitive type, their respective development being in a constant state of movement.[17]

Another reason is the adaptation of cooperation schemes and techniques to the special conditions of recipient countries, where, as for instance in many African countries, nationhood is still in the process of formation and political independence has underlined local differences within the geographical boundaries determined by the withdrawing colonial power.

The characteristics share one thing in common. In micro-cooperation, the essential element is the functional and day-to-day suitability of a given project to the mentality of the recipient. Here we find adaptation stemming from an experience already analysed, the aim being to evaluate the impact of modernism on indigenous human conditions. The analysis I have particularly in mind is that which developed in my country. In this field Israel has gained experience in tackling her own problems of development, and has established agencies to study the implications of her experience relevant to international cooperation.

I fully agree with all those who believe that Israel cannot be taken as an example of a typical developing country, because of the special social structure, its historical development and its particular sources of income and investment such as German reparations etc., which would fit with difficulty into the common patterns of economic structure and development of other developing countries. Many of the lessons which can be derived from Israel's experience in international cooperation can in fact be learned from its failures—usually in macro-cooperation. These failures are perhaps made more evident in a small country than in a big one. And it is from Israel's failures—rather than from Israel's successes—that I have drawn most of my present conclusions.

As a typical example of such failures, I shall mention Israel's past need for changing its cooperation policy in the field of training programmes for foreign students. The tendency to 'macro-cooperate' in the field of education, i.e. to offer high school and university grants, in spite of the difficulties of the Hebrew language and the difference in curricula, has gradually been overcome by a more appropriate system of educational micro-cooperation. Present study-schemes concentrate on the training of low and middle cadres—the future N.C.O.'s of national production and not the future generals—and are concerned with the problem of returning the student to his country of origin in the shortest possible time. As to the assessment of success, this is no longer done on the basis of the numerical quantity of participants but on their capability of finding a job on their return home. To this purpose a 'tracking service' has been established in order to follow up former trainees through correspondence.

Thus we have derived great advantage from the establishment of a centre for the study of African agriculture: through it, pass all the outgoing and incoming agricultural experts to be briefed on the basis of accumulated experience, and to be interrogated on every aspect of their personal participation in technical cooperation. Another institution which has done much towards better understanding of the problems of coexistence of the seventy odd groups or tribes which constitutes Israel's population today is the Institute of Applied Social Research (see note 6). Its chartered task is, *inter alia*, to advise and counsel Government offices and other public and private concerns in all matters touching upon research projects in social psychology and related disciplines, and to supply them with pertinent research material in an attempt to guide and improve their operations, which, of course, directly or indirectly influence the approach to projects of cooperation.

Among the subjects studied in the Institute of Applied Social Research are the following: public reaction to currency and the psychiatric attitude to medicine; standardization of food habits; the relation between bureaucracy and the public; job evaluation of blue and white-collar workers; and changes in moral ideology in the first and second generation of collective and non-collective settlers.

Another Israeli agency is the 'Afro-Asian Institute for Labour Studies' which has drawn much of its teaching experience from comparisons and rationalizations of Israeli and Afro-Asian labour experiences, as revealed by the very wide range of discussions and lectures provided by its curriculum. It is not my purpose to enter into the details of these operations, but I believe that the experience gained by the kind of research carried out by these institutions and comparable academic organizations in Israel has been a perceptible factor in Israel's success in training, proportionately, the largest number of trainees from developing countries: some 6000 of them in six years.

So much for exportable experience. But were all the experience in the world imported, it would not solve local problems; for the chief problem seems to me to be that of the rise of responsible national leadership capable of independent decision.[18] It is the beginning of a sequence of acts, sometimes extending over a long period of time, involving problems and people whose reactions can rarely be fully grasped and evaluated by a foreign planner.[19] It takes more than logic and technical knowledge to implement decisions; it takes enthusiasm, a lot of adaptation, and an insight going far beyond mere outside observations. Nehru once said that the only indispensable rhythm of progress needed for India was the one which was capable of 'crossing the threshold of hope'. Micro-cooperation is the operation which evaluates its experience not so much in terms of economic or statistical measurement as of its capacity for creating a contagious sense of enthusiasm, a 'risk-taking' mentality which a developing country can only derive from success, even if it is limited, so long as it is realized with indigenous forces.[20]

This infectious zeal, this effective creation of hope through micro-cooperation among developing states, is not the result of material success alone. It is also the result of a deeper understanding of mutual weaknesses. I am not speaking only of economic weakness, but of that, too, of the spirit. As an example of what I mean, I shall briefly mention that Israeli experience concerning the sensitive yet important subject commonly called 'witchcraft'.[21]

We have cases in Israel which involve what is usually described as an extra-human element. This is largely due to the fact that the majority of the present inhabitants of Israel come from regions—Asia, the Middle East, North Africa—where magic is still an active component of mass belief and culture. The cases range from a few murders committed under the spell of sorcery to family tensions or social frictions because of an imagined 'evil eye'. The subject is fascinating in itself, but the reason why I thought it might have some bearing on my present argument is that official recognition, in Israel, not of sorcery but of the fact that it exists among immigrant elements, has helped to solve, or at least to alleviate, a lot of tension and to assemble much data for the better understanding of the reactions of people who are representatives of different cultural patterns.

First of all, the possibility of committing a crime while under the spell of magic has not been overlooked by the Israel judiciary, not just as grounds for leniency, but as an accepted term of reference, much as, in the U.S., American legislation recognizes the influence of intoxicants, or in Italy, the Italian one of the influence of love and honour.[22] It has been discovered, empirically, that many tensions among the working class, attributed to magic, are just different ways of expressing psychological friction,—what in Western jargon might be called a complex.

In other words, a formidable concept full of unpleasant connotations is very often merely a traditional mode of expression which needs an intelligent and sympathetic dictionary to translate it into current western terms. It seems to me that one major characteristic of micro-cooperation is the common effort to interpret not only verbal labels, but actual states of minds, on the basis of comparative analysis and experience. Above all, to learn how not to shame others and not to feel ashamed.

In conclusion, I believe that the time has come to make a clearer distinction between macro- and micro-cooperation, two entirely different but closely linked operations. Neither should ever exclude the other or take its place. Ideally, they should operate in harmony, recognizing their respective limitations and seeking cross-fertilizations through a deeper and better planned exchange of information and through acceptance of the fact that in international cooperation, the most important experiences are those that never can be transcribed in scholarly reports. Above all, macro-cooperation should always be attentive to the essential truth and strength of micro-cooperation, the essence of which is that a locally-implemented scheme, however small, represents the triumph of will-power over psychological inertia. It represents the modest victory of the common man over the almost super-human temptation to vegetate.

We have a saying in Hebrew that the Lord created all things small to allow them to grow through man's hard work. All things except one: sorrow. Sorrow is born big, from the start, so that time, work and hope may reduce it in the heart of men with every passing day and make it lighter and ever lighter to endure.

REFERENCES

I am indebted to Prof. Joseph Agassi for his critical comments on the final draft of this paper.

1 Herbert Fies retraces in *Foreign Aid and Foreign Policy*, London, 1964 pp. 123-127 the pangs of USA foreign aid in 1947 and the disaster which the absence of foreign aid policies brought to the world before World War II. As for historical and statistical analyses of records of past USA aid, see Raymond F. Minesell: *US Private and Government Investments Abroad*, University of Oregon Books, 1962—J. P. Schlesinger in his remarkable study *The Political Economy of National Security*, New York, 1960, summarizes the various US theoretical approaches to international aid in relation to security and makes a clear distinction between what he calls the 'free enterprise approach' (based on economic motives but lacking in force) and the 'Millikan-Rostow approach' (no-strings-attached approach) full of humanitarian impulses but lacking in political realism, and the 'electric approach' based on no doctrine but on an American security consideration only (pp. 232-240).

2 World III—Overseas Development Institute, London, 1965, p. 94.

3 On changes of terminology in aid and international assistance see L. Dudley Stamp, *Our Developing World*, London, 1966, p. 175.

4 It is interesting to note that the expression 'technical assistance' does not appear anywhere in the UN Charter. See G. Fewe, 'Les Aspects Juridiques de l'Assistance Technique dans le Cadre des Nations Unies et des Institutions Specialisees', Paris, 1957, p. 16. On the myths and illusions of foreign aid see T. Mende, *Entre la Pour et Espoire*, Paris, 1958—p. 139 and Gabriel Ardant, *Le Monde en Friche*, Paris, 1958—pp. 30-39; Eugene Staley, *The Future of Underdeveloped Countries*, New York,

1954—p. 213. For L. Gardner, Vice President of the I.B.R.D., quoted by Staley *op. cit.* p. 204: 'the habit of thought and conduct are the most stubborn obstacles to development'. The 'January Report' of Frances Ministry of Co-operation, speaks only of the 'mirage des techniques' and of the 'dream of the possible transfer of know-how' —*La Politique de Co-operation de la France avec les Pays en Voie de Development*, Paris, 1963—p. 28, and states: 'L'etat d'esprit avec lequel un peuple se penche sur le sort d'un autre peuple est le produit de tout son passe' (ibid).

5 Jean Ziegler, 'Necessaire mais imparfaite la science du developement'. *Jeune Afrique*, 14 Aout, 1966.

6 'Africa is afraid to find itself a second time in a position of "school-children" ' writes G. Balandier in 'Afrique Ambique', Paris, 1962 (p. 305) and has some very pertinent remarks on the inefficiency of psychological tests when applied by the western social researchers on Africans (ibid, p. 40).

7 N. Sithole speaks at length of the problem of the relations between white supremacy and African nationalism and of the 'cracking myth' of white superiority. See chapters 3 and 12 in *African Nationalism*, Oxford, 1959.

8 F. Perroux in 'L'Economie des Jeunes Nations', Paris, 1962—has some very pertinent remarks on the mistake of believing that 'the economic references might be able to give a meaning to the multiplicity of the social contradictions' (p. 203) and on the fallacy of possible solutions of the under-development problems through the co-operation of 'experts'. 'The contact between the young and the old nations in the field of development is the contact of a double poverty' of experts (p. 214).

9 I am fully aware of the deep difference between the terminology I use and the similar distinction in the economic field. My choice has been guided by my concern to stress the fundamental differences which exist between a cooperation which deals primarily with development equipment, in the largest sense, and the one whose principal aim is to develop through common experience—the *virtutes*, the spirit, behind the development.

10 J. Ziegler, *ibid.*

11 Melville J. Herskowitz, 'The Role of Culture Pattern in the African Acculturative Experience'. Paper presented to the XXVth International Congress of Orientalists, Moscow, 9—12 August, 1960 and also 'The problem of adapting societies to new tasks' in *The Progress of Underdeveloped Areas* ed. by F. Hoselts, Chicago, 1952 (pp. 89-111).

12 Dr. Rosalba Terranova, Lecturer at the Milan Faculty of Medicine, whose summaries of preliminary researches, still to be published, have been briefly recorded by 'Note di Civilita Vive', Milan in various issues from March, 1964 to July, 1966.

13 See Andre Pautard, 'Formose et les Etats Africains', *Le mois en Afrique*, Dakar, No. 6.

14 Even in Israel, few systematic studies of international co-operation have been carried out in spite of the fact that cooperation with Africa, Asia and South America today constitutes a major and essential part of Israel's international projection. Only one study has grasped the full importance of Israel's technical co-operation as an example of micro-co-operation. I refer to that of Prof. Mordechai E. Kreinin, of Michigan State University: *Israel and Africa: A Study in Technical Co-operation*, Praeger Special Studies in International Economies, London, 1964.

Another effort has been made in this direction by Leopold Laufer, whose research study: *Mutual Aid among Developing Nations: The Case of Israel*, sponsored by the Twentieth Century Fund, due to be published soon, seems to measure 'Israel's experience in relation to the general question of mutual aid among developing nations'.

15 See also E. Staley—pp. 25 and 249 and J. R. Schlesinger *op. cit.* on the breaking of social 'cake of customs' p. 194 on the 'Psychology of the Beneficiary', pp. 220-230.

16 See Arthur Lewis, *The Theory of Economic Growth*, London, 1955, p. 65.

17 See M. Kreinin, *op. cit.*, p. 9 and the typical examples mentioned in the *Jerusalem Post* of 17 August, 1962, on carp-breeding: 'Israelis have been teaching the Yugoslavs more advanced and more intensive versions of methods they have themselves learned from the Yugoslavs'.

18 P. Mendes-France raised the problem in his essay, 'La Science Economique et l'Action', Paris, 1954, where he says *inter alia* 'La ligne motrice de toutes les solutions consiste a monter des mecanisms reflechis qui seraient la transposition—l'imitation presque des mecanismes naturels', pp. 211-254.

19 See the provocative remarks of a high ranking Senegalese official quoted by Justin Vieyra in his reportage on 'La Nouvelle Classe Africaine . . .' *Jeune Afrique* du 9 Septembre 1966.

20 C. Kumalo, *Il Mulino* No. 7-8, 1962, pp. 782-788, 'Aspetti Socioli Dello Suluppo Economico Africomo'.

21 I owe much of this part of my lecture to my distinguished friend Mrs. Phyllis Palghi, Chief Anthropologist of the Mental Health Department at the Israel Health Ministry, who was good enough to make available to me her lecture to the Tanganyika Cultural Society in 1963. (See also: Phyllis Palghi 'Comment from the Anthropological Point of View on the Subject of Experimental and Cultural Determination of Behaviour', paper presented to the joint meeting of the Israel Neuro-psychiatric Association and the American Psychiatric Association, Hebrew University, Jerusalem, May 1963; and 'Immigrants, Psychiatrists', Jerusalem, 1963).

22 It has been established that in Israel, where people from Afro-Asian countries have been brought in contact with people of Western culture, a 'double-standard' of attitude has been developed in many cases of psychical and mental illness or disorder. It is quite common, for instance, for a person to consult both a doctor and a traditional healer, and collaboration has frequently been established between the two specialists, the advice of one type of medical practice being sought by the other when there is a chance of securing a better understanding of the patient's problems by that means.

SOME THOUGHTS ON THE EVOLUTION OF EDUCATION AND SOCIETY IN AFRICA

by

G. E. A. LARDNER[1]

This paper begins with the proposition that in the world of today and of the foreseeable future the first object of education, in a sense we shall define later, is to enable a society or a community to acquire increasing awareness of changes in its environment and to make the best adjustments that it can to survive within that changing environment. The liberal interpretation of education associated, for example, with the United Nations Declaration of Human Rights is essentially related to the desirability and prospects of the individual human being securing the opportunities and the means of full self-development as a condition of that wholeness and roundedness which is the true essence of human existence. We will consider this the second objective of education in our era even though it is in the final analysis the more fundamental, since we must accept that, if the society or the community is imperilled, either from within or without, the individual's opportunities disappear. Before we pass on, it is necessary to note that the environment we speak of may be external to the community or it may be internal to it. To effect the necessary adjustments requires an elite equipped with perception (whether by natural gift or by study) and with the energy, patience and courage to persuade the community to recognize and appreciate the social, political and economic forces that demand adjustment. This elite must also perform the far more difficult task of permitting and participating in the steps that are required for survival and growth. Our main concern in this paper will be with education as a factor in the emergence and quality of this elite and with the conditions which facilitate or inhibit its performance. The instruments available to education may be broadly separated into two categories: command of social technology and command of material technology.[2]

In the search for effective forms of either category of technology it has become a conditioned reflex that Africans should turn to those societies which have succeeded in seizing world leadership and apparently achieving some of the objectives the new elite considers evidence of a capacity for survival and growth. The attitudes which determine the receptivity of the may be one of three: acceptance, rejection, adaptation.

The African elite seeking change begins with a black[3] crow perching on his shoulder—the widespread, much debated and much documented thesis that the African races are fundamentally inferior and come last in a divine ordering of human society which places the blonde Nordic at the top.[4] This thesis has been powerfully supported by two arguments of doubtful significance: the absence of the wheel and the dependence on the spoken rather than the written word. The struggle for political independence in Africa has been, at bottom, a struggle to gain command of material and social technology through which Africa would demonstrate its capacities as being no less than those of other races and thereby establish its claim to equality.

In his approach to the material and social technologies proffered by the 'advanced' countries the African appears not yet to have acquired enough of that scepticism which is the true basis of objectivity and rationality. Nor does it seem that either the scope of the challenges to African education or the totality of African responsibility is fully grasped:

> *But whether they like to or not, they are now confronted with the task of absorbing within a few generations movements such as rationalism, nationalism, and industrialism, which the western nations were allowed to develop within centuries—though often even then with doubtful success.*[5]
>
> *It is African perceptions that must now determine what are to be considered major educational problems, and African judgement that must determine the lines to be taken in dealing with them.*
>
> *But the attainment of that goal will not be an easy matter. It is not enough to have the power to decide. The ability to judge ends and means shrewdly is also essential for the making of poor decisions can only be disadvantageous.*[6]

The educational systems in Africa derived from outside suffered from at least two major defects: they came from self-proclaimed master races and they were initiated through the agency of religious institutions. The most outstanding feature of religion, especially in its organized form, is unquestioning acceptance of dogma and doctrine. This inhibits the development of a spirit of curiosity, free enquiry, creativity and innovation—the qualities most essential for growth and change.[7] Moreover, it has been argued that the Christian religion has itself been intensely informed with the master race thesis[8] and is almost everywhere powerfully allied with ruling classes. The master race content of education is obvious from the most cursory inspection of school syllabuses from the primary to the university level in Africa. History syllabuses in particular are full, until today, of the conquests, heroisms, tragedies and betrayals of former metropolitan countries. So powerful has the impress on African minds been that until quite recently—and in some cases even now—African educational authorities resisted suggestions or attempts to modify contents, teaching methods and educational organization in the firm belief that this would weaken the efforts of their communities to gain command of the material and social technologies essential for achieving equality with, and commanding respect from, 'superior' races.[9]

We must also not overlook an earlier 'model'. F. Musgrove, after years with the British colonial education service in Uganda, describes this 'model' as follows:

It is customary for Englishmen in East Africa to deride the African for aping European ways, and to charge the schools with producing imitation-Europeans'. Educationalists themselves have often shared this view and have sought to keep school curricula and activities in some way essentially African'. They have failed to take advantage of the tendency in their pupils which makes them supremely educable; they have been inclined to deplore and discourage rather than to exploite the African's capacity for imitation. They have placed increasing emphasis on vernacular instruction without ascertaining whether pupils are interested in, and gain personal fulfilment from, learning the vernacular rather than English; they have revived native legends and given the pupil old and familiar models in history and literature without attempting to discover whether his imagination in fact receives greater excitement, his outlook greater breadth and his sympathies greater depth from the study of the unfamiliar figures of a different culture; they have sought to confine geography to the African continent without considering whether Timbuktu has a greater relevance to the Mukiga of Uganda than Tientsin; they have, in some cases, introduced a tribal setting and duly expurgated tribal activities into the schools without reflecting that their pupils might be thoroughly bored with what was only too familiar. They have failed to see that a truly 'African' and original character will emerge not by limiting the scope for imitation but by enriching it as far as possible with a wide diversity of models. There has been a tendency among European teachers to assume that anything with a tribal flavour must interest the African pupil, and this oftten leads to a form of bogus tribalism in the school. In order to discourage 'imitation-Europeans', a school may be more tribal than the tribe itself: a dead and even imaginary past may be fossilized in order to keep the African truly African'.[10]

Factors of this kind have greatly influenced the degree to which the African reforming elite have chosen either acceptance, rejection or adaptation.

There is, however, a fourth attitude which is a compound of the other three, but provides a new dimension which can best be illustrated by an excerpt from a speech by President Nyerere:

We in Tanganyika do not believe that mankind has yet discovered ultimate truth in any field. We do not wish to act as if we did have such a belief. We wish to contribute to man's development if we can, but we do not claim to have a solution; our only claim is that we intend to grope forward in the dark towards a goal so distant that even the real understanding of it is beyond us—towards, in other words, the best that man can become.

This means that the people who anxiously watch to see whether we will become 'communists' or 'Western democrats' will both be disconcerted. We do not have to be either. We shall grope forward, and it may be that we shall create a new synthesis of individual liberty and the needs of man in society; freedom for each individual to develop the spark of divinity within himself at the same time as he contributes bebefits from his membership in the community.[11]

This approach demands certain significant and rare qualities: perception by which is meant the ability to evaluate particular forms of experience for their relevance and adaptability to African needs; courage in resisting open and covert forms of persuasion to accept models without discrimination;[12] a considerable degree of understanding of the factors affecting equilibrium and change in one's community. More than this it calls for the development of autonomous forms of social and material technology and it is at this point that we return to the problem of educational reform.

It is essential for Africans to recognize more fully than they do the fallacy of claims to universal homogeneity, rationality and efficiency in the group models presented by countries of the advanced world from whichever sector of the globe, or of crediting these qualities to individual models.[13] Everywhere there is a crisis of political, social and economic doctrine which profoundly affects these—in many respects now synthetic and romanticized—models. The main weakness of the African approach here seems to be a marked uncertainty which could be resolved with some imaginative effort. For example, virtually every new university established in Africa today includes a Department of African Studies. Important as the study of Africa's present and past is in order to create that self-confidence implied in Nyerere's thesis, and essential though it is for approaching foreign models or forms of experience, there seems to be a tendency not to give full attention to the need for European, Asian and Latin American studies *in depth* in order to provide the critical equipment required for evaluating not only educational but also political, social and economic models and forms of experience. The expression 'in depth' is used to distinguish the kind of studies required (i.e. from the African viewpoint) from the synthetic, romanticized versions African institutions have inherited from European scholars writing about European history and society.

The mere fact of the growing inter-dependence of member countries of this world and the responsibility for making contributions of substance to the development of world order demands such study and research.[14] Emotional reaction is not enough.

One of the oldest features of higher education in Middle Africa is the singular absence or neglect of the subjects which are critical for accelerating economic development and, in particular, for effecting genuine changes in the structure of the African economies. This has received considerable attention in the Economic Commission for Africa,[15] and a few illustrations might help. In a region in which technological adaptation is expected to play a crucial role, the absence of at least one school of materials science and technology is difficult to understand. No serious adaptation can be undertaken without great emphasis on design engineering production, industrial chemistry, cost accountancy, management, industrial engineering and industrial economics. Soil science, water resources technology, textile technology, electronic engineering, transportation, fuel science and technology, are all conspicuous by their absence or inadequacy. The models chosen by or pressed upon governments in Middle Africa appear to be selected from among those of Western Europe in the inter-war years. In the field of agriculture, the deficiencies are ludicrous and potentially tragic. Those who are best fitted to help are content with exhortations (often wrong-headed) or with pious gestures. The prospect of developing any kind of autonomous material technology adapted to the current and foreseeable needs and material resources of Africa appears remote.

The social technology that Africa needs for rapid transformation is yet to take shape and to free itself from intrusions of European and American cultural biasses and habits of thought. For example, land tenure is not, with few exceptions, a serious limit on agricultural production. Yet for years advisers, thinkers, and commentators, from advanced countries, imbued with a strong sense of the significance and rightness of land tenure reform in their own history insisted that this should be the highest priority in agricultural development policy in Africa. Not only was this technically inadmissible, it was also sociologically unsound.

For many years developing countries were urged to sink a considerable part of their scarce resources in mass literacy campaigns in rural areas. This was based, quite obviously, a on remarkable and unforgivable ignorance of social dynamics in rural Africa.[16] Another sterile debate, conducted in the face of mounting agricultural export surpluses produced by African peasant farmers with the minimum of effective social and technical change, centred on the capacity of farming communities in Africa to respond to market incentives.

Much more recent is the growing emphasis on what may, for brevity, be described as educational technology: programmed learning, educational television, video-tapes and, other audio-visual techniques. These are in process of becoming part of the educational technology in Africa without adequate research evaluation. There are two aspects of this problem. Firstly, it seems obvious to a non-educator and a non-scientist that the adoption of these forms of educational technology should be accompanied or preceded by continuous research to determine what adaptation in contents and methods are required to make them genuinely effective in the African context. Secondly, it seems equally obvious that such research cannot, as a matter of scientific reasoning and commonsense, be separated from research and experiments, in curricula, text books and teaching methods. Nevertheless, this is what happens.

It will be recalled that we have spoken of elite in Africa in charge of reforming social and educational processes, but that we have attempted neither to define the concept (in the belief that a definition is unnecessary for this particular audience)[17] nor to describe the characteristics of the existing elite in Africa today. To attempt a description would involve too far a digression into political and social structures; moreover, the rapidity of change and the surprisingly quick succession of elite in the recent past make such an attempt of doubtful value. We assume for the purposes of this paper the emergence ultimately of an elite inspired by President Nyerere's thesis. It is sufficient to note that the pace and direction of change and growth, and the dominant and recessive features of social development of any moment, reflect the power situation of particular types of elite their qualities and their objectives.[18]

We now ought to give some attention to the kind of problems which confront the reforming elite in Africa, especially the challenges which confront

African education. The economic aspect is simple to outline. The following passage is taken from a document[19] prepared for the Working Party on Manpower and Training, organized by the United Nations Economic Commission for Africa in:

The population of the African Region is rising at an estimated rate of between 2.6 and 3 per cent per annum and demographers estimate that it is likely to rise, in absolute figures, from some 280 million at present to well over 600 million by the end of the Century. The most striking aspect of the demographic trend is the very high dependency ratio: 40 per cent of the population is estimated to be under fifteen years of age compared with 25 per cent elsewhere.

The African Region is exceptionally endowed with both mineral and agricultural natural resources, the full extent of which is unknown to its governments and peoples. In the field of agriculture there has been strikingly disparate advance. With minor modifications in technology and in social structure, Africa has considerably raised her exports, through peasant farming, of oil-seeds, natural fibres, natural rubber, cocoa, coffee, tea and other traditional agricultural export products. On the side of food, Africa's efforts to feed herself is a record of failure. One of the many consequences of this is the utilization of scarce foreign exchange on imports into the Region of food which Africa could, by a determined effort at transformation of the agricultural sector, provide amply for herself and for export to assist in mitigating a threatened world food crisis.

As regards industry the Region depends, with little exception, on the initiative of foreign private enterprise. The most cursory study of the geographical direction of flow and the enterprise preference of private foreign investment indicates the limitations of this source of support for accelerated industrial development in depth and on a broad front.

Studies of the experience of advanced and semi-advanced countries reveal that the key factors in accelerated development are not, as is often claimed, physical or financial capital, however great the importance of these, but the capacity acquired by the people, through education, training and research, to apply science and technology (including management) to their resources for potential development.

The enormous and grwoing burden of the working population to:

(a) *maintain the existing low levels of living;*

(b) *improve it by modest increases;*

(c) *provide, over and above* (a) *and* (b) *the additional resources for further growth; and finally*

(d) *effect a structural transformation of the whole economy, including permanent self-sustaining growth of the industrial sector,*

calls for a transformation of education, training and research scarcely yet comprehended.

On the social side we can only indicate a few of the most striking problems. First is the question of promoting internal social cohesion and stability among the conglomerate of communities which the intrusion and withdrawal of European powers has confined within artificial 'national' boundaries. Second is the necessity of carrying through this process of integration without seriously impairing the possibilities of close co-operation between the mosaic of new states—a co-operation recognized by African elite, at least in theory, as crucial to the larger problems of survival and growth. Third is the problem of accommodating the rapidly growing urban proletariat, fed by a steady and increasing discharge from the rural areas. These proletariats are hungry or under-nourished; either totally illiterate or illiterate in the sense of having received an 'education' which denies them the capacity for self-employment or for productive activity, and haunted by a deep psychological sense of being dispossessed and unwanted.[20] Their sense of futility and growing anger is strengthened by their inability to participate in the enjoyment of the goods and services lavishly displayed in the urban area and the equally clearly observable growth of a privileged class which enjoys high levels of living by virtue of having obtained, in one way or another, a higher level or more relevant form of education and competence. Fourth is the problem of securing the commitment of the population as a whole—in particular the vast rural sector—to a massive effort towards change and development. Fifth is the need to achieve these objectives within a framework of effective planning and plan implementation requiring the design and provision of adequate instruments and institutions.

On the level of multi-national co-operation, new problems arise. Territorial disputes over national boundaries bedevil understanding; empathy is inhibited by the heritage of four great streams of language, culture, political and economic influence from Western Europe: via Britain, France, and Belgium, Portugal and the Middle East. The language problem extends beyond the borders of Africa. The need to secure the commitment of the people as a whole to the struggle for national independence led to the adoption of forms of expressing liberal democracy as the object of the struggle, such as 'African socialism'. These aroused deep hostility from advanced nations who had taken up rigid stances in the cold war and were unable to grasp that African political leaders and intellectuals, unable to invent a language to describe the concept of the new civilization they wished to build in Africa, had been forced into the inevitable semantic error of adopting terms highly charged with cold war overtones. The failure in communications has led to consequences sometimes tragic and sometimes comical and exasperating.

What should now be apparent is that, as Mannheim puts it,[21] the choice before Africa—as before more advanced societies—is not between 'laissez faire' and planning but between good planning and bad planning. This requires the direction of energy 'towards finding a combination of social controls which would determine how far individual liberties should be left unrestricted in order to preserve both the freedom of the invidual and the efficiency of the community.'

The present and future reforming elite is thus faced with the necessity of continually making choices in response to often unexpected situations and of making such choices with foresight and wisdom. Whence are the foresight and the wisdom needed for the making of such choices to be obtained? Our answer is from education: not merely from the primary school to the university, not merely formally organized but in as wide a variety of ways, including reflection, as are open or can be devised.

It is at this point that we return once again to the desirable characteristics of an educational philosophy and practice appropriate for Africa. John

W. Gardner[22] writing on 'Renewal in Societies and Men' discusses the problems which confront a mature, i.e. an advanced society, and the constant need it has of providing mechanisms for recharging its vitality. He draws attention to the enormous accretion of routine and precedent, custom and convention, powerfully organized vested interests, and their effect in paralyzing creativity, vigour, enthusiasm, and what Alva Myrdal calls 'fungibility', i.e. the readiness to accept change and to act with purpose.[23] Gardner's thesis applies with equal force to societies in Africa. The dangers he foresees and warns against are concealed in precisely those social, political and economic characteristics inherent in societies in Africa. The fashion of referring to 'new nations' tends to obscure the fact that Africa is comprised of old, i.e. well-established social groups and cultural systems. Gardner makes two points about an elite capable of revitalizing societies: they must be able to perceive and understand the challenges confronting the society; they must possess creativity. He then adds a final point of great significance for our education policy-makers and practitioners: the need for a balance between specialization and versatility. The uncontrolled development and expension of specialists at the expense of that form of versatility embodied in the many-sided individual, the generalist, the polymath, is a short-cut to social atrophy. Alvin Eurich, in his visionary article on the probable lines of development of higher education between 1960 and 2000 observes:

> *We are just now beginning to take seriously Ortega y Gasset's insight set down years ago in his 'Mission of the University'. The need to create sound syntheses and systematization of knowledge, to be taught in the 'Faculty of Culture', will call out a kind of scientific genius which hitherto has existed only as an aberration, the genius for integration. At Brown University, President Barnaby Keeney was one of the first to initiate an Institute for the Synthesis of Knowledge.*[24]

If, as we said at the beginning of this paper, the first object of education is to enable societies and communities to survive and grow—recalling that nothing in biological history provides an assurance that survival and growth are automatically guaranteed to any living species—and if we are considering Africa of the future, we are in effect considering those policies and actions which, today, will determine the characteristics of the members of the future elite. We educate now not only for 15 to 20 years ahead but for the active lifetime of those we educate. In the next few paragraphs we shall consider some current problems and policies which affect the emergence of these elites composed of the generalist and the specialist, capable of creativity, able to communicate with the rest of the community and of inducing innovation.

In the economic sphere, we now recognize that the essence of development lies not in physical assets such as factories, or even in natural resources or in finance capital, but in the men and institutions capable of generating self-sustaining growth. It is the capacity to create wealth and income that lies at the heart of the development process, not the immediately quantifiable increment in the volume or quality of goods and services per head of the population at any one period.[25] Indeed development in this sense may occur in conditions of static or even declining levels of *per capita* income. It has taken two decades at least of intense debate and dispute to discover this obvious fact and it has yet to be widely acknowledged or accepted as a guide to development planning and policies. Man, as the agent of production and distribution, occupies the pivotal position in the development process.[26] A casual glance at the African scene reveals, not merely the paucity or absence of such men and institutions, but a failure fully to recognize this crucial defect. The institutions of higher education established in Africa within the past decade, on the advice of large numbers of experts from advanced countries and in virtually every case with aid from the same sources, display an unbelievable conventionality of design and inspiration—or perhaps lack of inspiration. The subject structure appears to have, as its main but probably unconscious aim, the further extension of that classicism which has bedevilled lower levels of education in Africa in the past and from which advanced countries are making the most valiant efforts to escape. The subjects or aspects of subjects which today provide dynamism for development are conspicuous by their absence or inadequacy. Educational authorities and even senior university staffs appear unconscious of the need for radical reforms in subject structure, content and teaching methods. Without these reforms, undertaken as a matter of urgency, reasonably rapid economic development and structural transformation in Africa must be dismissed as a romantic dream.

The process of reform in general encounters the mystique of book-learning, reflected in many fallacies underlying the case for universal free primary education and for eradicating mass illiteracy. It would help to clarify matters at this point by drawing attention to what Mannheim describes as the three levels of thought.[27] The first is thought of the level of chance discovery which forms the basis of social and economic life in backward societies. It is chance discovery of social and physical fact through painful experience that produces the web of prescriptions and taboos so characteristic of pre-literate societies. At the much higher level (that of sophisticated modern societies), until the inter-war years thought at the level of invention prevailed and still constitutes the basis of the proud claims with which developing societies have been repeatedly battered. The third level of thought, that of planning, is yet to be mastered by even the most sophisticated of the developed societies. Societies in Africa, faced with the necessity to move from the first to the third level, cannot afford an educational system which puts the emphasis on efficient memorizing rather than on the capacity to reason and to face unfamiliar problems with confidence.

The primary object of making significant contributions to modern civilization can only be met if reforms include the study and devising of the means of identifying a promoting creative capacities. The current debate on this subject in the advanced countries is indecisive. The questions to be answered appear to be: How can a society or community most efficiently detect, as early as can be, the individuals who are endowed by nature with creative ability of specific types? How are their gifts to be nurtured through education and training?[28] Creative capacity may be of two kinds: the process of patient, independent reasoning through what one might call linear or collateral association of ideas. It is currently often organized as group activity, the form most suited to the growing complexity of modern science and technology, and is frequently summarized in the expression 'a brilliant team'. The other and less readily apprehended form of creative capacity is the ability to perceive valid and significant relationships between apparently unrelated phenomena. This 'flash of insight' capacity accounts in the main for the really great and fundamental advances in man's understanding of the physical and social environment.

But it is not enough to have, dispersed in society, men *and women* of great creative potentiality or even to identify them and nurture their gifts. It is also essential to provide the bridge between creative thinking and innovation.[29] We need only to bear in mind that the really open scientific and technological society in which identification and development of creative thinking and free conditions of innovation exist is only now in process of emergence in even the most advanced countries. Creative thinking is individual but innovation must, to be truly effective, be social.

In the search for the means of developing the elite of the future we must bear in mind three great problems: firstly, the risk of sustaining the 'two cultures' dichotomy. C. P. Snow's arguments may be subject to modification in the context of advanced countries but he would undoubtedly have more easily won his case by basing his study on Africa.[30] Secondly, much more co-ordinated and intensive effort needs to be directed to the determination of the means by which the education and role of women may be more efficiently designed to enable them to make a fuller contribution to the pattern and texture of a new civilization in Africa.[31] Present efforts are conventional, spasmodic and feeble. The corollary is, of course, an increase in the scale and enlargement of the variety and scope for employment of women, especially talented women. The third great problem is that of convincing and devising the means of producing teachers with the special qualities required to help develop the character and potentialities of the elite Africa needs for the realization of President Nyerere's thesis.[32]

Our concern with elites may have suggested an elitiste, i.e. aristocratic, concept of society. Whilst it is true that no developing society functions without elites it is also true that social efficiency is not sustainable without a measure of individual self-fulfilment at every level and in every sector of the community. This brings us to the second and more fundamental object of education. It would add too much to an already long paper to examine the implications of education for the average and those judged below average. What is obvious is that educational systems at the primary and secondary levels in Africa are modelled on those of the former metropolitan country (sometimes touched with a minor daring innovation or two from elsewhere) and make little or no distinction between different kinds of gifts or different rates of potential growth. The dominance of the concept of the 'average' child or student in the structure of African education is terrifying to observe. As Eurich argues:[33]

> *Television provided the medium for mass instruction; programmed learning provided the ultimate in individualized instruction. Within this range, including other devices and procedures, such as motion pictures, filmstrips, language laboratories, and increased scope for independent study, a new diversity was added to the educator's repertoire. These resources enabled us to break the ancient framework that for so long had held college education in a rigid pattern. No longer do we have to divide the school day into fixed fifty-minute periods; no longer do we measure a student's progress by the number of credit hours he has banked, no longer do we march all students through the same series of lectures and classes.*

The emergence of these new instructional resources provides an institution preoccupied with Africa's social, political and economic development, such as the Organization of African Unity, with extraordinary opportunities for genuine architectonic contributions to such development. It is also not uncommon for the true meaning and purposes of education to disappear easily under the stress of coping with the mechanics of systems and procedures. Regrettably, those who profess to be helping Africa often approach the problems of 'built-in institutions of inventive research applied to social as well as to material technology' in an ill-organized and fragmentary way.[34] They are often informed with a desire to score over rivals rather than to co-operate in making optimum use of scarce resources or to solve crucial problems, charged with undertones of political or economic interest and hampered by the struggles of 'organization men' to protect or enlarge their boundaries of authority within aid-providing institutions, whether bilateral or multi-lateral. There seems to this writer to be no alternative but for African policy-makers to realize the extent to which no one else can, or is truly going to develop Africa for Africans. The corollary or this is that African policy-makers must now decide that where aid is not forthcoming for the design and establishment of the kind of institutions to which Staley refers, they must be prepared to forego relative inessentials (which still amply figure in African import statistics) in order to undertake the work themselves.

Another of the great tasks confronting African educators and policy-makers, if a genuine recognition (in action as well as in theory) of a common destiny is to emerge, is the symbiosis through education of the four major streams of political, social and economic influences, to which we referred earlier, that have profoundly affected Africa.

Designing the institutions that are required calls for an intellectual and social effort and self-discipline which is far from being realized. Indeed some critics doubt the ability of Africans to perceive the nature and extent of the 'challenge of modernization' and to exercise the will to meet that challenge.[35] This brings us to a brief description of 'Africa and the Rest of the World'. For decades the advanced nations most intimately associated with Africa have successfully built up, partly out of careless thinking and partly in justification of themselves as the model for political, social and economic development, what the author has recently described as the 'Theory of Relative Costless Development'. The following passage is quoted from the original without allowance for diplomatic finesse:

If developing countries were politically allied to the 'right' side; if they adhered to an open door economic policy (including the unfettered inward and outward movement of capital); if they freely granted generous concessions to foreign private enterprise; if they remained politically stable (an exhortation to which it is hard to give meaningful operational content); if they eschewed unsound monetary and financial policies; if they rejected/accepted economic planning; if they resisted the temptation to embark on industrial development; if they left all in the hands of the private sector; if they obeyed the rules of somebody else's games; if x, *if* y, *if* z, *development would proceed with ease and little friction or cost in terms of suffering, frustrations, social upheavals, etc. This relatively costless theory with its ever-changing nostrums, has not only failed to work but is chiefly responsible for the growing political and social instability in the developing world arising mainly from the failure of the development process as prescribed.*

Africans, reformulating the dynamics of political, social and economic development, need to resist this form of utopianism derived from, 'a romanticized, rationalized and synthetic interpretation of European and American history'. Insofar as current models of the all-comprehending variety are concerned, the African elites of today are in the fortunate position of being able to observe their limitations and defects in practice. All this does not imply 'rejection' as we spoke of it much earlier in this paper but adaptation and experiment in search of new autonomous solutions.

In their search for experience which may be relevant and adaptable, African policy-makers have displayed a marked degree of self-inhibition. For development and growth one would think that, setting aside cultural, ideological and other similar impediments, African policy-makers and educational thinkers would currently be making intensive studies of such countries as Japan, Australia and Canada, Scandinavia, the U.S.S.R., and Eastern Europe as well as the two Chinese Republics. It is a mistake to assume that this will be organized by anyone for Africa or if organized at all will be satisfactory in terms of African understanding of Africa's needs. This is work of a far-reaching nature which, an institution such as the OAU could very profitably undertake.

It is striking that, whilst increasing attention is being paid to all these matters in advanced countries, not much effort is being made to construct, in the field of education, new designed structures to replace the bug-ridden and sketchy buildings inherited from former colonial regimes.[36] It seems currently fashionable to prescribe outmoded material and social technologies as appropriate for curing backwardness! If African policy-makers fail to face the problem of educational reform and to face it very soon, we may, expect the situation described in the following passage:

There are two immediate implications of the developments in the advanced countries to which attention should be drawn. The first is that the prospects of closing the education gap in qualitative as well as in quantitative terms is diminishing and the effect is likely to be a rein-

forcement of the steadily widening gap between levels of economic and social development in advanced and in developing countries. In effect, therefore, what may be an evolutionary change in education and manpower development in advanced countries requires a revolutionary change in a developing region such as Africa.

A second implication is the unlikelihood of the advanced countries being in a position to produce, in the quantities and qualities and in the professional mix required, the supply of teachers essential to complement the grossly inadequate indigenous African supply to bring about this revolutionary change. This limitation extends with almost equal force to teaching and training facilities available in the advanced countries. The developments in the advanced countries and the causes which gave rise to them reflect what has been described as an educational crisis extending with few, if any, exceptions, from the USA and Canada to Japan. This makes it less easy for such countries to provide, in terms of the realistic needs of the whole developing world (that is with the object of accelerated development and structural economic change which takes reasonable account of population growth and living standards)the equipment, teachers and training opportunities which the advanced countries themselves require to meet their own rapidly expanding needs.[37]

There seem to be reasonable prospects that Africa will continue for quite a while yet to be 'the land where the Jumblies live'.

REFERENCES

1 Although the author of this paper is a staff member of the United Nations Economic Commission for Africa, the views expressed are entirely his own and should in no way be attributed to the Commission or its Secretariat.

2 See E. Staley, *The Future of Under-developed Countries*, New York, 1961.

3 For the international social significance of 'black' as indicative of evil, see 'Colour, Racism and Christianity'—Roger Bastide—Seminar on Race and Colour; Congress for Cultural Freedom and American Academy of Arts & Sciences; Copenhagen, 1965. See also Pitirim Sorokin, *Contemporary Sociological Theories*, New York, 1928.

4 It is interesting to note that according to some authorities no major civilization emerged in Northern Europe spontaneously and that the most striking characteristic of the Northern European races was an inclination to destroy civilizations they encountered but could not understand—Sorokin *op. cit.*, p. 276.

5 Robert Ulich, *The Education of Nations—A Comparison in Historical Perspective*; Harvard University Press, 2nd Edition, 1954. See also the passage quoted from Document E/CN.14/WP.6/3/Add. 1 on pp. 11-12 below.

6 Karl Bigelow in *Educational Foreign Aid*, Harvard University Press, 1965, p. 44.

7 'Scientific Growth: A Sociological View', Joseph Ben-David; Minerva, Vol. II, No. 4, 1964.

8 Bastide—*op. cit.*

9 See L. Gray Cowan, 'British and French Education in Africa: A Critical Review' in *Post-Primary Education and Political and Economic Development*, Eds. Don Piper and Taylor Cole, Duke University Press, 1964. *African Universities and Western Tradition*, Eric Ashby, London, 1964.

10 F. Musgrove, '*Education and the Culture Concept*,' Africa, Vol. XXIII, No. 2; April, 1953, pages 110-125.

11 Address on the opening of Kivukoni College, Dar-es-Salaam, 29th July, 1961, quoted in '*The Politics of African Nationalism—Challenge to American Policy*', George W. Shepherd, Jr., Praeger, 1962.

12 *The Chinese Model*, Warner Klatt (Ed), Hong Kong University Press, 1965, L. Gray Cowan—*op. cit.* See also F. Musgrove quoted above.

13 Recent literature on the defects in educational systems in advanced countries is far too vast to be cited in detail. The reader's attention is drawn to the series of reports by Government committees in the United Kingdom, the *Times Educational Supplement;* issues of *New Education;* the *Times Review of Industry and Technology;* issues of the *New Scientist*, etc. A searching note on some basic defects in the United Kingdom is provided by A. P. Rowe: 'A Beeching for the Dons' in the *Times Review of Industry and Technology;* July 1963. As regards the United States, the works of James Bryant Conant should be consulted, also issues of the quarterly magazine, *The Educational Record*, published by the American Council of Education, Washington; annual reports of the Ford, Carnegie & Rockefeller Foundations are also valuable. There are also a large number of eductaional magazines which should not be overlooked but are too numerous to mention. For Western Europe some ideas may be gained from the following:

'Recommendations of the Science Council for the Development of Scientific Institutions in Western Germany' Minerva, Vol. I, No. 1, Autumn, 1962; 'A German View of the Robbins Committee's Report—Ludwig Raiser, Minerva, Vol. II, No. 3, Spring, 1964; The Educational Value of Science, Kurt Mothes, *ibid.;* Heretical Remarks on Professor Aron & University Expansion, J. G. Weightman, Minerva, Vol. II, No. 4, Summer, 1964; Swedish University Policy, Minerva, Vol. VI, No. 1, Autumn, 1964; Scandinavia's Response to the Science Boom, A. C. Vaigo, *New Scientist*, 2.6 1966.

14 For there is no assurance that barbarism, whether backward or modern, has yet disappeared from the world scene. Nor should sight be lost, in the effort to achieve equality by successfully demonstrating capacity in terms of criteria set by advanced countries, that Africa has social values she has contributed and is contributing to human civilization (these are already obvious in music, art and literature). These values imply a set of criteria for, and a challenge to, advanced countries no less than those Africans now strive to answer. To lose sight of this is to fail, *in limine*, in a very profound sense.

15 See, for example, documents E/CN.14/INR/113, E/CN.14/LU/DCOP/9, E/CN.14/WP.6/3/Add. 1, E/CN.14/AS/IV/9, E/CN.14/WP.6/4, E/CN.14/WP.6/7, E/CN.14/363.

16 See the author's contribution to: 'Development and Adult Education in Africa, (ed.) Carl Widstrand; the Scandinavian Institute of African Studies; Uppsala, 1965. 'A nation engaged in something as delicate as social change wants to work in the clear light of facts' (p. 176) . . . 'A developing country cannot afford to waste resources on unsuccessful or inefficient campaigns' (p. 177)—Wilbur Schramm in *Mass Media and National Development*, Standford University Press, 1964.

17 It should be obvious that the term is used in a sociological rather than a popular 'social' sense.

18 See Karl Mannheim, *Man and Society in an Age of Reconstruction* — London, 1940; pp. 82ff.; Robin Marris: *The Economic Theory of 'Managerial' Capitalism*; London, 1964—pp. 1 & 14. On current types of socio-political structures in Africa and their elites, see Shepherd, *op. cit.*

19 Document E/CN.14/WP.6/3/Add.1 of 26 August, 1966: 'Recent Developments in Education and Training: comment by the ECA Secretariat'. The passage quoted does not pretend to be a comprehensive statement of the problem. An interesting and pessimistic view is set out in the address by Mr. Philippe de Seynes, Under-Secretary of Economic and Social Affairs of the United Nations in New York, on 'The Outlook for African Economic Development' to the Conference on Legal Problems of Investment and Development in Africa, at New York University; March, 1966.

20 The absurdity of pressing an abstract, disembodied literacy on rural communities whilst the urban 'literate' find no opportunities for productive employment is easy to perceive.

21 Mannheim, *op. cit.* page 9.

22 Presidential Statement, Carnegie Corporation of New York—see Annual Report for 1962, pp. 3-13.

23 Alva Myrdal, 'The Power of Education' from *Education in World Perspective*, New York, 1962, p. 140.

24 Alvin Eurich, 'Higher Education in the 21st Century', Atlantic Monthly Vo. 211, No. 6 of June 1963, pp. 51-55. Eurich imagines himself writing in the year 2000 and surveying developments in the preceding forty years.

25 Hans Singer, *International Development—Growth and Change*, New York, 1964, p. 19. Robin Marris, *op. cit.*

26 Singer, *op. cit.;* Staley, *op. cit.*, pages 202-3, 230-244.

27 Mannheim, *op. cit.* pp. 147-152.

28 Cyril Burt, Foreword to *The Act of Creation*, Arthur Koestler, London, 1964. Burt points out that the existing methods of teaching, the examinations system, etc., are all designed to select the efficient learner rather than identify the truly creative child. He also observes 'that the greater the number and variety of genuinely creative minds a nation can produce and cultivate, the faster will be its rate of progress'.

29 See, for example, Everett M. Rogers: *Diffusion of Innovations;* Glencoe Free Press, Scotland, 1963; also Peter F. Drucker: 'From Progess to Innovation', Ch. 2 in *The Landmarks of Tomorrow*', London, 1959.

20 See Rowe, *op. cit.*

31 W. E. F. Ward, *Educating Young Nations*, London, 1959—pp. 109-110.

32 This expression is employed as a shorthand for summing up what Africans, the author feels, are really pursuing.

33 Eurich, *op. cit.*

34 Staley, *op. cit.* p. 249.

35 I. R. Sinai, *The Challenge of Modernisation;* London 1965. Sinai speaks with the bitterness of exasperation. A less pessimistic view was taken by contributors to 'The Progress of Underdeveloped Areas'—Harris Foundation Lectures; University of Chicago Press, 1952.

36 The term 'structures' is used to cover education systems. It is important to stress that the essentials of an effective educational system are: good teachers, good equipment and willing students and a well-thought out philosophy, and that the enormous investment in 'fancy' buildings which swell education budgets is mostly a costly irrelevance.

37 Document E/CN.14/WP.6/3/Add. 1.

Justice would not be done nor our purpose served without reference to the monumental path-breaking Reports of the United Nations Advisory Committee on the Application of Science and Technology to Development: documents E/3866 of 1964, E/4026 of May 1965, E/AC.52/R.3/rev. 1 of Nov. 1965, E/4187 of May, 1966 and E/AC.52/L.27 of Nov. 1966, obtainable from United Nations Headquarters, NewYork.

EDUCATION FOR TOMORROW IN AFRICA: A PROJECT FOR AID

by

G. C. LAST

My work in Africa over the past eleven years has carried me through three cycles of thought on basic educational policies. I arrived on the continent convinced that education was a basic human right and that nothing should stand in the way of its very rapid extension. I felt that roads and hospitals and all the other paraphernalia of civilization were fine in their way but the most urgent task was to provide the population at large with the fundamental tools of reading, writing and basic calculation. I argued that without these tools, it would be difficult for citizens in emerging and developing societies to participate effectively in national and local decision making and so take part in the creation of a new and better life. The alternative, it seemed, was decision-making by the few on behalf of the many. This had been going on far too long in Africa and the only decision which the few had the right to take was to destroy their own monopoly of literate ability and share this basic facility with all.

I soon learned, of course, that those in power knew differently. Governments compete, not only on the basis of the percentage of literacy but also in terms of national airlines, iron and steel mills and broad-laned boulevards. Slices from the national cake should be reserved for these activities since a blueprint for the developed society has already been in wide circulation and includes all these desirable things. Education must, then, take its place in the cake queue. Education becomes in fact a means and not an end. In my experience even the economists came to realize that education had to do with human beings but, unfortunately, they began to classify human beings as natural resources and education was granted crumbs from the cake provided that this in turn resulted in the ability to bake a still larger cake. We were in the manpower era and I too was seduced by sweet arguments about productivity, input and output and the place of education in economic growth. Only those educational institutions which would produce young people for jobs (or for further training for more highly skilled jobs) defined and projected in national economic plans would be tolerated and financed. It is certainly important that young people who spend years addressing themselves to textbooks should find some rewards at the end of this process. But, unfortunately, something went wrong with the educational equations. In the first place the products were not always acceptable for employment (this was largely the fault of the educators who still thought that they were in a cultural milieu which demanded knowledge of the past rather than the present); in the second place, apart from those who struggled on through university and further scholarship to a level where they could make their own decisions and their own demands upon society, many of those favoured few who managed to complete their elementary or secondary school courses found no jobs waiting for them. This was the fault of the economists who forgot that 'plan' does not mean 'implementation' and who chose to ignore the fact that most of the decision-making leading to job creation took place outside their control and very often outside their society. Strange to say, the activities of economists sometimes resulted in an actual reduction in the volume of employment available as new, modern, capital-intensive factories and highway construction machinery came into being. We found then, suddenly, that we were producing the wrong amounts of the wrong type of people at the wrong level. What was needed was a smaller number of people, with much higher qualifications able to control this complex machinery. So we have the paradox to which our chairman, Mr Gardiner, has drawn attention, that 'while we are suffering a genuine man-power shortage, we have only to look around us to see growing numbers of school leavers, idle or under-employed, in all our major urban areas. But what seems a paradox may well turn into a tragedy, for these people are, for the most part, unemployable, because they have acquired none of the skills that would fit them for a part in the economic transformation of their society.'

So—not only was the education system not geared to precise economic requirements but the economists themselves do not seem to have managed to bake the kind of cake that would give all of us a larger slice.

We cannot however blame everything on the economists (or even on that curious hybrid, the educational economist), for the educationalist, both national and expatriate, is also at fault for accepting and applying a pattern of education which is almost entirely 'western' or 'developed' or what you will, but certainly external in concept. True, there has been a great deal of talk and a certain amount of action to 'Africanize' the curriculum of studies but this curriculum has been placed in the same old boxes of classrooms, taught by the same old teachers with much the same old methods, using the same old style of text-book with students writing the same old notes and keeping the same old school hours in the same sort of academic year as we did in good old Europe in those distant times between the two world wars! Such techniques as group teaching, study halls, taped lessons, programmed learning texts, radio and television education and language laboratories exist and have been proved to be both economical and educationally more effective, but how far have they been applied in Africa's schools? Particularly at secondary school level, and more so at university level, where the teacher is not only a very expensive item but also an extremely scarce commodity, effective substitutes for day long teaching and proven aids for the sub-standard teacher should have received immediate attention. To a certain extent at secondary school level and much more at university level, rigid time requirements which hold back the outstanding student should have been relaxed. There is an urgent need for the trained man, but do we allow him to train as rapidly as he can, or do we stick to outworn educational procedures? We construct expensive buildings, fill them with expensive equipment, and then keep them open only half the day—and close them entirely for almost one third of the year! Does this make sense in an era of scarce resources? It makes even less sense when we discover that so-called advanced countries with more abundant resources at their disposal are introducing all these measures in the interests of educational efficiency. Yet in reality, in Africa in 1966 these techniques are essential tools rather than interesting novelties.

Fortunately in one sense, we have been experimenting with only a very small proportion of the youth of Africa. Most of them have never managed to get near a school. This is because economists and educators, together with those citizens who really mattered, have not been thinking in terms of a broad national development at all. They *talked* about comprehensive planning and balanced programmes, but what they really meant was industrial development and the requirements of urban communities. This is very strange when you look back on the statistics and see that perhaps 5% of the citizens were being supported in schools by about 18% of the national budget which was largely derived from the 80% of the population who farm the land and yet the students themselves are perhaps 60% urban in origin.

Clearly something must be done about the African rural scene:

(a) from the economists' point of view—since agriculture provides the bulk of income on the continent and yet this is the sector of the economy where productivity is lowest.

(b) from the social point of view—since the gap between town and country is widening and the drift to the towns is increasing.

(c) from the point of view of education—since rural literacy followed by general education to give self-confidence and stimulate initiative and by specific training to improve agricultural techniques is the only way to increase agricultural productivity and break away from subsistence type economies.

Here then is the third cycle in basic educational policy. We must, of course, continue to try and meet skilled manpower requirements in the new sectors of the economy. At the same time, we must return to the concept of mass education. This will necessarily be in rural areas since this is where the mass of Africa's population is located. Now, however, we can justify the application of economic resources to the education of a much larger number of people in a relatively short time, because we have the clear evidence that African economies are not expanding at a rate which will take account of both expansion in population and the demands being made by more sophisticated social and economic developments.

Fortunately, at this moment in history, man has developed a tool which will enable him to undertake this gigantic task. Educational television together with educational radio services, but most particularly educational television, enable effective education to be developed in remote areas. Perhaps more important, they make possible a much more even geographical distribution of educational facilities than is feasible or economically possible by the use of more traditional methods.

The great difficulty is to get at these rural communities. Over wide areas in Africa communications are rudimentary and population densities are low. In some parts of the continent, for example in Ethiopia, the nature of the landscape will make it difficult, and certainly expensive, to construct local roads at any time in the future. The provision of a traditional structure of education covering a variety of needs and providing a network of instruction through rural areas would be a super-human task involving an enormous drain on resources. Fortunately, at this moment in history, science has given us television. It has also given us, as a by-product of more martial preoccupations, the television satellite relay system. Here is a tool which will enable us to undertake this gigantic task.

There are many who have not yet come to accept this medium as a very practical tool capable of a complete transformation of educational processes. No doubt, there were similar reactions in the past to the potential effect of printing and the textbook on education. Yet the advent of educational television can have a revolutionary impact on our educational problems. It can ensure a more equitable distribution of educational facilities. In doing so, it can begin to reverse the trend which has created a widening gap between town and country. It can ensure that students of all types all over the region—people seeking literacy, farmers seeking an insight into new agricultural techniques, students in locations where it would be most uneconomical to establish high schools and people working in remote locations who wish to continue part-time education—receive regular instruction. Educational television can solve the problem of maintaining quality in education since it can ensure that the best type of instruction is available to all regardless of location. It can also make a significant contribution to the problem of quantitative expansion, since, properly organized, it can result in a saving in expensive teaching staff. It may even permit qualitative expansion to take place since qualified and experienced teachers for all classrooms, particularly at secondary and university levels, are very difficult to find.

For this to take place, two things are necessary. First, African countries themselves and their advisers must come to regard educational television not as a fringe benefit, not as an additional cost to education, not as a gadget in a facade of superficial progress, but as a basic educational medium around which supplementary educational services must be built and without which general progress is bound to be slow if not impossible.

Second, more advanced countries which have these techniques at their disposal must understand that the creation of these services would be the greatest contribution they can make to education and to general social and economic progress on the continent of Africa. Vast sums of money have been spent on the scientific research which has resulted in television transmission and the development of satellite communication. It would be better for mankind if the benefits from this expenditure could include the immediate development of an educational service for the less developed regions of the world. At least this should bring some satisfaction to scientists who have been engaged in the technical development of these media. They will be able to see their creations serving more basic human needs than the dissemination of pop cultures over television services, the perfection of military communications through the use of satellites, and the creation of destructive weapons through rocket research.

It is true that, in many respects with regard to its detailed application, educational television is still in the experimental stage, but the proven basic results and possibilities are so clear that we can stop arguing about its validity. It is also true that a number of embryonic educational television systems exist in various parts of Africa. They have, however, taken several years to reach the present small scale of development; they are largely still serving urban rather than rural areas; they face technical difficulties through insufficient aid for development and they are still regarded as ancillary rather than basic operations. They are also technically backward in attempting to expand and provide services to more remote areas; they are having to rely upon outdated ground installations rather than space techniques which have already been proved feasible.

Hence, the project:

PROJECT FOR MAKING A REALITY OF EDUCATION FOR THE MASS OF PEOPLE IN AFRICA

Addressed to: The scientifically advanced world which has relatively more resources at its immediate disposal.

Title of Project: To create and provide the technical services for a continent-wide system of television distribution satellites which will enable African countries to reach educational 'take-off' point within the present generation.

Cost: Minimal when compared with the high cost of present international and bilateral aid to education in Africa—in terms of the salaries and expenses of expert personnel and the provision of traditional materials and equipment, which are resulting in the creation of conventional educational processes in Africa capable of serving only a small fraction of the population and which will establish a rigidity in educational institutions, structures and methods which may well be regretted by Africa within the present century.

Time: Immediate.

Advantages: Unlimited, but specifically,

(a) in the short run, the project will ease the impossible situation which is developing with regard to the provision of teachers for Africa's schools and will enable the best resources to be concentrated so that their effect can be spread over the whole system;

(b) in the long run, it will be possible to ensure more even educational and therefore social and economic development over the continent to the benefit not only of Africa but of the whole world in terms of developed human and economic resources.

Contributions from African States:

(a) A national plan which will emphasize the need for the rapid and positive involvement of the mass of the population in economic and social development; which will ensure a balanced development of both agriculture and industry and both rural and urban areas.

(b) An educational plan designed primarily to satisfy the objectives in (a) above; built on an assumption that the most modern techniques will be employed and that standards can be maintained and raised through the use of these techniques;

(c) An educational programme that will define courses of study and teaching methods appropriate to the immediate requirements of African development and regardless of curricular assumptions formulated in more remote times for use in different cultures.

THE PRESENT ROLE OF THE EXPATRIATE SCIENTIST IN AFRICA

by

H. C. PEREIRA

There is a great deal of rather emotional discussion in newly independent countries in Africa about the necessity to 'sever the umbilical cord' and to terminate all dependency on the older countries of Europe. In science, the many specialists supplied from the countries which were formerly colonial powers play a critically important part in the economy and development of emergent African countries. It is important that such essentially objective and non-political scientific staff should not be lost as accidental casualties in the political strife, thereby seriously delaying the attainment of economic independence which alone can make a reality of political independence.

Since I can claim twenty years of close personal knowledge of that varied group of scientists concerned with Africa's natural resources, the following remarks refer specifically to that economically vital field. Science, in Africa, for half a century has lain in the slow historical phase in which the critical studies were founded and carried forward by a very small number of adventurous enthusiasts from overseas. They were supplemented by an even smaller number of locally born students sent overseas for scientific training. The last decade has seen a dramatic emergence from the rapidly increasing universities of Africa of a substantial force of locally born scientists. These are reinforced by the rather small numbers of local men and women, educated in friendly countries overseas, who return to practise science in Africa.

This long awaited stage in the evolution of the continent should have produced an all-round acceleration of the scientific progress which is so urgently needed to meet the 'crisis of expectation' among our fellow citizens. As scientists we ourselves recognize the harsh fact that this very necessary reinforcement has been eliminated by the simultaneous wholesale loss of expatriate scientists and technicians. With them have gone many thousands of man-years of hard-won experience of the natural resources of Africa. This migration has been far more acute in the English language countries than in the French-speaking communities, as a result of a basic difference in organization of science to which I will refer again later.

Some degree of loss was of course inevitable, since human personalities vary widely in their powers of adjustment to changing circumstances and to patterns of life. The overall loss has been far too heavy and expensive to the continent as a whole. I believe that much of it was unnecessary and that because it has been so recent, a substantial amount of this precious research experience under the field conditions of Africa could still be won back again. While the locally born and locally educated scientist must increasingly learn to carry the main burden of the scientific task in Africa, the magnitude and urgency of that task is so vast that every possible reinforcement and every available man-year of research experience in the tropical environment is needed in the field now.

The Lagos Conference, organized by UNESCO in 1964 to assess the scientific task in the development of the natural resources of Africa, reached some grave conclusions. After noting that all the more advanced countries of the world employ very large numbers of trained scientists, of an average order of one thousand per million of population, it was estimated that Africa has at present less than forty per million. At the same time the urgent drive to catch up with the standard of living of more advanced countries overseas can be sustained only by the rapid development of our natural resources and of the commerce based thereon. Products must be developed not only for home consumption but for export in exchange for all the many things Africa needs from overseas. Such products must be able to compete on equal terms in a world market ever more selective and insistent on quality. Agricultural and forestry produce will be for some time the mainstay for most countries in Africa. Export quality in livestock, crops and timber is achieved only by relentless scientific efficiency in production.

The growing of crops of competitive export quality at competitive prices needs accurate agricultural guidance, based on quantitative scientific knowledge as well as on skill. Much of this knowledge has indeed been won over the past half century and extension staffs throughout the continent are battling with the dead weight of tradition and ignorance in order to translate this knowledge into field practice. Only successful crops will carry conviction about new methods. For success in the many complex biological problems facing them, the extension staff must have the close support of trained and experienced specialists for diagnosis, advice and instruction. In this role alone we could use every available biological and agricultural scientist in Africa today, and also several hundred of the experienced specialists who have recently left.

Protection of crops and livestock from the pests and diseases which spring up so readily from the rich ecological environment of Africa, to multiply at least as fast as we can develop agriculture and forestry, involves both field experience and technical knowledge. The modern armoury of chemical weapons is complex, ever-changing and very expensive, so that the most up-to-date expert advice is continuously necessary to maintain high quality, undamaged products—without bankrupting the producer in the process. The world is facing the need to replace chemicals by biological controls, and this must have continuous close study from competent entomologists and pathologists.

Rigorous inspection and control of the marketing systems is essential for modern world trade. This again can be done effectively only by trained staff. Phytosanitary protection at the ports in a world of rapidly increasing transport facilities is itself a growing problem needing evermore trained staff. All possible recruits, both the experienced and the newly qualified, are needed for this vast task of applying the knowledge already won.

There are, however, all too many problems as yet unsolved; soils in which crops do not respond as expected to fertilizers; or areas in which cattle do not flourish. These are the really difficult problems calling for intensive research work in which training and experience are of critical importance. As we carry agricultural and forestry development into new areas, new problems arise with an endless succession of new scientific tasks. New techniques are developing rapidly overseas. We must have research staff energetically seeking to improve existing methods and to test out methods reported from elsewhere. It is no exaggeration to say that in very large measure the expectations of the millions on this continent will depend for their realization on the efforts of the comparatively small number of scientists in the field of natural resources.

Paradoxically, the expansion of educational facilities in Africa to produce more local scientists is in itself absorbing an increasing proportion of the qualified practitioners. Another source of loss is into the administrative field, where opportunities for advancement are exceptional in rapidly developing countries.

For the next twenty years we shall need in Africa every competent scientist whom we can train for ourselves or borrow from the outside world. Beyond that span, we can look at the most advanced countries for a forecast of the position. In spite of their high annual output of thousands of scientific graduates, they are still competing for the services of each other's scientists.

The position which I have outlined is cold fact, not political theory. Why, then, have the African countries failed to convince their experienced expatriate scientists that they are still wanted? In the pressure for 'localization' very many of them, to my personal knowledge, have been made to feel that they remain on sufference, for as brief a time as possible. As a result, the 'relay race' of research, in which each individual puts in his main effort and then hands on the baton to his successor, has become disorganized and scores of the scientific batons have been dropped.

I believe that the forces of nationalist politics have shown confused thinking on this issue. We should be using our new African scientists to expand our scientific force, not to replace it. Scientists with invaluable experience of Africa's natural resources have not been invited to continue their careers, but have instead been offered ludicrously short contracts with the openly-expressed hope that they will not be needed for more than a year or two. Faced with a need to rebuild their careers elsewhere, they have inevitably chosen to do so at once. At the Lagos Conference African countries had an excellent opportunity to appeal to the outside world for the loan of scientific staff, but failed, for political reasons, to do so. I have heard fears expressed as to the prospects of finding posts for African students now training overseas. Such fears are based on absurd miscalculations.

The remedy is a major change of policy. We have an excellent object lesson in the system which the French have operated with such success. Given the elementary security of a home-based post, the more adventurous scientists from the developed countries can be attracted by Africa's wide research opportunities to undertake major tasks here. More particularly, in the research fields complete groups, based on a single overseas centre, can give an impetus to scientific life in Africa and provide foci for the attachment of newly graduated African staff. There are so many urgent problems to choose from, and the need of the whole community for the outcome of a research programme offers the stimulus and challenge which is not easy to find in the vast research complexes of the advanced countries.

We could win back much of the precious field experience of expatriate scientists who have recently left Africa if we offer them the right form of organization. This will not happen unless African countries face up to the situation and ask clearly and unequivocally for this form of help.

SOCIO-DEMOGRAPHIC DISPROPORTIONS OF AFRICA IN THE MODERN WORLD

by

DR. L. YABLOCHKOV

The theme of our symposium is extremely wide in scope, not only because it embraces the whole continent with its various problems and the rest of the world closely watching African events, but also because it permits various approaches.

One such approach to the theme of 'Africa and the World' has yet to be adequately elucidated in the studies of Africanists. I have in mind the study of the social evolution of African peoples as an integral part of the modern history of mankind.

In our narrowing world there are no longer any isolated social phenomena. African society has developed within the common evolution of humanity. I do not think that one should repeat here the truism that there are general laws of social development. Correlation and interaction of neighbouring societies are factors which exist beyond any doubt.

Proceeding from this assumption it would be of great interest to analyse how the European industrial (or in Marxist terminology, capitalist) society has influenced traditional African society, characterized as this is by diversity of social and economic structure with strong survivals of communal life.

The social relations introduced by a commercial money economy have considerably changed the tempo and the trends of development of African society. They have impelled an accelerated disintegration of the rural community, accompanied by the growth of towns.

By itself this process is not absolutely unique and can be retraced in the history of all nations. In Africa, however, where traditions of rural communal life are rooted more deeply than anywhere in Europe or even in Asia, the colonial economy deformed social stratification in an unprecedented way.

It might be said that in tropical countries, as much as anywhere else, society is gradually dividing itself into opposing classes of land owners and peasantry, employers and employed, while it remains true that in some regions the ancient communal relations between tribal chiefs and commoners still prevail. One may doubt whether any of these opposing social pairs shaped the face of colonial society in most of the African countries. But there was one more specific pair of opposing social layers—the African administrative élites and the urban poor—both generated by the specific conditions of the colonial structure.

Since the system of private enterprise in tropical Africa had not developed from within but was mainly introduced by foreign companies, the colonial society was socially unbalanced. The layer of employed was not confronted by a corresponding African layer of employers. Instead, there appeared an increasing number of clerks, officials, secretaries, etc. This intermediate social layer gravitated more towards foreign activities than towards the domestic environment. Many of these white-collar employees received higher education abroad. Implementing the foreign will, they had no independent importance in economic life and by no means expressed the interests of local African populations. On the contrary, they tried hard to fence off traditional society, and copy the way of life that was typical for European administrators. In fact they were scornful about the 'savage' customs of the village.

They were identified as élites, or colonial élites, for they enjoyed some special privileges. A specific state of mind and peculiar psychology were characteristic of them.

Not all the representatives of the colonial élites participated in the liberation movement, though this particular social stratum provided the anti-colonial struggle with some devoted national leaders. Yet today you cannot find a single tropical African country previously under long colonial rule, that does not have remnants of the former élites in its state machinery.

In colonial times, another peculiar layer of urban population appeared in Africa. It is rather difficult to find anything similar in European social history. As a result of the urban growth and the relative deterioration of the village, the colonial towns were flooded with people who severed their ties with the rural community but could not find employment, and who lived at the expense of their kith and kin. Even the colonial élites did not dare to disregard the ancient custom of supporting relatives. Besides that, the generous nature of tropical countries provided a guarantee from starvation for those who otherwise lacked employment and support.

These people were neither migrant labourers, nor were they temporarily unemployed. Thousands of young men who had definitely lost any hope of finding employment and had no occupation at all were closer to the classical category of papers. They were alienated from the village community that had strictly regulated their behaviour in accordance with the customs of their forefathers. Their ideal became the way of life of the colonial élites upon whom they depended, and whom they envied and hated.

During the transition period from colonial status to complete independence, the social relations that took shape earlier have been an influencing factor and will remain so for some time. They have survived foreign rule, and the colonial mentality appeared very hard to get rid of. The former colonial élites find their official position now gainful in many ways other than a high rate of salary. Instances are known when officials in some African countries invested money accumulated in this way in real estate: land, building etc. For them the African revolution has come to an end.

And what happens now to the numerous urban paupers? It is an established fact that this layer has not lost its tendency to grow. The increase in urban population now in tropical Africa is far from equal to the growth of the number of jobs in production. The degradation of the rural community continues; the cities are still flooded by thousands of new young men who are far from being absorbed by the existing industrial capacity and cannot find any useful outlet for their energies.

In recent years, many school leavers have joined this totally or partially unemployed mass. They have no opportunity of going into administration or business. The jobs that correspond to their qualifications and aspirations are lacking.

This situation is different from that of Europe in the period of the industrial revolution, when special measures were taken to alienate the peasants from their land so as to enlarge reserves of labour for urban industrialization.

In contemporary Africa, the discontented mass of unsettled urban dwellers is known to be a breeding ground for different forms of instability. And it does happen that the opposing political groups use the deep-rooted (though understandable) dissatisfaction of the urban paupers against one another.

Now that we know the origin of the poor urban population in tropical Africa let us examine the possibilities for their future adjustment.

The national governments are aware of the need to provide employment for the growing masses of these socially displaced persons. It might appear that the easiest way would be to invite more foreign investments into national economies. But experience shows that this does not solve the social problem—post-colonial socio-demographic disproportion still remains. Some administrations have tried labour armies for public works on a national scale. Others have forced the development of the state sector. There are in evidence attempts to facilitate the expansion of the small private sector.

All these efforts to find employment for the mass of urban dwellers are not sufficient to effect a drastic change in the trend. Soon it may become necessary to concentrate attention on the very source of population influx: the African village.

If we recognize the fact that the productive capacities of the African village lag behind modern methods of production, if we recognize that the old communal structure is passing away, then there should be some hopeful prospects for switching the development of the post-colonial African village on to new socio-economic rails, instead of vainly trying to find an ideological basis in the weakening womb of the traditional way of life, while the town enjoys priority. In the last analysis, the direction in which tropical African countries develop will largely depend on an ability to fill the yawning gap between the levels of social standing of the town and the village. After all, rural dwellers will comprise an overwhelming majority in tropical countries for many years to come.

Having localized the most pressing issue of social development in the African tropics, it is only natural to pre-suppose that a greater degree of international assistance should be provided for village development. In harnessing the experience of developed nations, one can now feel a certain disproportion in the amount of attention paid to African urbanization.

As far as world Africanist sociological thought is concerned, this should obviously transfer its emphasis from endeavouring to reconstruct the African past, to searching for optimum models so as to speed up the modernization of the tropical village, collecting and adapting the experience acquired by humanity in other countries and regions.

If the inherited socio-demographic imbalance is to be diminished in tropical Africa, then the scientific and technological achievements of the modern world should be used with the energy equal to the efforts in industrial development.

The end of the colonial era in Africa has immensely influenced the world. Africa has really become an integrated part of international life. That is why the internal processes of African social development are now of fundamental international concern. The crucial problems of the African village form as important an international issue as any other problem of the socio-economic development of mankind.

For some ex-colonial powers it might be considered to be their moral duty to help African socio-economic equalization. For other nations this help is considered to be a manifestation of their international doctrine. Be that as it may, African development is now more than ever interwoven with the general socio-economic evolution.

REPORT ON THE SOCIAL AND EDUCATIONAL SITUATION

COMMISSION C

The Conference recognized the new challenges presented by the attainment of independence in Africa and took note of the difficulties that Africa will have to face in order to achieve the development goals which she has set for herself. These goals cannot be achieved unless full consideration is given to the masses of new Africa and the new values that must be inculcated in a widespread manner amongst her people.

It is not only economic development that will give to this new Africa the values that she has set out to achieve. Educational development will help Africa to acquire material progress by providing skilled manpower, but it should also help Africa to appreciate her human values, especially by developing a sense of belonging to both the African and the world context. To achieve this it is suggested that revolutionary thinking in education is required. At present education in Africa is suffering from conservative ideas. Patterns of development copied or inherited from other societies are now being followed. Such new ideas as have been adopted and implemented have not shown any indication of dynamic departures from old practices. The approach must be more fundamental and should be rooted in the idea 'that the heritage of pre-colonial Africa, with its richly various cultural patterns and political, social, economic and artistic achievements, must be called upon to play a full part in the work of continental reconstruction'.

A new approach to education in Africa must pay particular and urgent attention to the following:

CURRICULUM AND CONTENT

Although it is noted that certain African countries have already started to Africanize their curriculum independently, it is felt that these countries would have been able to move more rapidly and effectively towards new objectives if they had worked in cooperation with other African countries. The curriculum should be organized so that the role of education as a tool of social, economic and political change is emphasized. Curriculum development should also be based on the assumption that it is important to provide education not only to children of school age but also to the adult working population, which forms the productive nerve of Africa's development. There must be less emphasis on conventional primary education leading to further education. More emphasis must be placed on primary education appropriate to producers in the agricultural and the modern sector, whose education in present circumstances cannot go beyond the primary stage. This may entail the re-direction of resources, including a new way of using mass communication media.

TEACHERS

Teachers are the direct means through which education takes place. Teachers in Africa need a new deal through a fresh appreciation of their services and an improvement of their status in African society.

The first step in the new approach of education in Africa should be made by the teacher-training institutes. Even though African countries now rely heavily on expatriate teachers, and will continue to do so for some time to come, they should aim at self-sufficiency in the future. In the meantime, care should be taken when recruiting teachers from abroad to ensure that selected candidates possess not only adequate professional training but also constructive personal attitudes which will enable them to contribute more effectively to the goals of African development. Not only should teachers be carefully selected (the emphasis being on African requirements), but when recruited, should also be offered a period of orientation to adjust themselves to their new environment and the demands of their new curriculum.

NEW TECHNIQUES

African educational development must take full advantage of modern mass media educational techniques for which massive external assistance should immediately be sought (on the assumption that the use of these techniques will remain in African hands). The Conference also felt that many opportunities exist for cooperation in the production and use of educational programmes.

African educational development must make use of modern mass media on a sufficiently large scale. The full economic and cultural advantages of these techniques are to be realized.

RESEARCH

The successful implementation of a new programme for education in Africa will depend ultimately on adequate research, and must be accompanied by adequate scientific evaluation. Institutes for educational research are still insufficient to meet pressing needs, and national and international action to develop and extend these facilities would be welcome.

Finally the Conference was convinced that this new and dynamic approach, which should make it possible to accelerate the speed of development, depends on adequate financial investment in education, and a bold policy to encourage those engaged in it. Education has a paramount role to play in the social, economic and political reconstruction of Africa, a role that is by no means beyond the ability of African educationists.

NOTES ON CONTRIBUTORS

BELAI ABBAI, Economic Affairs Officer, United Nations Economic Commission for Africa, Addis Ababa.

1955-60 Director-General, Imperial Ethiopian Government Technical Assistance Board.

GERMA AMARE Ph.D. *Southern Illinois*, Unesco Senior Lecturer in Education, School of Education, University of Zambia.

1964-7 Assistant Professor of Education, Faculty of Education, Haile Selassie I University; 1959-62 Assistant Dean, and Dean of Students, University College, Addis Ababa.

PAULOS ASRAT B.A. *Addis Ababa*, M.A. *Michigan*, Assistant Minister, Ministry of Education and Fine Arts, Addis Ababa.

Chief Education Officer, Governerate General of Eritrea, Asmara. Dean of Students, Haile Selassie I University, Addis Ababa. Director of Teacher Training Institute, Harar. Assistant Director and Teacher, Medhane Alem Secondary School, Addis Ababa.

DAN V. AVNI-SEGRE, Associate Professor of Political Science, Haifa University College.

1967-9 Research Fellow, St. Antony's College, Oxford. 1968 Ford (Visiting) Professor, M.I.T., Cambridge, Massachusetts. Former Israeli diplomat.

Publications include: *Israel, Society in Transition* (in preparation); *A Political History of Africa* (in Hebrew) 1967, 'Madagascar: An Example of Indigenous Modernization of a Traditional Society in the 19th Century' *St. Antony's Papers - African Affairs No. 3,* 1969.

GWENDOLEN M. CARTER B.A. *Toronto*, M.A. *Oxon*, Ph.D. *Harvard*, Melville J. Herskovits Professor of African Affairs and Director, Program of African Studies, Northwestern University. Professor of Political Science.

1943-64 Smith College, Northampton, Massachusetts; 1942-3 Tufts College, Medford, Massachusetts; 1941-2 research associate, Bureau of International Affairs, Harvard University; 1938-41 Wellesley College, Wellesley, Massachusetts; 1932-5 McMaster University, Hamilton, Ontario, Canada. Honorary degrees from eight universities; Achievement award of the AAUW, 1962; Medal for Distinguished Achievement, Radcliffe College, 1962.

Publications include: *The Politics of Inequality: South Africa since 1948*, 1958; *Independence for Africa*, 1960; *African One Party States*, 1962; *Five African States*, 1964; *National Unity and Regionalism in Eight African States*, 1966; *South Africa's Transkei: The Politics of Domestic Colonialism*, 1968; *Expanding Horizons in African Studies*, 1969; *Government and*

Politics in the Twentieth Century, 2nd ed., 1967; *Government of the United Kingdom*, 2nd ed., 1968; *Government of the Soviet Union*, 2nd ed., 1968; *Government of France*, 1968; *The British Commonwealth and International Security, 1919-1939*, 1949; *Politics in Europe: Five Cases*, 1965; *Politics in Africa*, Six Cases, 1966. Also pamphlets and articles in professional journals.

B.T.G. CHIDZERO M.A. *Ottawa*, Ph.D. (Political Science) *McGill*, Director, Commodities Division, United Nations Conference on Trade and Development, Geneva.

1963-8 Resident Representative, United Nations Development Programme, Nairobi, Kenya; 1960-3 Economic Affairs Officer, United Nations Economic Commission for Africa, Addis Ababa, Ethiopia; 1958-60 post-graduate research, Nuffield College, Oxford; 1957-8 Teaching Assistant in Comparative Government, McGill University; 1955-8 graduate student, McGill University,

Publications include: *Tanganyika and International Trusteeship*, 1961.

J.H. DALTON AB, Ph.D. (Economics) *California*, FAO Agricultural Planning Economist, Ministry of Agriculture, Ethiopia.

1968-9 Agricultural Economic Affairs Officer, Research Division UNECA Addis Ababa; 1967-8 UN Agricultural Planning Adviser, Ethiopia Ministry of Planning; 1962-8 Agricultural Economic Affairs Officer ECA-FAO joint agriculture Division UNECA; 1955-62 Assistant Professor, Economics, University of Maryland; 1953-5 Instructor, Economics, San Francisco State College; 1951 Lecturer, School of Business Administration, University of California.

BASIL DAVIDSON M.C., Bronze Star (U.S.), Hon. Major, British Army.

Publications include: *Old Africa Rediscovered*, 1959; *Black Mother*, 1961; The *African Past*, 1964; *Which Way Africa? The Search for a New Society* revised ed. 1970; *The Liberation of Guine*; *Aspects of an African Revolution*, 1969; *The Africans, An Entry to Cultural History*, 1969; many articles, papers, essays.

A.F. EWING, UN Co-ordinator of External Aid, Prek Thnot development project, Cambodia. Since 1949 member of United Nations Secretariat.

1966-8, Director, UNECA Sub-regional Officer for Central Africa; 1964-6, Special Advisor to the Executive Secretary, UNECA; 1961-4 Director, Industry Transport and Natural Resources Division, UNECA; 1952-61 Director, Steel Engineering and Housing Division, UNECOE; 1946-8 Assistant Secretary, in change of Building Materials, Ministry of Works Great Britain; 1943-6 Principal Private Secretary to successive Ministers of Works.

ROBERT K.A. GARDINER B.A. (Economics) *Cambridge*, M.A. *Oxon*, Executive Secretary, United Nations Economic Commission for Africa.

1962-3 Officer-in-Charge, UN Operations in the Congo; 1961-2 Director, Division of Public Administration, UN New York; 1961, Member, UN Mission to the Congo; 1959-60, Deputy Executive Secretary, UNECA; 1957-9 Head, Ghana Civil Service; 1955-7 Permanent Secretary, Ministry of Housing, Ghana; 1953-5 Director, Social Welfare and Community Development, Ghana; 1949-53 Director, Exeramural Studies, University College, Ibadan, Nigeria; 1947-9 Member, Trusteeship Department, UN, New York; 1943-6 Lecturer in economics, Fourah Bay College, Sierra Leone.

Honorary Fellow: University of Ibadan, Nigeria; Selwyn College, Cambridge. Honorary Doctorates: Civil Law, University of East Anglia, 1966; Philosophy, University of Uppsala, 1966; Laws, University of Ibadan, 1967; Sciences, Kumasi University, 1968; Laws, University of East Africa, 1968; Civil Law, University of Sierra Leone, 1969; Civil Law, Tuskegee Institute, 1969; Bradford University, 1969.

Member of: International Honorary Committee, Dag Hammarskjold Foundation; Society for International Development; Board of Trustees, International Legal Center; International Advisory Council, Haile Selassie I Prize Trust; UN Fund for Population Activities. Chairman, Commonwealth Foundation.

Publications include: *The Development of Social Administration* (with H.O. Judd), 2nd Edition, 1959. *A World of Peoples*, 2nd edition, 1965.

G.C. LAST, Advisor for Social Studies in the Department of Curriculum and Research, Ministry of Education and Fine Arts, Imperial Ethiopian Government, Addis Ababa. Also concerned with physical planning for educational development programme. 1957-63 Headmaster, Medhane Alem School, Addis Ababa; 1949-57 taught geography and economics in London and Addis Ababa.

Publications include: *A Regional Survey of Africa*; *A Georgraphy of Ethiopia*; *Social Studies Atlas for Ethiopia*; *Beginning Secondary School Geography*; *A Pictorial History of Ethiopia* (with R. Pankhurst)

G.E.A. LARDNER, Director, Division of Natural Resources & Transport United Nations Economic Commission for Africa, Addis Ababa, Ethiopia.

1964-5 Chief, Natural Resources Section, UNECA; 1961-3 Permanent Secretary, Ministry of Economic Development, Nigeria; 1960-1 Economic Commission for Africa; 1949-60 Assistant Secretary and Senior Assistant Secretary, Government of Nigeria; 1947-8 Principal, Olu-Iwa Secondary School, Western Nigeria; 1940-4 Junior Service, Government of Sierra Leone.

Graduate of Universities of Durham and London; post-graduate studies, University of Oxford; Visiting Fellow, Institute of Development Studies at Sussex University.

C. LEGUM, Africa and Commonwealth Correspondent of *The Observer*.

1945-7 Chairman of Johannesburg Housing Committee and Johnnesburg General Purposes Committee; 1942-7 Member of Johannesburg City Council; 1944-6 Editor, Labour *Illustrated Bulletin*: 1939-44 Editor,

Labour Weekly *Forward* and *The Minework*; 1936-9 Political Correspondent, Johannesburg Sunday and Daily Express.

Publications include: *The Bitter Choice*, 1968; *Africa Hand book*, 1963 & 1966; *Lumumba "My Country"* 1961; *South Africa: Crisis for the West* 1964; *A Short Guide to Pan-Africanism*, 1962; *Congo Disaster*, 1960; *Bandung Cairo and Accra* 1958; *Must we Lose Africa*, 1954.

DURI MOHAMMED, Assistant Professor of Economics, Haile Selassie I University, Addis Ababa.

R. PANKHURST Ph. D. *London School of Economics*, Director, Institute of Ethiopian Studies and Professor of Economic History, Haile Selassie I University, Addis Ababa.

1952-6 Lecturer in London University, and Research worker National Institute of Economics and Social Research; co-editor of the *Journal of Ethiopian Studies, Register of Current Research on Ethiopian and Horn of Africa*, and *Ethiopia Observer*.

Publications include: *Introduction to the Economic History of Ethiopia, Economic History of Ethiopia 1800-1935*; *Travellers in Ethiopia*, and *A History of Ethiopia in Pictures* (with G.C. Last).

H.C. PEREIRA B.Sc., Ph.D., D.Sc., F.R.S., Director of the East Malling Research Station, Kent, and also Chairman of the Agricultural Research Council of Malawi.

1961-7 Director of the Agricultural Research Council of Central Africa, and helped to set up research laboratories in Malawi, Rhodesia and Zambia; 1955 Deputy Director of Laboratories, Physics Division, EAAFO; 1952 started the Physics Division of the East African Agriculture and Forestry Organisation; 1948 helped to set up the Kenya Coffee Research Station. Wartime service in Western Desert with Royal Engineers.

1966 Haile Selassie award for African Research. 1969 elected a Fellow of the Royal Society.

E.A.A. ROWSE, formerly Co-ordinator and Planner, Technical Agency, Imperial Ethiopian Government, Addis Ababa.

1937-40 and 1947-52 Principal of the School of Planning and Research for National Development, London; 1929-33 Senior Lecturer in Town Planning and Architecture, College of Art, Edinburgh; since 1927 private practice in development planning in various parts of the world.

DUDLEY SEERS, Director, Institute of Development Studies, University of Sussex, England.

1964-7 Director-General, Economic Planning Staff, Ministry of Overseas Development; 1963-4 Director of Economic Development Division, UNECA 1963 Leander UN Economic Mission to Zambia; 1961-3 Visiting Professor of Economics, Yale University; 1957-61 Chief, Special Studies Group, Economic Commission for Latin America; 1955-7 UN Statistical Advisor to Eastern Caribbean; 1953-5 Research Economist, United Nations Headquarters; 1947-53 Research Economist, later Senior

Lecturer in Economic Statistics, Oxford University; 1945-6 Research Economist, Prime Minister's Office, New Zealand.

Consultant to governments of Malta, Jamaica, Trinidad, Ghana and the World Bank.

Publications include: 'The use of a modified input-output system for an economic programme in Zambia' in *Theory and Design of Economic Development*, ed. Adelman and Thorbecke, 1967; 'International Trade and Development - the special interests of Africa' in *African Primary Products and International Trade*, ed. Stewart and Ord, 1965 *Cuba - the Economic and Social Revolution* (ed) 1964; 'Inflation and growth: the heart of the controversy' in *Inflation and Growth in Latin America*, Yale University, 1964; and many articles in leading economic journals.

L.D. YABLOCHKOV, Head Department of Foreign Relations, African Institute of the Academy of Sciences U.S.S.R.